A Guide to Renovating

the

South Bend® Lathe

Models
10L • 13" • 14 ½ " • 16"

Published By

ILION Industrial Services, LLC

Printed in the United States of America by Instantpublisher.com

ISBN: 978-0-578-07869-4

South Bend® and South Bend Lathe® is a registered trademark of South Bend Lathe Company

Index

Topic	Page

Lathe Parts Identification

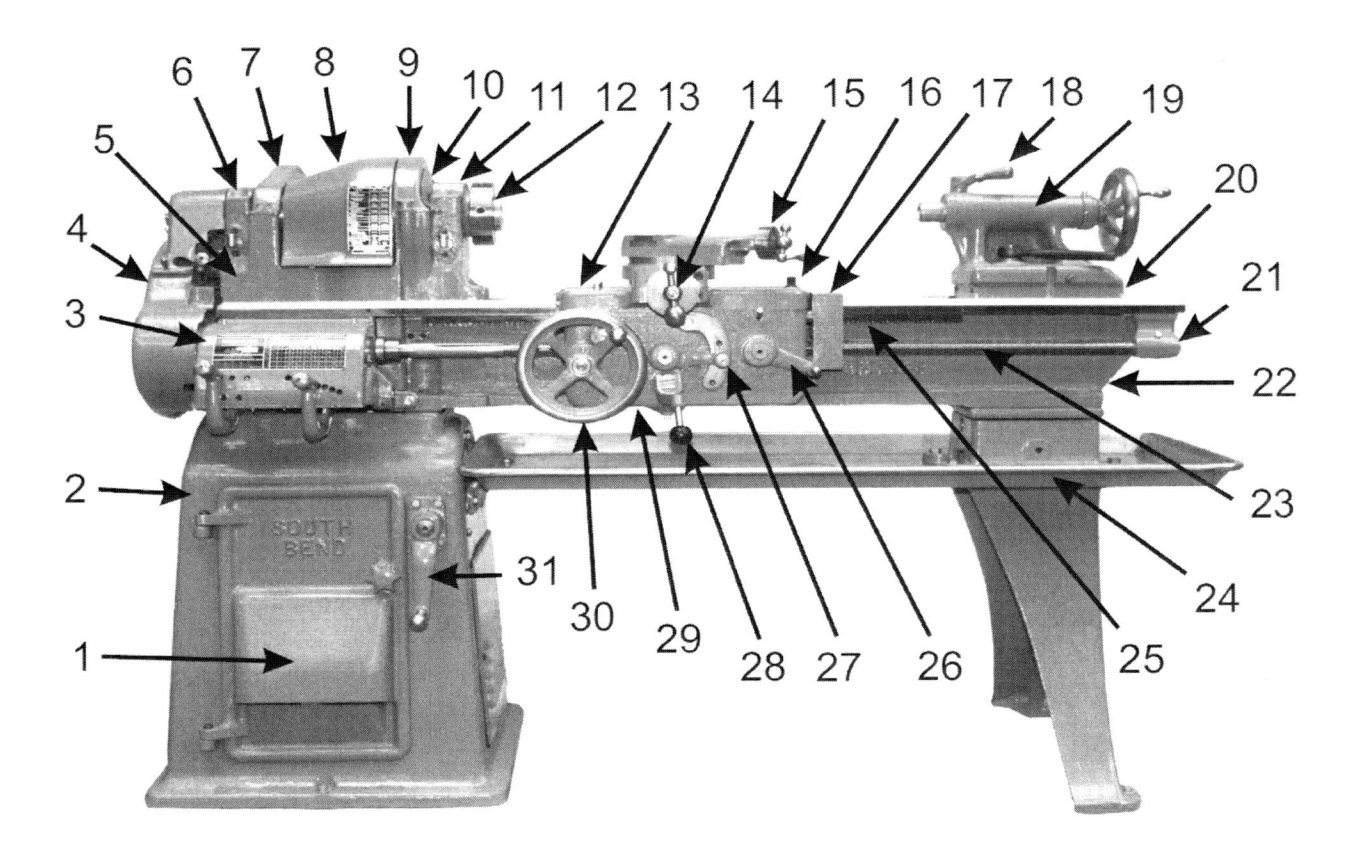

1	Drive Access Door	11	Large Bearing Cap	21	Lead Screw Bracket
2	Cabinet Base	12	Spindle	22	Bed
3	Gearbox	13	Saddle	23	Lead Screw
4	Primary Gear Guard	14	Cross Slide	24	Chip Plan
5	Headstock	15	Compound Slide	25	Rack
6	Small Bearing Cap	16	Saddle Lock	26	Half Nut Cam Lever
7	Quill Guard	17	Threading Dial	27	Shifter Lever
8	Spindle Cone Cover	18	Tailstock Quill Lock	28	ClutchLever (Star Wheel)
9	Bull Gear Guard	19	Tailstock	29	Apron
10	Bull Gear Plunger Guard	20	Tailstock Set-Over Base	30	Apron Handwheel
				31	Belt Tension Crank

The 10L, 13", 14 ½" & 16" South Bend® Lathe Disassembly and Servicing Guide

Forward

Having received so many positive comments from users of our previous manual on the 9" series of workshop lathes, we are humbled and pleased to be able to offer a brand new shop manual which provides illustrated step-by-step guidance for disassembling, refurbishing and re-assembling the industrial versions of the 10", 13", 14.5" and 16" South Bend® Lathe. The information presented here comes from many sources plus direct experience in working with these high-quality American lathes, but it is in no way intended to be an authoritarian or an OEM sanctioned guide. The target user of this manual is someone who is considering an acquisition or has already acquired an older lathe and simply needs a little guidance on the path toward making their old iron serviceable once again.

The original South Bend Lathe Works was in operation for over 100 years and during that time a number of modifications were made to their wide selection of lathes during the normal course of product development. This guide focuses on the industrial series of heavy duty lathes which were manufactured in large quantities from the 1930's through the late 1980's. Among the industrial lathes were many variations such as the tool-room model with taper attachment, the turret lathe, etc., but the basic machine is the same throughout. The company was very practical in how they approached the design of their industrial lathes and if you look closely you will see that the 10L, 10R, the 13", the 14 ½" and the 16" are all essentially the same design except for the scale. For instance, if you look at the gearbox or apron on a 10L and a 13" lathe of similar vintage, you will see that the design is the same and that only the scale of the corresponding parts is different. They have the same layout, same gear configuration, same bolt pattern, same functionality… the parts are just larger on the 13". We primarily use the 10L and 13" floor-mounted lathe with a double tumbler gearbox for demonstration purposes in this manual. Note that there are many small differences between older and newer models (such as the single tumbler and double tumbler quick change gearbox), but if the fundamental machine design is understood then these small differences are well within the capability of even a "first-timer" to manage with minimal anxiety. We have included a new section in the book devoted entirely to the single tumbler gearbox for those who have an earlier version lathe.

On the subject of major restorative services such as the regrinding and scraping of the bed or other bearing surfaces, we feel that these operations are beyond the scope of what the typical small shop or home machinist is able to handle alone. Unless you have an older gantry style metal planer in the garage or a surface grinder that can handle a 6' work piece, there is just no way to accurately correct a badly worn, twisted or damaged bed by yourself. If you encounter severe wear or damage on critical surfaces such as these, it is strongly recommended that you consult with a qualified machine shop that can perform and warranty the repair work.

For a lathe in normal use, it is recommended that you completely disassemble it every 7-10 years to clean the metal chips out of the inner workings, degrease it, and clean or replace consumable items such as wicks, gaskets, belts, etc. With respect to aesthetic restoration, we have had many requests for reference material on refinishing techniques so we have added a small section to the appendix on how to handle the stripping, filling, and repainting operations. A stiff brush, a good degreaser, and high-quality industrial enamel paint will go a long way unless you are restoring a museum piece, so there is no need to agonize over the finish. These lathes were made to be used in industrial applications, and with proper care and maintenance we can expect them to last much longer than ourselves.

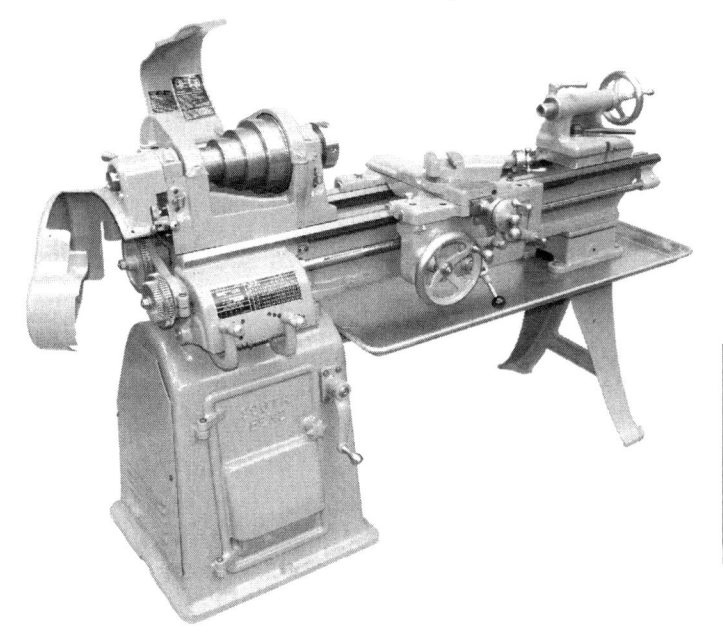

Late Model 13" Lathe that came from an industrial school shop in Wisconsin. (Vintage 1981) Among the last of the 13" lathes produced in South Bend, IN.

The 10" – 16" Lathe Models

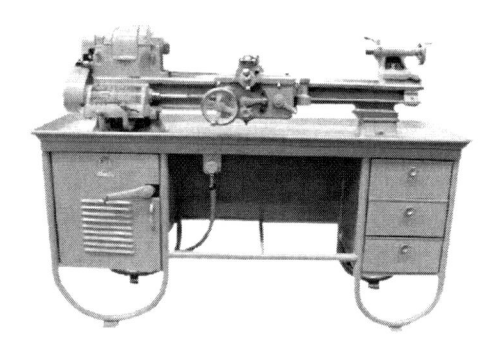

The 10L Lathe or "Heavy 10" was the workhorse of the industrial series and aside from the 9" workshop and 10k series of lathes; it is the machine most often found on the used market. There was also a 10R version sold with a smaller spindle bore and 2A (11/16") collet capacity instead of the larger 5C (1-1/16") collet capacity of the 10L. The 10" came mounted on several different bases including a cast iron pedestal and several sheet metal variations.

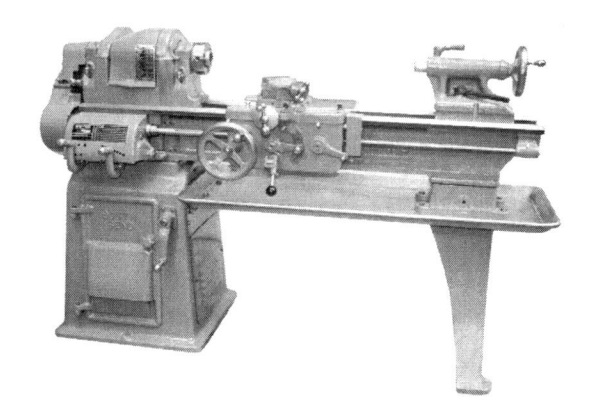

The 13" Lathe was one of the more versatile lathes produced and was in production up until the early 1980's. A great compromise between swing, turning horsepower and bed length. The 14 ½ " lathe was very close in scale to the 13" but it is not often seen in the used machinery market.

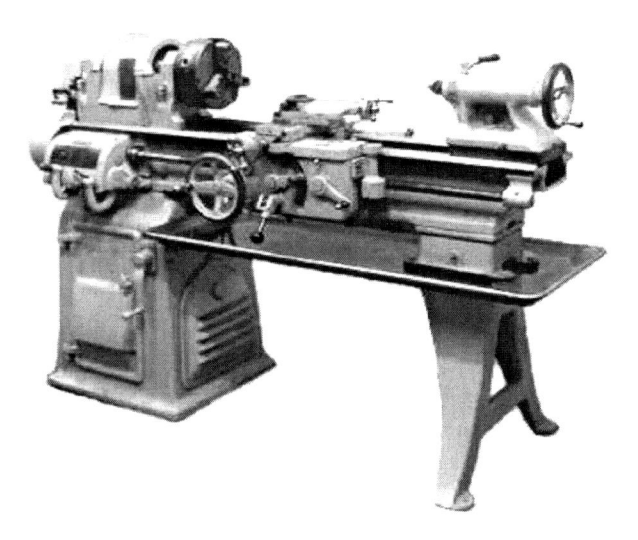

The 16" Lathe was the "Big Daddy" of the line and could be extended to a 24" swing with the addition of 4" Spacers beneath the headstock, tailstock & compound. A real beast.

The Industrial South Bend® Lathes came in four basic sizes with minor differences such as the tool-room and standard models. The only lathe that had an atypical designation was the 10L or "Heavy Ten" to differentiate it from the later 10k or "Light Ten". The 10k is very similar to the 9" lathe.

Gearbox Variations

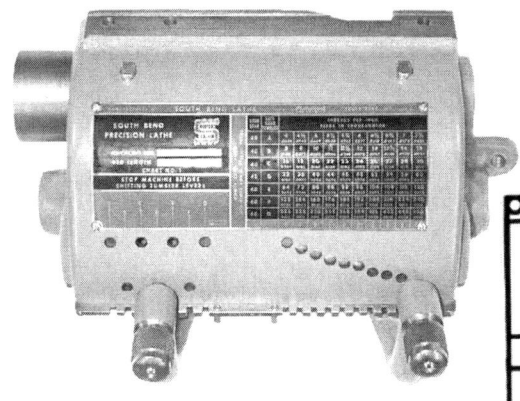

The 10L Wide Range, Double-Tumbler Gearbox

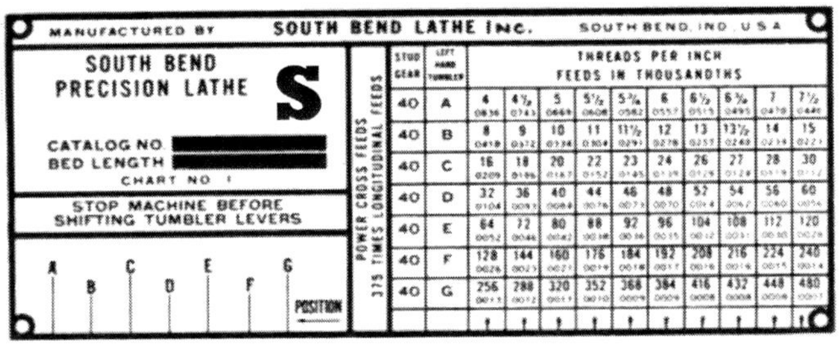

Threads for Double Tumbler Gearboxes

10"

Threads per inch and carriage feeds per spindle revolution

Wide Range Gearbox Only

4 .0836	4½ .0743	5 .0669	5½ .0608	5¾ .0582	6 .0557	6½ .0515	6¾ .0495	7 .0478	7½ .0446
8 .0418	9 .0372	10 .0334	11 .0304	11½ .0291	12 .0278	13 .0257	13½ .0248	14 .0239	15 .0223
16 .0209	18 .0186	20 .0167	22 .0152	23 .0145	24 .0139	26 .0129	27 .0124	28 .0119	30 .0112
32 .0104	36 .0093	40 .0084	44 .0076	46 .0073	48 .0070	52 .0064	54 .0062	56 .0060	60 .0056
64 .0052	72 .0046	80 .0042	88 .0038	92 .0036	96 .0035	104 .0032	108 .0031	112 .0030	120 .0028
128 .0026	144 .0023	160 .0021	176 .0019	184 .0018	192 .0017	208 .0016	216 .0016	224 .0015	240 .0014
256 .0013	288 .0012	320 .0011	352 .0010	368 .0009	384 .0009	416 .0008	432 .0008	448 .0008	480 .0007

10", 13", 14 ½ " & 16"

Threads per inch and carriage feeds per spindle revolution

4 .0841	4½ .0748	5 .0673	5½ .0612	5¾ .0585	6 .0561	6½ .0518	7 .0481		
8 .0421	9 .0374	10 .0337	11 .0306	11½ .0293	12 .0280	13 .0259	14 .0240		
16 .0210	18 .0187	20 .0168	22 .0153	23 .0146	24 .0140	26 .0129	28 .0120		
32 .0105	36 .0093	40 .0084	44 .0076	46 .0073	48 .0070	52 .0065	56 .0060		
64 .0053	72 .0047	80 .0042	88 .0038	92 .0037	96 .0035	104 .0032	112 .0030		
128 .0026	144 .0023	160 .0021	176 .0019	184 .0018	192 .0017	208 .0016	224 .0015		

Threads for Single Tumbler Gearbox

SOUTH BEND LATHE WORKS		**S**	SOUTH BEND, IND., U. S. A.							
	QUICK CHANGE		GEAR LATHE							
SLIDING GEARS	TOP LEVER	SCREW THREADS PER INCH USING HALF NUTS								AUTOMATIC CROSS FEED EQUALS .375 TIMES LONGITUDINAL FEED
IN	LEFT	2	2¼	2½	2¾	2⅞	3		3¼	3½
	CENTER	4	4½	5	5½	5¾	6		6½	7
	RIGHT	8	9	10	11	11½	12		13	14
OUT	LEFT	16	18	20	22	23	24		26	28
	CENTER	32	36	40	44	46	48		52	56
	RIGHT	64	72	80	88	92	96		104	112
	AUTOMATIC FEEDS THROUGH FRICTION CLUTCH									
	LEFT	.0208	.0185	.0166	.0151	.0144	.0138		.0128	.0119
	CENTER	.0104	.0093	.0083	.0075	.0072	.0069		.0064	.0059
	RIGHT	.0052	.0046	.0041	.0037	.0036	.0034		.0032	.0030

Gearbox Variations

Extra Pair of gears on screw gear and central shaft to provide wider range

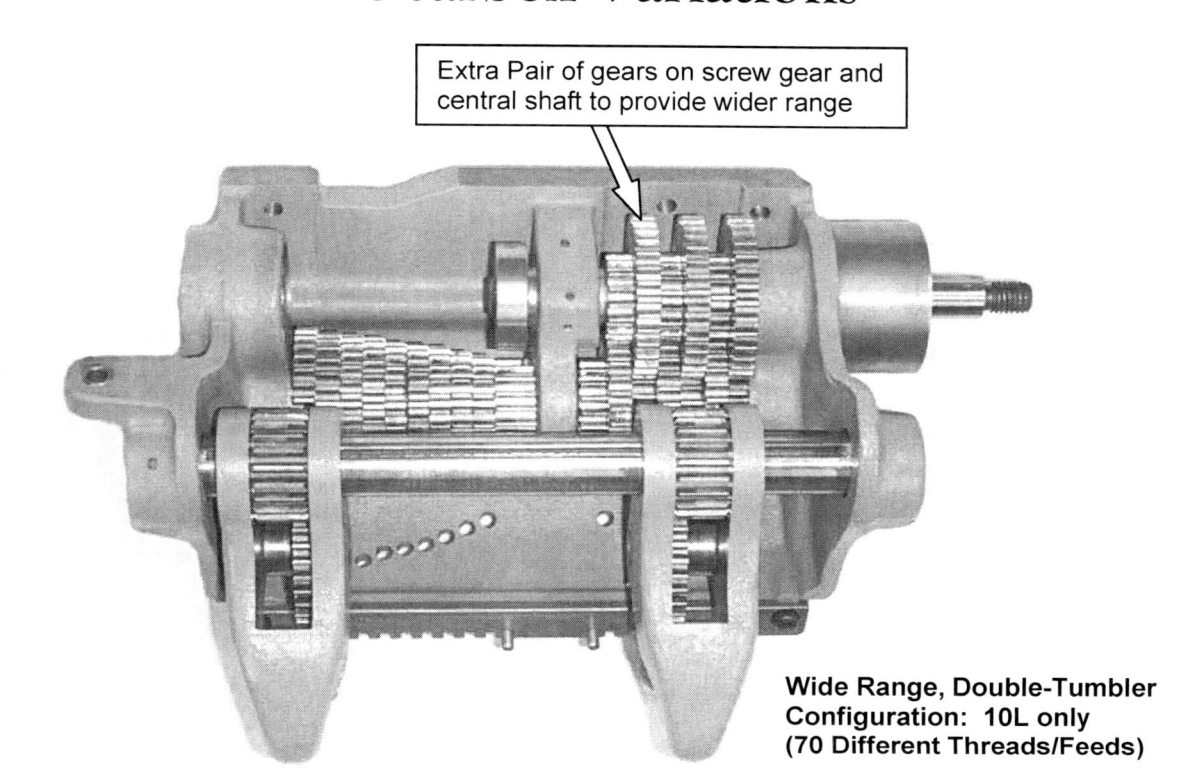

**Wide Range, Double-Tumbler
Configuration: 10L only
(70 Different Threads/Feeds)**

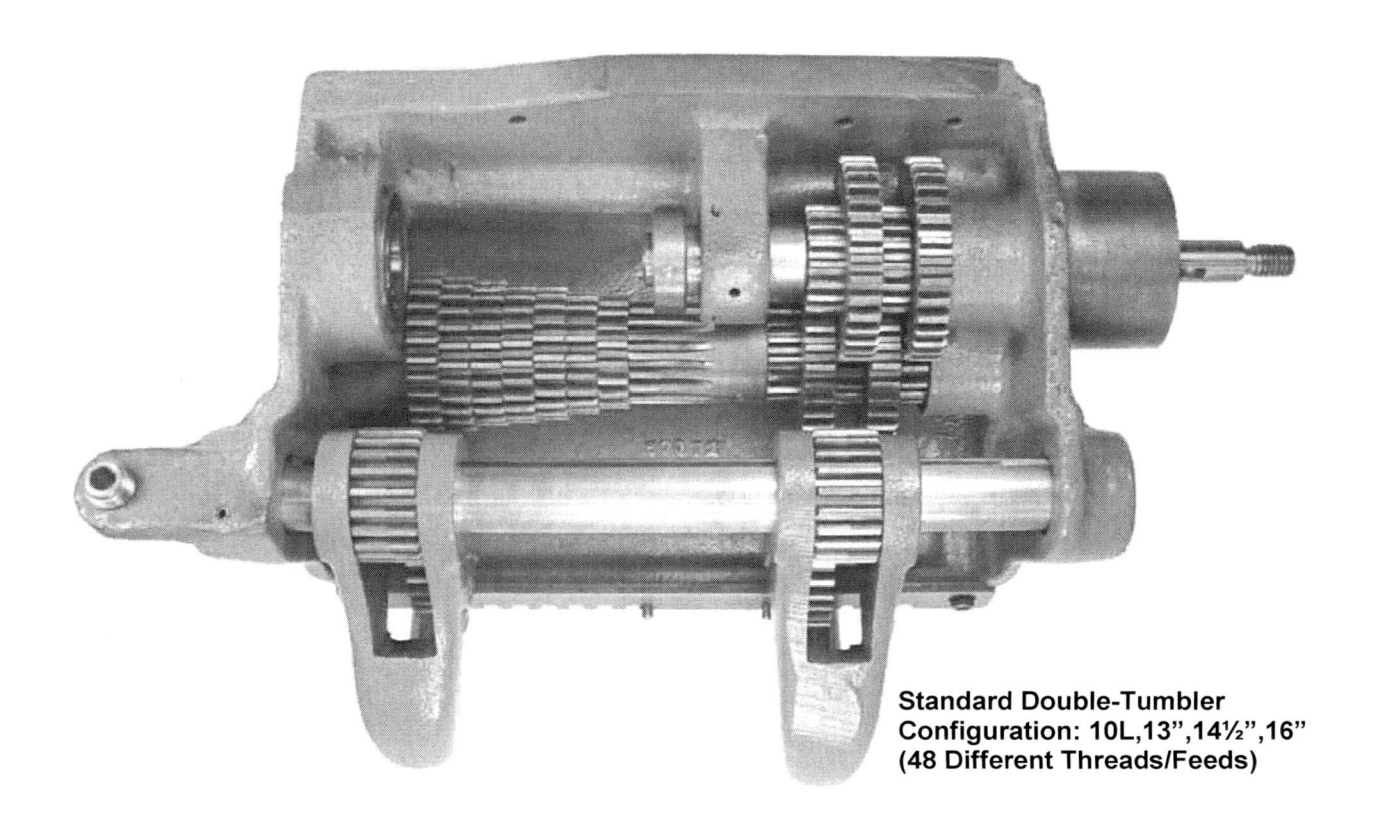

**Standard Double-Tumbler
Configuration: 10L,13",14½",16"
(48 Different Threads/Feeds)**

Comparing the Different Size Lathes

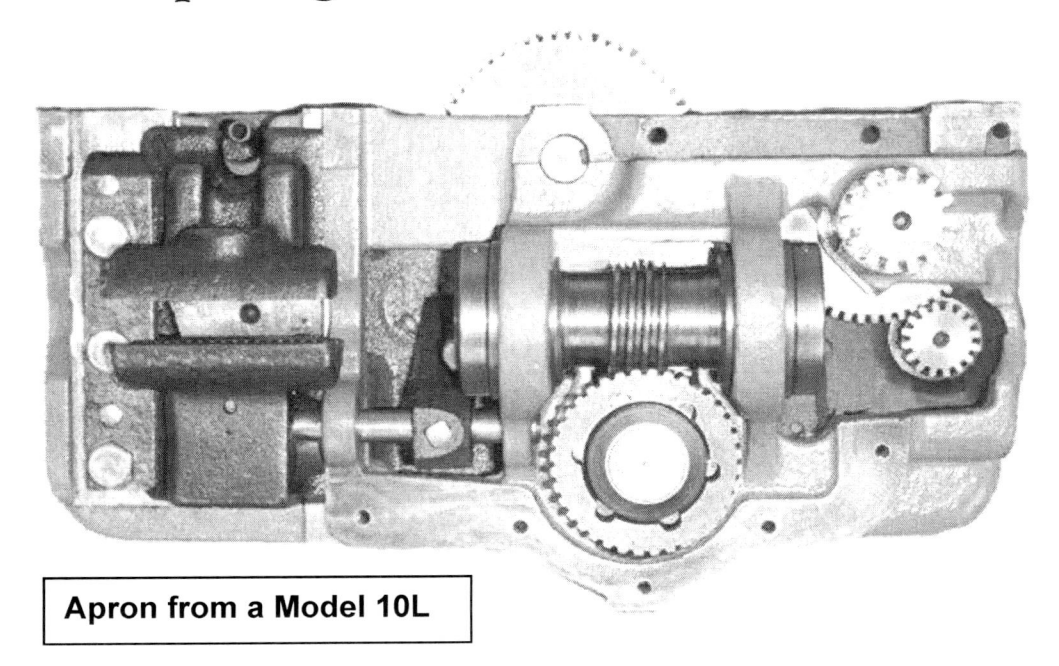

Apron from a Model 10L

Apron from a 13" Lathe

With the exception of the overall size, the 10L, 13", 14 ½" and the 16" lathe are essentially the same design. Compare the rear view of the aprons above and you'll see that the configurations are identical.

Assessing and Purchasing a Used South Bend® Lathe

If you are not lucky enough to already own one of these fine pieces of American iron, then locating and evaluating a used lathe can be a real challenge. Depending on the part of the country you reside in, it can be surprisingly easy or amazingly difficult to find a suitable used South Bend® available for local sale. Time and patience will generally be rewarded, so do not jump on the first lathe that you come across. Machinery auctions, business liquidations, machinery dealers, government auctions, ebay® and craigslist are all good sources though it is best not to purchase based on photographs alone if at all possible. If the machine has just exited service and can be inspected under power, that's about as good as it gets. You will be able to get a very good idea of the machine condition, how it was used, and how it will perform before making the purchase.

The Cost

Cost creep can be especially dangerous when buying a piece of used machinery since there can be other "not-so-obvious" costs to consider. The basic machine, transportation, accessories, parts and repairs must all be considered carefully since they can easily turn a sweet $500 purchase into a $1200 money pit. Starting with a basic model 10L with hard bed, the prices for a lathe in good condition (as of the time of printing) ranged from approximately $900 to $2100 depending upon the market and available accessories such as tooling, steady rests, follow rests, chucks, tool posts etc. Generally the newer models command much higher prices but they can also be had at a reasonable price depending upon the circumstances. The later 13" models with hard beds in good condition generally fetch between $1200 and $2800 depending on the vintage, condition and accessories. 14.5" and 16" models range between $1500 and $3000. The 10L bases varied between a cast iron pedestal and sheet metal cabinets according to vintage but for the larger lathes the cast iron pedestal designs remained constant over the years. On the price, you may always get lucky at an auction or fire sale so the above estimates are only provided for general guidance. We've seen "cherry" lathes that were purchased new in 1954 "and used only by a little old lady who turned plastic on Sundays" go for $8k+ but they are rare and are not a practical investment for the non-commercial user. A 50 year old South Bend® with moderate wear and .020

backlash on the feeds can still be made to cut tapers and turn to within .0005" over 12" so part of the accuracy equation is the machine and the other part is the machinist. If you are purchasing a lathe from a source that is not close to home, preparation and transport must also be considered. Crating and shipping is usually expensive on 1000 lbs - 2000 lbs of iron, so it is best to try and purchase locally if at all possible. Some common carriers will not accept machinery that has not been fully crated so figure $150 to $250 for crating just to get it onto a common carrier and then figure the freight & delivery. If you are purchasing from a machinery dealer, you can generally negotiate the crating and get the best quotes on freight but you can also do reasonably well by using an automated online freight booking service like freightquote.com. Most used machinery will ship by freight class 85 so use that class when pricing on line. If you are picking the machine up locally then it can be done with a heavy-duty lift-gate rental truck and a pallet jacket if the machine has been skidded. You will need someone to assist you so do not do attempt this alone.

The Vintage

It is fairly easy to determine the approximate age of a lathe by comparing the serial number to the online resources listed in the appendix. The serial number is stamped on the top of the bed on the far right end. There tends to be a considerable amount of attention paid to serial numbers when evaluating machinery but a serial number is just an indication of the machine age and not of its condition. While it is true that a 70 year old lathe may have seen longer service and may have had a greater *opportunity* for wear or abuse, it does not mean that you should expect the tool to be in poor condition just because it is old.

Ways

The bed ways are the most critical element to examine first since they are the most visible. Before the introduction of flame hardened ways (indicated by a "Flame Hardened" tag shown above) South Bend® Lathes were primarily "soft beds" which meant they were ground, scraped by hand for accuracy and then had geometrical "flaking" applied to the bearing surfaces of the bed to provide recesses for oil retention (and it looked good too). When viewing an older machine, if you can still see the original flaking on the bed and it is somewhat uniform, then the rest of machine will probably be in good condition as it was either well maintained or it was little used. (see the reference photos below) The depth of this scraping is only about .001" so it is a good wear indicator. For comparison, look at the ways on either side of the headstock since these ways rarely contacted the carriage. If you can see the scraping there, then you can compare the wear pattern along the bed. It is not unusual to have little or no scraping remaining on a lathe with some age but then it becomes important to look for severely uneven wear or a "sway back" bed. Check the area just beneath the chuck since that is the part of the bed that is most used during operation. If there is excessive wear you will see it here. Excessive wear is usually indicated by a deep groove or scored metal on the front and rear V-ways. Most often, damage from dropped chucks is found on the inner ways which are only for the tailstock, so damage there is not as critical. Focus on the outer two V ways. Damage or grooves on these ways will affect the accuracy so if it is bad, you should probably keep looking. If the work zone looks fairly clean, run the carriage to the far right end of the bed. Tighten the square carriage locking bolt lightly by hand until it just touches the underside of the bed. Note the position of the bolt head. Now run the carriage to the left and stop in front of the chuck. Now turn the bolt down again by hand until the lock just touches and note the relative position of the bolt head. Most bolts are 7/16-14 thread so a 1/4 turn will indicate about .018" of wear between the two measured locations. This value is probably the limit for acceptable wear. Important Note: Hard-bed lathes were typically not scraped, but you should still check for wear grooves and damage. If the bed is good, move to the headstock & spindle.

  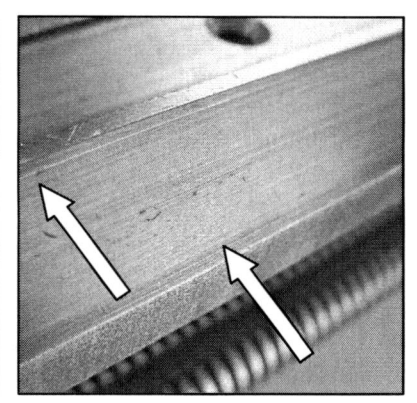

Fig. A: Soft Bed "As New"   Fig. B: Normal Wear   Fig. C: Wear Grooves

The Headstock, Spindle, Feed Screws

When checking the headstock, remove the chuck, collet or other tooling from the spindle if possible. Feel the inside of the spindle and taper for deep scoring or rough spots. Most Industrial South Bends used the threaded spindle nose on early models or the cam-lock spindles on the later models. Check the external threads and chuck registration collar for burs, chips, cracks or other damage. Check the two headstock oil cups to see if oil is present. If it is bone dry and the spindle feels tight, it may have been run dry and there may be bearing damage so it is best to keep looking. If oil is present in the bearings, loosen the belt, disengage the reversing gear from the tail of the spindle, and turn the spindle by hand. Test for rough spots and uniformity of rotation. This is done by feel so it is somewhat subjective. Spin the free cone pulley by hand. 1 to 2 full rotations is good.

If the lathe is under power, tension the belt, turn it on and listen for unusual noises in the bearings, motor or pulleys. Go through all speeds paying particular attention to how the lathe sounds at high speed. Stop the machine and check the back gear. Lift the bull gear cover and rotate the spindle until the bull gear locking pin is visible. Rotate the eccentric lever on the rear of the head until the back gears mesh. Release the bull gear from the pulley by pulling the locking pin out then down. Turn the pulley by hand and check that the rotation is smooth and that there are no missing teeth on any of the gears. Often, operators incorrectly use the back gear as a spindle lock, and the repeated stress from stuck-chuck removal can break off the teeth so check carefully for this condition.

Lubrication: South Bends typically lose some oil during operation which is normal, though you should not see huge puddles of oil around the headstock or apron. Lubricants tend to attract dirt over time so a dirty machine may also have been very well lubricated. Not a problem.

Lastly, check the feed screws for excessive play or "backlash". Typical minimum backlash is between .005 and .010" on the dial. High backlash is greater than .030" and indicates wear *may* exist or that other adjustments are required. Lastly, engage the threading half-nuts on the apron (lever up) and using the hand wheel, move the carriage back and forth to check the amount of backlash there. If you can rock the carriage left and right by more than 1/16" then there may be severe wear on the screw or half-nuts.

Other Items to Check

Check for general damage to the tool that may result in unwelcomed "Easter Eggs" being discovered later. For instance, cracked and re-welded gear covers, broken tumbler levers on the gearbox, broken or bent handles on the hand wheels, etc. If a machine has been tipped over or dropped during a move, usually these are the items that get whacked first. Dropped tools are generally the ones that get parted out on ebay®, but some are sold "as-is" so be careful. There are a number of other items to consider, however most of these are secondary in nature:

- Quick Change Gearbox
  The older lathe models had only a single tumbler handle with a spring loaded plunger on the front of the gearbox as opposed to the later models which had two tumbler levers. Double tumblers are a bit more robust in design and easier to use. There was also a "wide range" gearbox offered on the 10L which had 70 threads available instead of the typical 48, so consider these differences when pricing.
- Tailstock: Sometime lathes are sold without the tailstock because it was taken off and misplaced. Figure an extra $250 for a used tailstock if it is missing. Check the tailstock quill taper for any abuse or damage (Especially from spinning drill chucks)
- Motor: Many industrial tools are outfitted with 3 phase motors. If the lathe has a 3 phase motor and you do not have 3 phase power, figure $175 to change it to single phase. If you buy without a motor, make sure that you get the motor pulley if it is available. South Bends used very specific configurations and they are sometimes hard to find.
- Tooling: If a steady rest, follow rest, quick change tool post, thread dials or chucks come with the lathe it is a huge bonus . $300 each for a steady or chuck adds up quickly so ALWAYS ask about additional tooling up front and consider this when negotiating a price.
- When evaluating 10" or 13" lathes check the bore diameter of the spindle to see if it has the 1" diameter bore or the larger 1-3/8" bore. The 10R and early versions of the 13" had the smaller bore with a less common 1-7/8" x 8 TPI threaded spindle, sized for 2A collets instead of the more common 2-1/4" x 8 TPI sized for 5C collets. It is harder to find collets, chucks and face plates for the small bore.

One Last Thought Before You Begin

The refurbishing process described in this manual is not a Saturday afternoon task. It will take plenty of time and patience to perform all of the operations described here so if you do not have the luxury of time or if you are not comfortable undertaking the entire operation at once, it is possible to segment the operations and only do one section at a time. The drive unit, the headstock, the apron, the gearbox and the saddle are all areas where the work can be divided up cleanly. Lastly, there are many companies that specialize in selling refurbished lathes so if you're not presently up to the task; at the very least this manual will help you understand what questions to ask and how to approach the purchase of a refurbished lathe. The only word of warning on "rebuild" services is that there are some unscrupulous dealers that sell what is lovingly referred to as a "Spray-Paint Rebuild". Degreasing a machine, repainting it, cleaning up the machined surfaces with scuff pads, filing off the wear grooves on the bed and then adding some hand-scraping on the ways will often pass for a rebuilt machine to the uneducated buyer. Always look for a rebuilding service or machinery dealer that is happy to furnish you with customer references. The best self-defense is in knowing what to look for and what questions to ask.

Preparation

1. **Before you start:** Prior to disassembly of your lathe, it is essential to familiarize yourself with the components of the machine since they will be referred to many times in the accompanying text. See the diagram on page 4 of this manual. As the components are disassembled, it is very important that care is taken to identify each part and to keep all parts grouped together during cleaning and reassembly. Clear zip-lock freezer bags work especially well for collecting and protecting small oily parts, and the name of the sub-assembly can be written on the bag's white panel with a felt-tip marker for easy identification. It is highly recommended that assemblies be kept together such as "apron parts", "saddle parts", etc. Once you have your lathe in pieces, the screws, bolts & pins will all start to look the same and it is very easy to mix them up. An important goal is to complete the project without having any surplus parts left over. It should be

noted that since these lathes are not currently being produced, not all of the major components can be purchased easily, so it is important to take your time and never apply unnecessary force when taking your machine apart as there are some pieces that can be easily broken or damaged. Some parts are still available through the new South Bend Lathe Co.®, or can be found as used parts on eBay® so consult the appendix for additional information.

2. **Proper tools**:   Essential to the disassembly of your lathe is the use of the proper tools for the job. It is recommended that at minimum you have a very good set of screwdrivers which have hollow ground tips so that they do not slip out of a slotted screw head and damage it, a complete set of Allen wrenches up to 3/8", a good set of pin punches (steel and brass) from 1/16" to 1/2", a set of box wrenches up to 1-½ ", a rubber-faced dead-blow hammer, a ball-peen hammer, inner/outer snap ring pliers, ¾" brass rod, an old ½" wood chisel, a needle file, a bench vise, an arbor press and an abundance of patience. Penetrating oil may be useful for freeing up rusted or sticking parts but it should rarely be needed. CAUTION: SAFETY GLASSES ARE HIGHLY RECOMMENDED for the entire process. Compressed air is not recommended for cleaning operations.

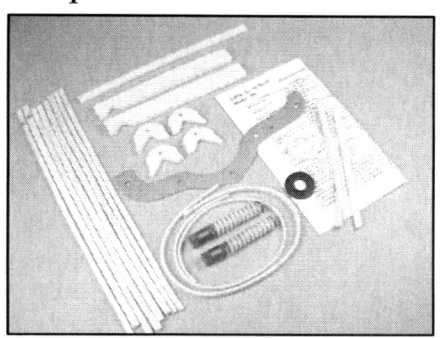 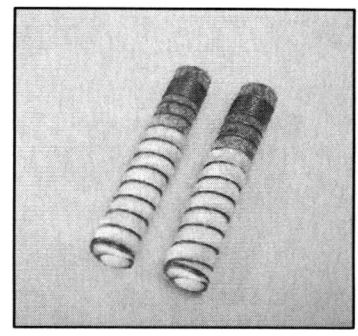 

3. **Consumables**: It is recommended that you obtain the necessary consumable parts for your lathe prior to disassembly. The most common items such as felt wicks, gaskets, way wipers, capillary oil wicks, belts, etc. can still be obtained for your South Bend® Lathe. See the appendix in the back of this manual for available sources.

4. **Cleaning Materials:** Solvents should be used with care and only outdoors. A one gallon can of automotive carburetor cleaner works very well for removing oil and grease that has solidified on small parts and most brands come with a small parts basket that helps keep all of the smaller items together during the soak.

Sequence of Operations

...or "how to eat the elephant". The disassembly sequence for the lathe is divided into 4 main sections and is performed in numerical order to avoid minor conflicts with other assemblies but the order is not absolutely critical. Do what works best for you. The index in the front of the book is also listed by section for ease in locating particular operations. Note that on some 10L lathes the headstock must be removed before the gearbox because of an obstructed mounting screw. See the instructions for details.

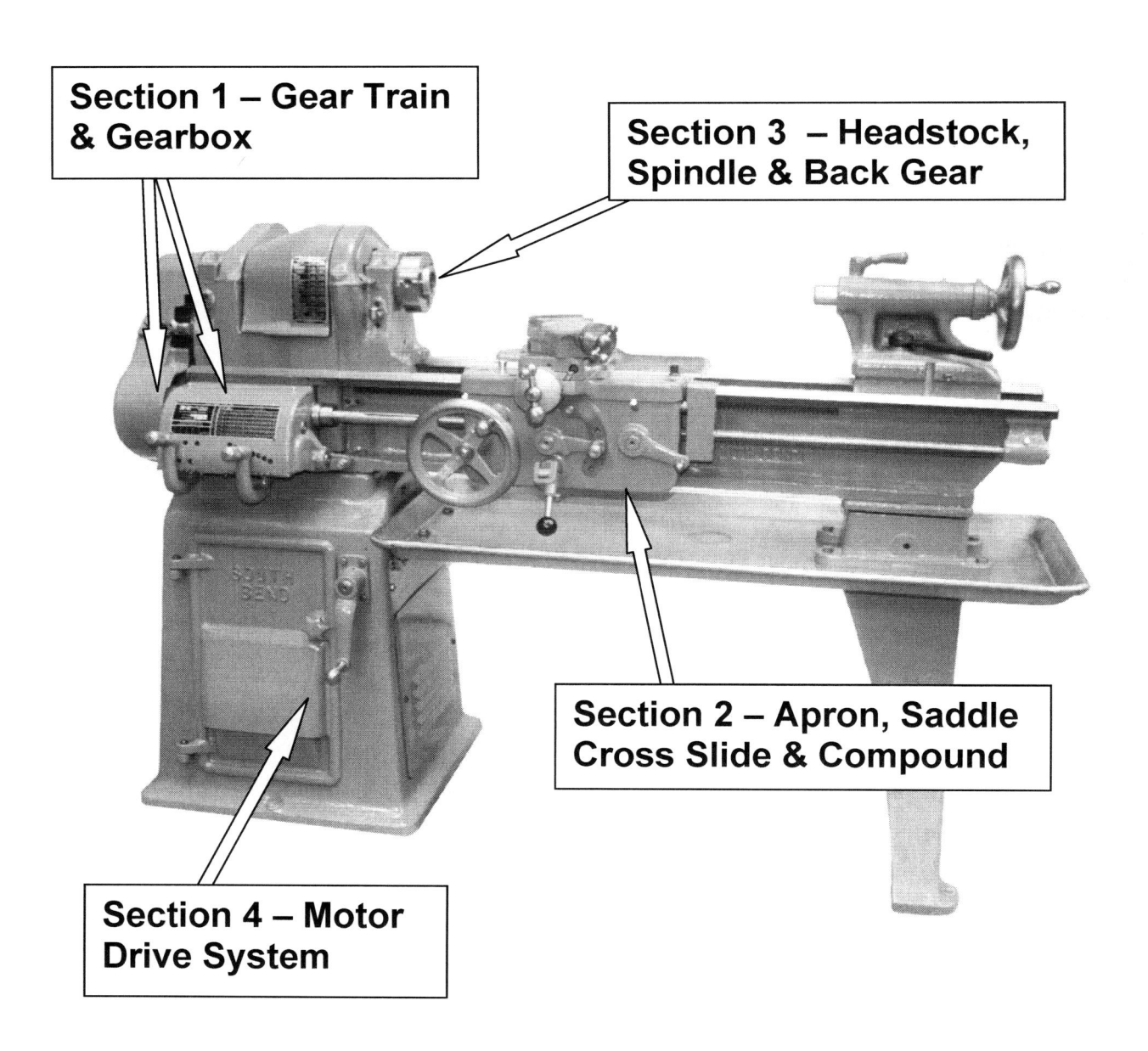

Section 1 – Gear Train & Gearbox

Section 3 – Headstock, Spindle & Back Gear

Section 2 – Apron, Saddle Cross Slide & Compound

Section 4 – Motor Drive System

Lathe Disassembly

Machine Preparation

To prepare the lathe for disassembly, the power source must be completely disconnected from the lathe. Note that all fasteners are right-hand thread **unless noted**. (Technical terms: Righty Tighty, Lefty Loosey)

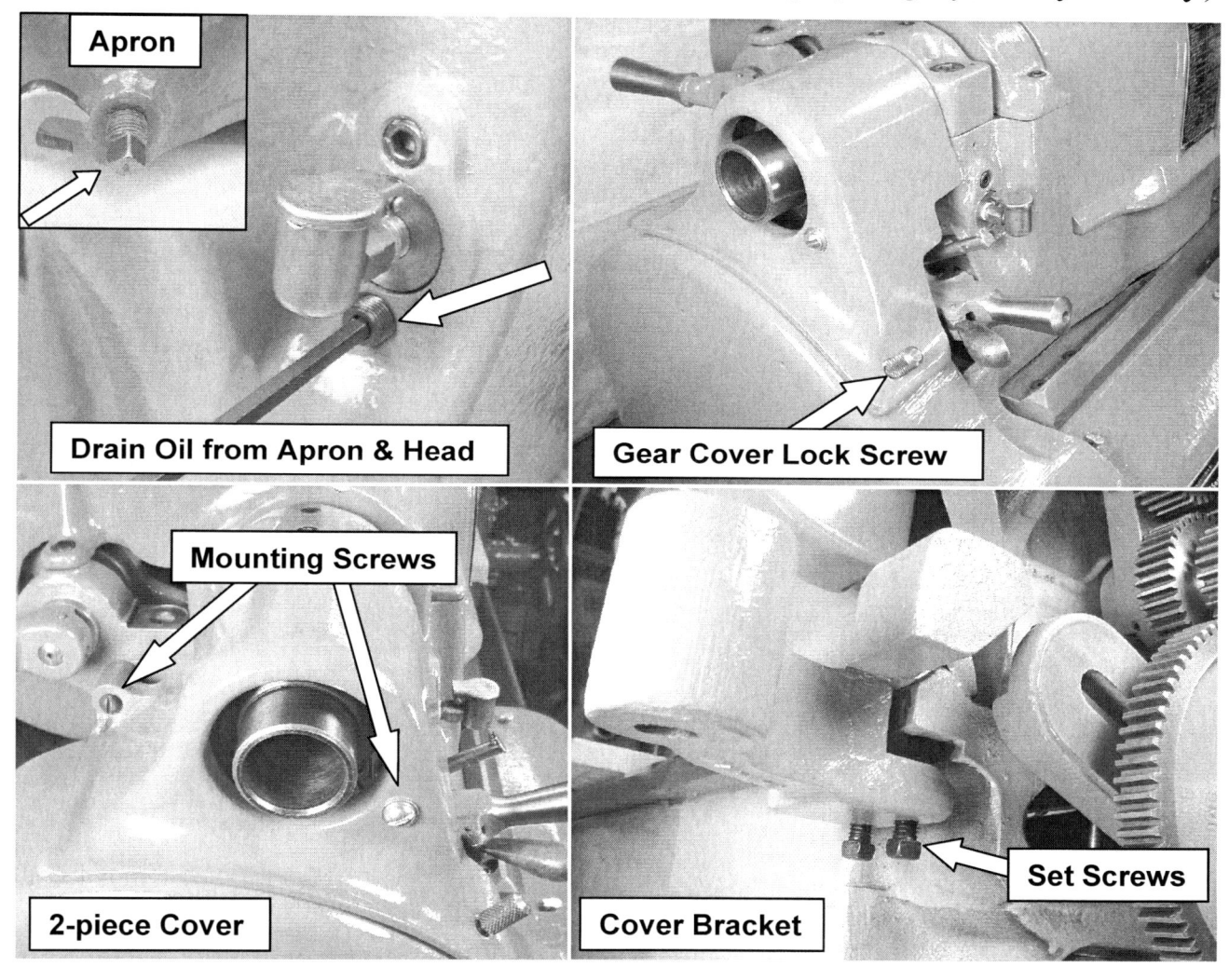

Apron

Drain Oil from Apron & Head

Gear Cover Lock Screw

Mounting Screws

2-piece Cover

Cover Bracket

Set Screws

1. Remove the oil drain plug on the bottom of the apron and drain the oil into a cup. Repeat for the two lower drain plugs on the headstock. Remove the gear cover lock screw, swing the cover open and lift the hinge pin off of the cover bracket. To remove the cover bracket loosen the two square head set screws on the bottom of the bracket and slide it off of the bed. If your lathe has the gear bracket bolted to the cover bracket, see step 4. On lathes with a 2-piece gear cover, take off the upper cover by removing the two machine mounting screws securing it to the headstock.

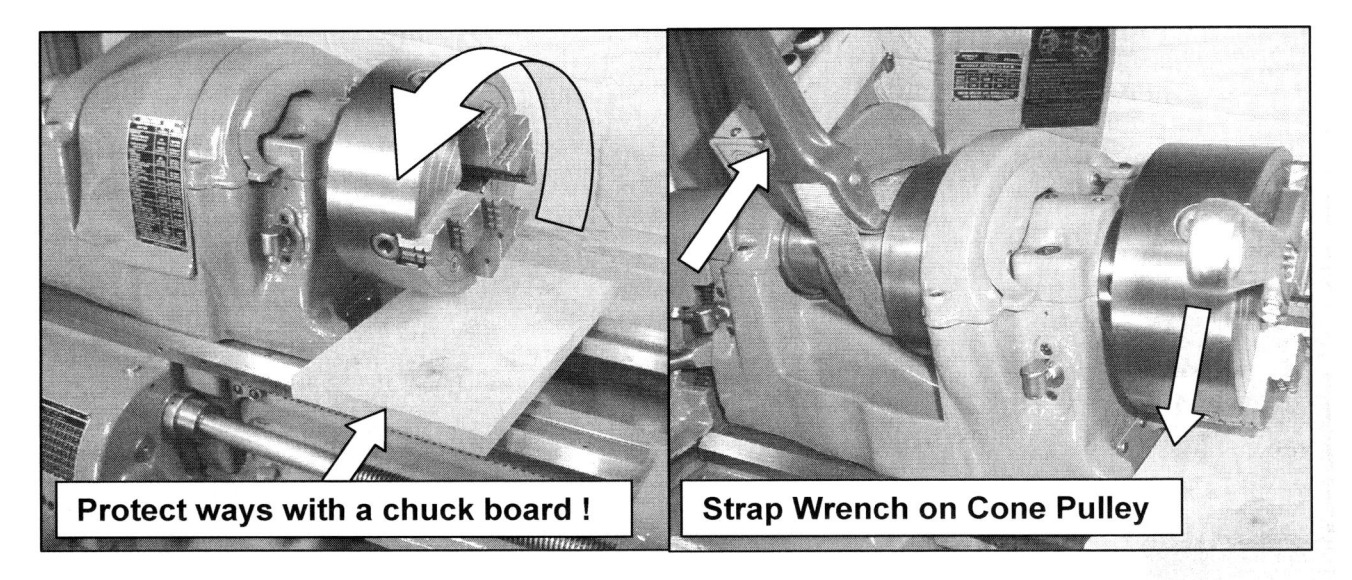

Protect ways with a chuck board ! | **Strap Wrench on Cone Pulley**

2. Remove the chuck from the spindle and any other accessories such as carriage stops or rack mounts from the bed of the lathe. If the spindle has a threaded nose and the chuck is seized, place a large strap wrench on the cone pulley as shown. Mount a piece of hexagonal stock in the 3-jaw chuck and unscrew with a large wrench. *DO NOT* use the back-gear as a spindle lock as the stress can result in broken teeth on the gears. To remove a cam-lock style chuck, rotate the 3 square socket cams to the "unlock" position.

Serial #

Lead Screw Bracket

3. Loosen the tailstock locking nut and slide the tailstock off of the bed. Remove the right-side lead screw support bracket by removing the two machine screws on the top of the lathe bed and sliding the bracket off of the lead screw. Note that the lathe serial number is stamped on the bed in this same location. We're now ready to remove the gear train.

Section 1: Gear Train

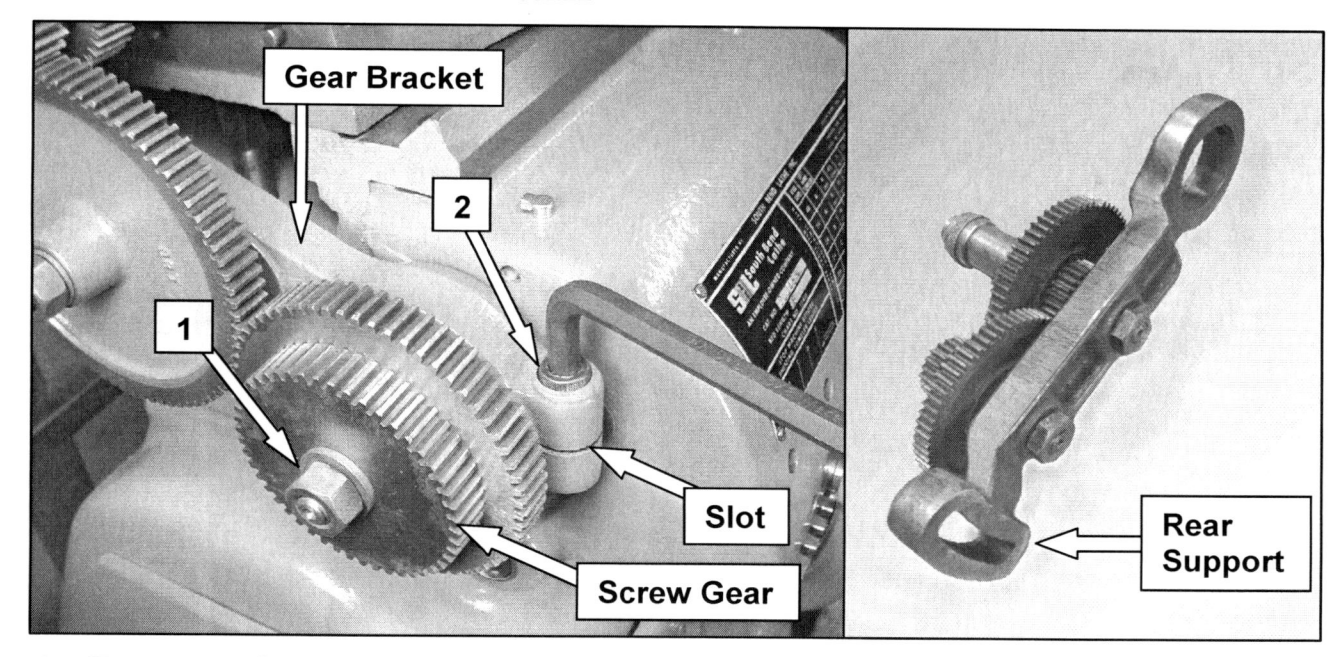

4. Remove the screw gear nut (1) and the screw gears from the left end of the gearbox. Loosen the gear bracket locking bolt (2). If the bracket has a rear support (above right) remove the bolt securing it to the bed mount. Slide the gear bracket from the gearbox mounting hub. It may be necessary to lightly wedge a screwdriver in the bracket slot to loosen the bracket.

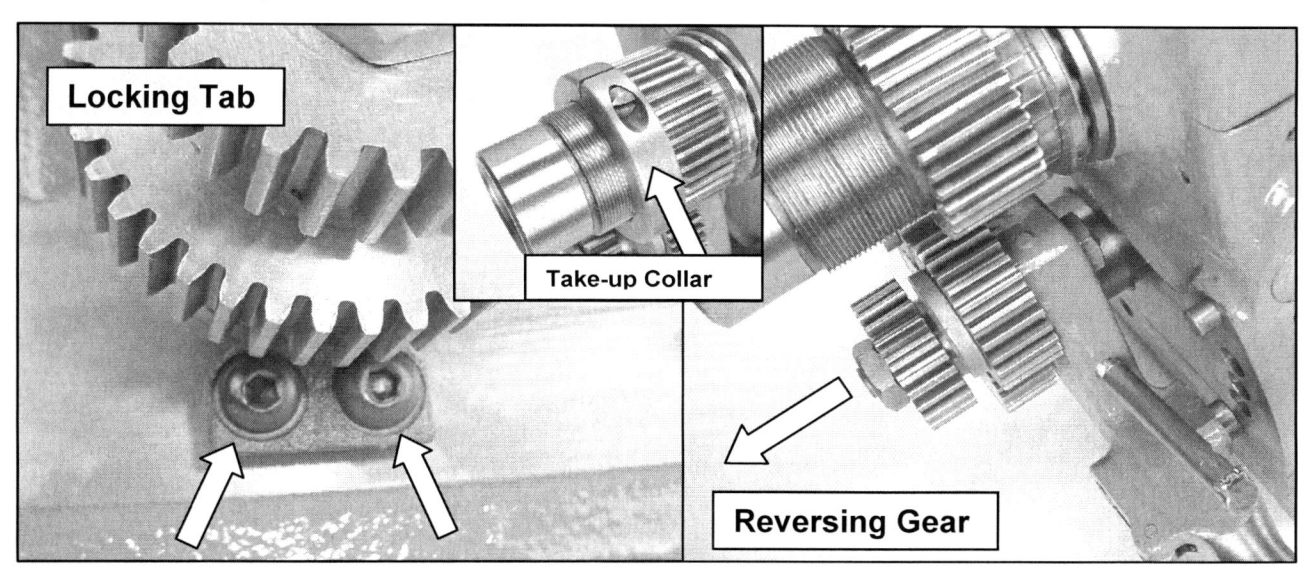

5. Remove the reversing gear bracket by first removing the two cap screws and locking tab below the bracket. If the spindle has an outboard take-up collar as shown in the photo, loosen the lock screw and unscrew the collar. Now slide the reversing gear assembly out of the headstock.

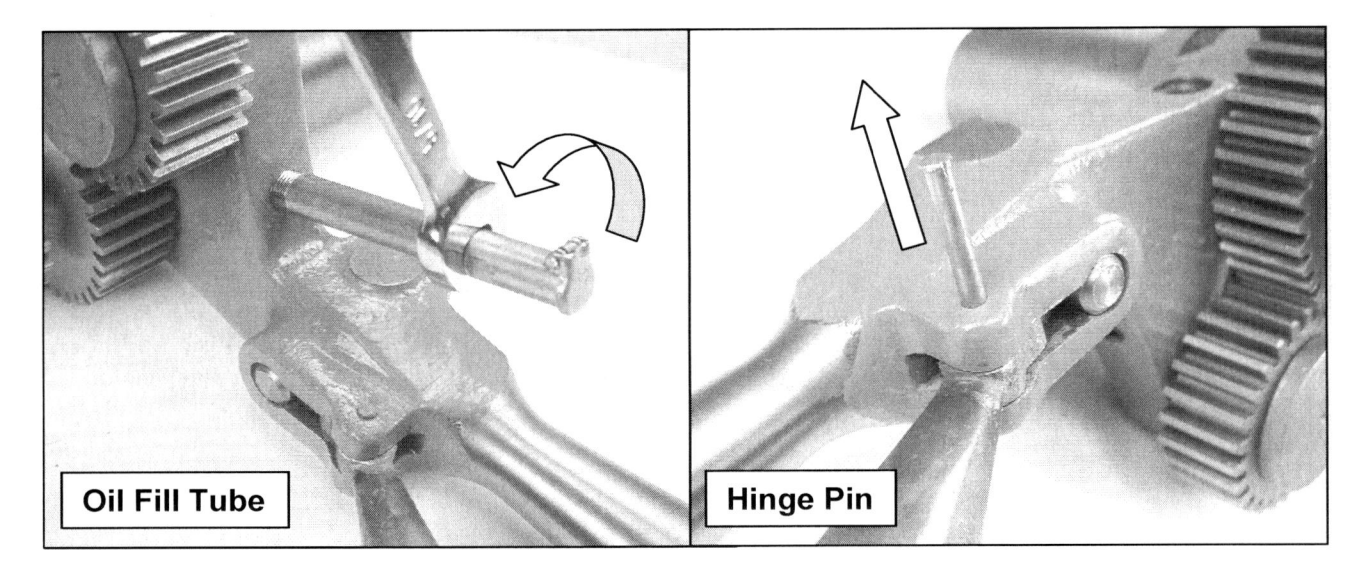

Oil Fill Tube

Hinge Pin

6. **Reversing Gear Disassembly:** To avoid damage, first remove the threaded oil fill tube from the reverse bracket body by using a box wrench on the tube flats. If there are no flats, use soft-jaw locking pliers to grip the tube (be careful not to crush the tube). Remove the bronze reverse latch by driving the hinge pin out with a 3/32" pin punch.

Reverse Latch

Stud Gear

7. Slide the reverse latch out of the slot in the latch plunger and push the plunger out of the reverse bracket. Remove the stud gear from the main reverse shaft by inserting a strip of hardwood into the gear teeth to hold the gears static, and then remove the stud gear locking nut. Slide the stud gear off of the shaft. If tight, it may be necessary to use a gear puller.

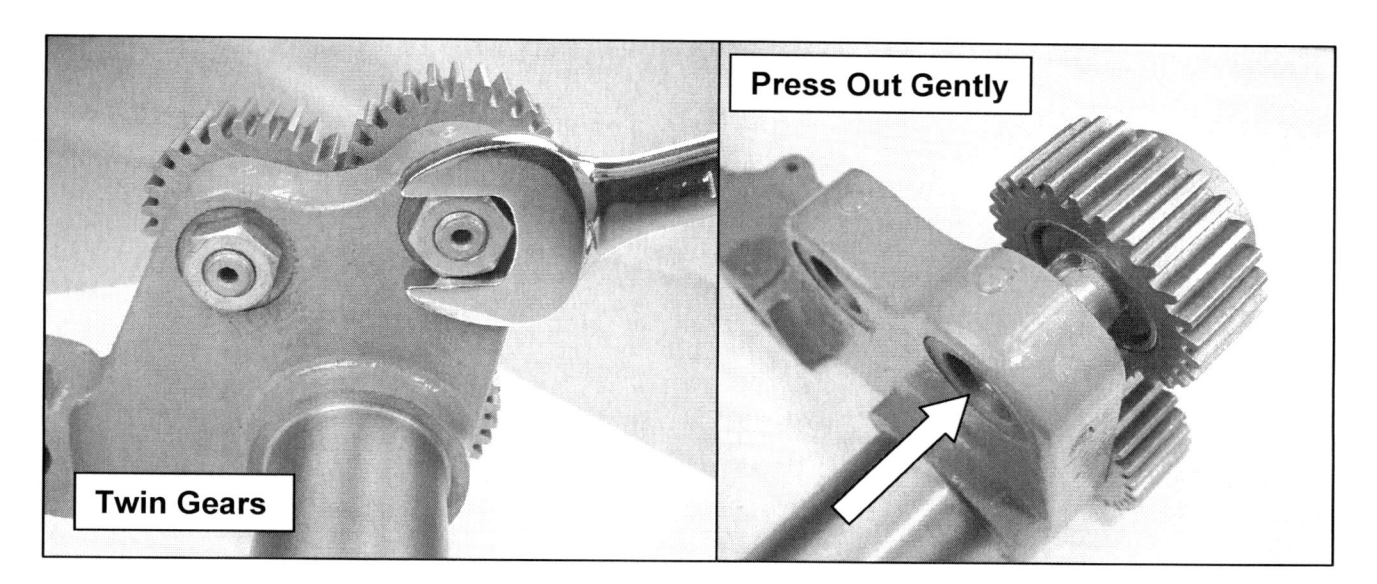

8. Remove the "twin" reversing gears by first removing the two locking nuts on the rear face of the bracket. Use an arbor press to gently press the two twin gear shafts out of the bracket. It is easy to damage these shallow threads so be especially careful not to ding these up during removal.

9. The main reversing shaft is keyed to the reversing gear and is a tight press fit. Do not try to drive the shaft out with a punch or hammer as the threads can be damaged easily. Place the entire assembly into an arbor press, insert a brass disk to protect the threaded nose and then press the reversing shaft out of the reverse gear bracket. Now that the bracket has been stripped, remove the old felt from all of the oil passages using a stiff wire with a hook on the end and a small pair of forceps if available.

Set Screw

Drill out plug & tap hole

Dowel Pin Plug

10.   **Reversing Gear Assembly:** Clean all parts thoroughly in a suitable solvent making sure all oil passages are clear. In order to fully access the oil passages for cleaning and wick installation, we typically drill out the thin metal plug on the underside of the reverse bracket. Depending on the bracket size, this hole may then be tapped 3/8"-16 or 7/16"-14 thread to accommodate a short socket set screw which serves as a removable plug. Use Teflon® tape on the threads to seal the reservoir. Drive the small 1/8" dowel pin plug (shown above) all the way through the hole and out of large shaft opening using a long pin punch. This pushes out the old wick as well.

11.   Install new Type 3 felt (Type 1 on 10L) in the twin gear shaft grooves as shown, slide the gear over the felt and then trim the felt flush with the inside face of the gear. Lubricate the end of the felt with several drops of Type C oil and turn the gear a few times to distribute the oil film.

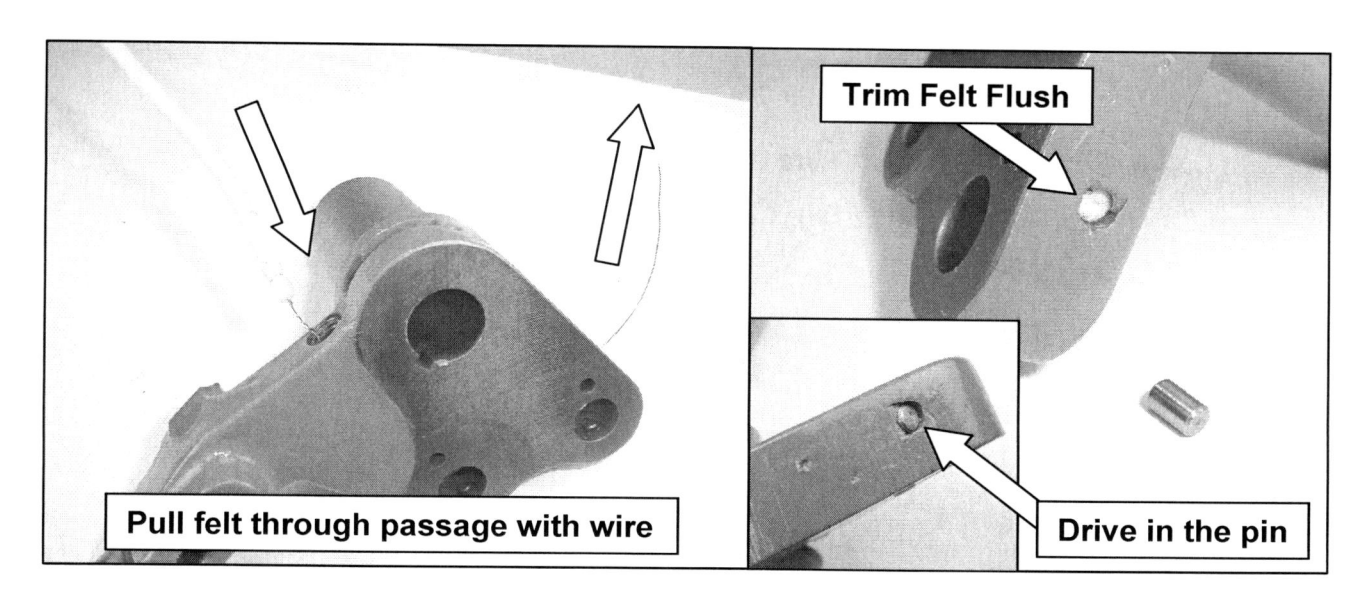

Trim Felt Flush

Pull felt through passage with wire

Drive in the pin

12. Feed an 8" length of flexible wire through the small dowel pin hole and fish it out through the larger hole that was threaded earlier. Twist the wire tightly around the end of a 3" length of Type 7 round felt wicking. Pull the wire and felt through the passage and trim off flush with the face of the bracket. Drive the small dowel pin back into the hole so that is it just flush with the surface. The felt tail will hang down into the reservoir.

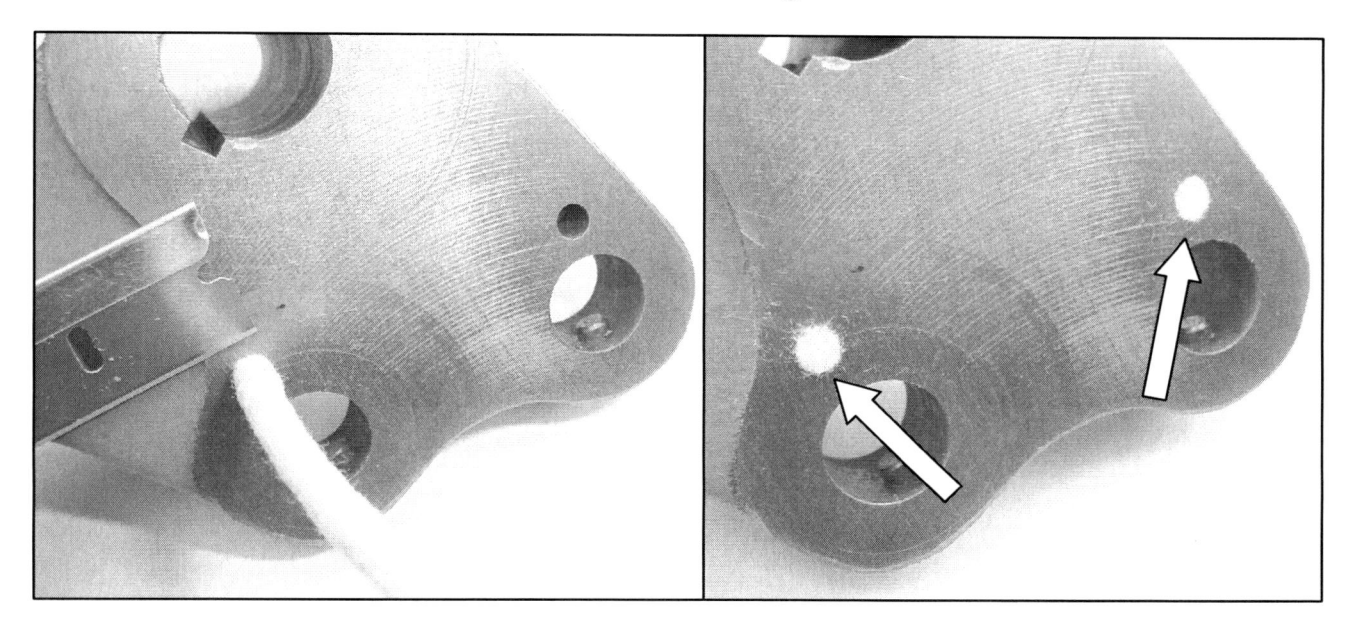

13. Twist a length of Type 7 felt into the two holes in the face of the reversing bracket. These two plugs lubricate the twin gears and feed oil from the felt you just installed. Once the felt has bottomed out against the felt inside the passage, trim the end off flush with the face. A sharp razor blade works well here.

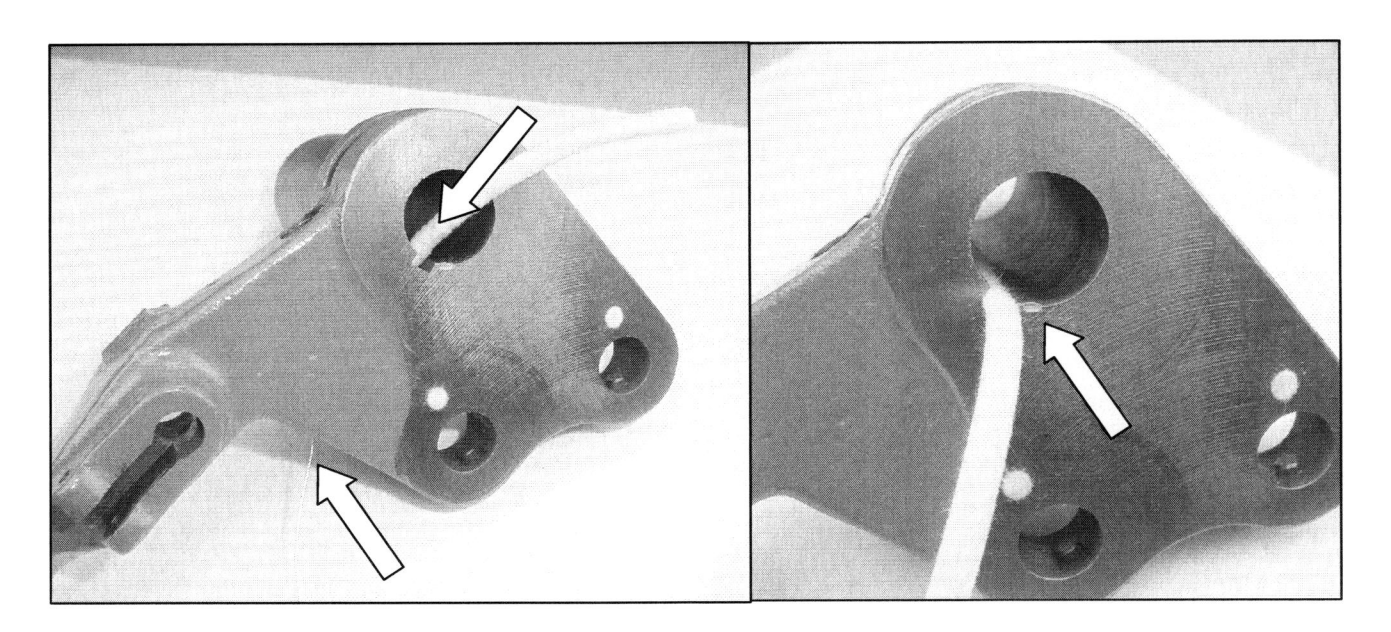

14.   Now tie another length of Type 7 felt to a wire and pull it through the hole which is located in the keyway adjacent to the main shaft. Pull until the end is flush with the keyway surface and trim the opposite end flush with the hole that is used for the oil fill tube.   Insert a length of Type 3 felt into the keyway. Leave the wick long on the twin gear side.

15.   Insert the reversing gear shaft into the bracket being careful not to catch the wick. Trim the wick flush with the machined surface. Install the stepped key as shown above. Lubricate the wick with Type C oil and turn the shaft several times to distribute the oil.

 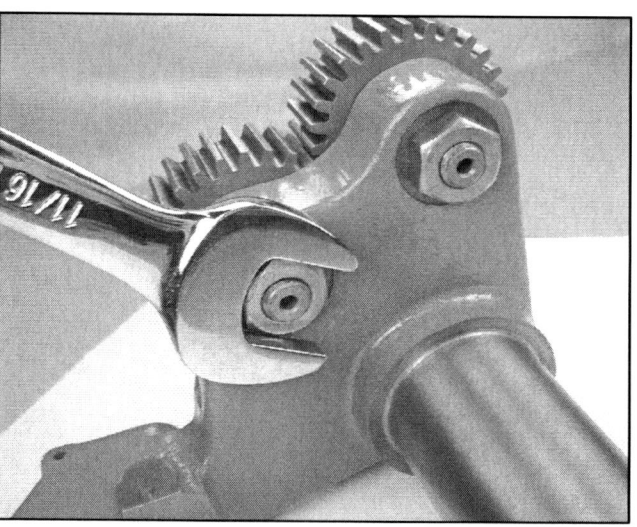

16. Press the reversing gear onto the shaft with an arbor press. Make sure that there is clearance between the gear face and the back of the gear and that it turns freely. Align and install the twin gears in the reverse bracket. Tighten the lock nuts.

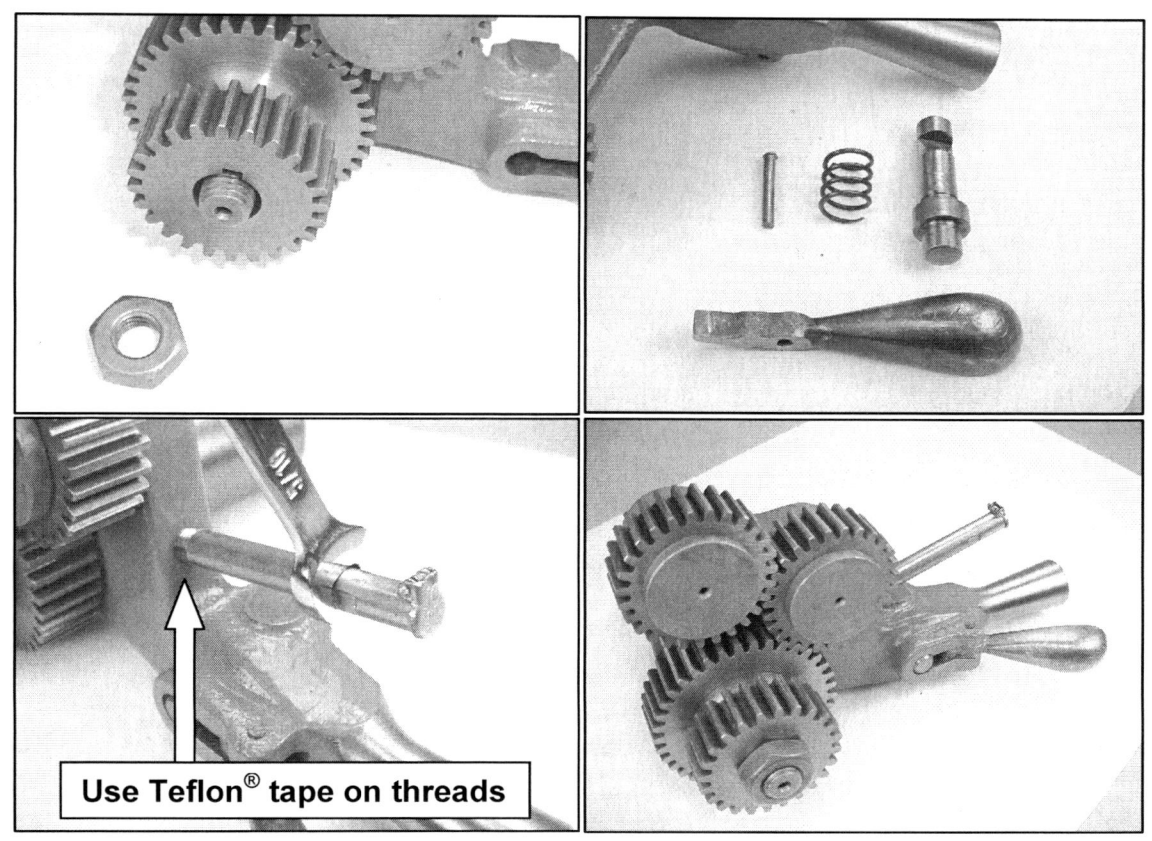

Use Teflon® tape on threads

17. Mount the stud gear & lock nut. Reassemble the reversing latch. Thread the oil fill tube into the body and align the cap so that the hinge is at the top. Fill the reservoir with Type C machine oil to soak the wicks.

Double Tumbler Gearbox - Disassembly

18. Rotate the lead screw so that the keyway is pointing down. On the lower right side of the gearbox, remove the gearbox mounting bolt first and then the threaded support bushing. Hold the gearbox securely and remove the 3 screws securing it to the bed. Note: On some model 10L's, the gearbox cannot be removed prior to the removal of the head because of one partially obstructed mounting screw as shown. If such is the case, jump to section 3, remove the head and then return to this step.

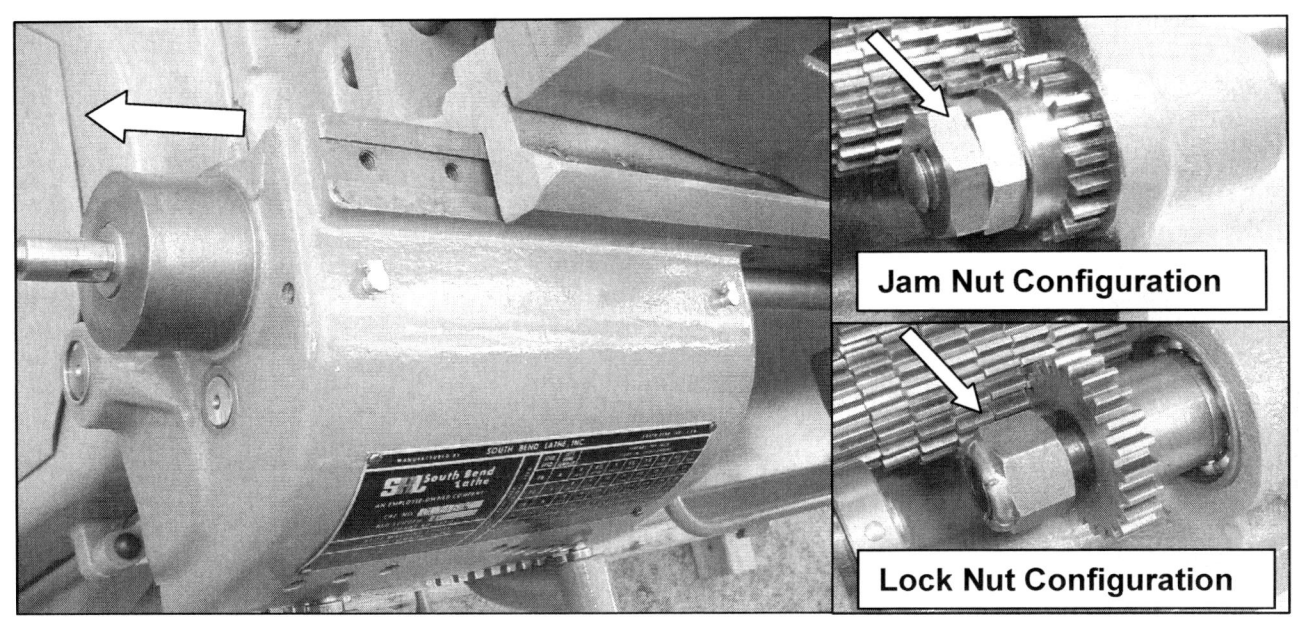

19. Slide the gearbox to the left until the lead screw exits the worm gear in the apron. Place the Gearbox front side down on a soft surface. Using two box wrenches, remove the jam nuts from the lead screw (or a single nut with thread locking collar) and slide it out of the gearbox.

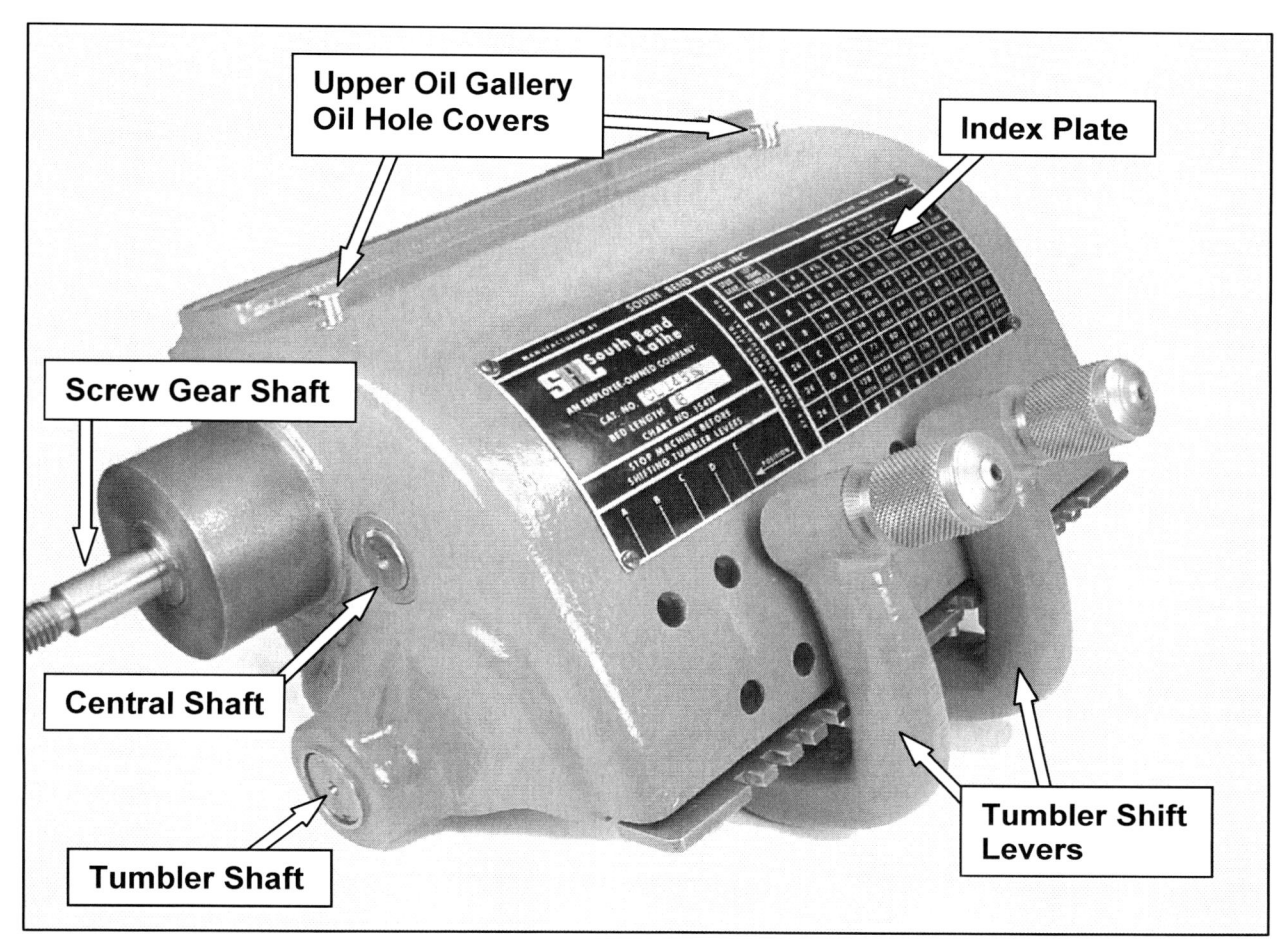

20. The double tumbler quick change (QC) gear box. Note terminology. Remove the screws holding the index plate. If drive screws are used see step 43 for additional details on how to remove the drive screws safely.

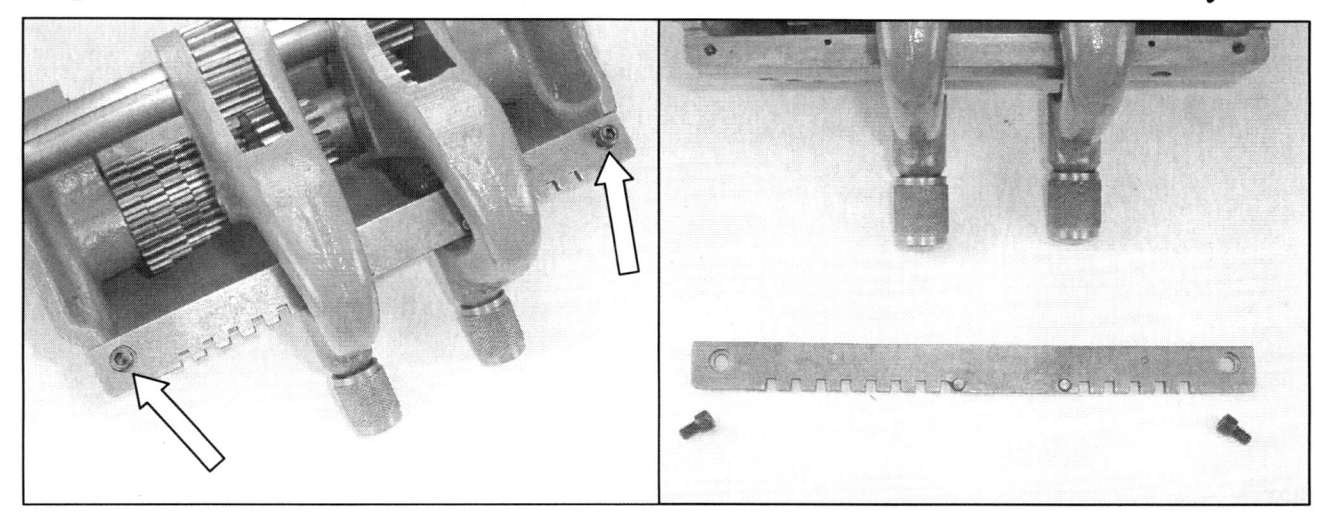

21. From the bottom of the gearbox, remove the two screws holding the tumbler lever guide bar to the base. Some screws are slotted, some are socket cap screws. Do not remove the two small dowel pins in the guide.

Felts

Drive Out This Direction Only!

22.   Using a 3/32" pin punch, remove the straight dowel pin from the left bearing boss which retains the tumbler gear shaft. Remove the 2 felt oil wicks from the slots in both sides of the shaft. Drive the shaft out the **LEFT** side of the casting (the side with the retaining pin) and remove the tumbler levers. The shaft cannot be removed through the right side because the keyways in the shaft are not cut the entire length of the shaft. Do not try driving it out in the opposite direction or damage will occur.

Gear Tree

Taper Pin

Felt Wick

Drive Out This Direction Only!

23.   On the central gear shaft, rotate the gear tree to find the small end of the **taper pin** located in the widest pinion gear. Using a 1/8" pin punch, drive the pin out partially. Rotate the shaft 180° and pull out the pin. Remove the felt oil wick on the end of the shaft. Drive the shaft out of the **LEFT** side of the casting using a 3/8" brass punch. Keep gears in the original order and position by stringing them together on a length of wire.

Drive Shaft Out This Direction Only!

24. Turn the gearbox around. For the screw gear shaft, remove the taper pin from the collar. Insert a brass rod through the hole for the lead-screw in the right side of the casting and tap the shaft out through the left side of the casting. It can only be removed in this direction.

25. If the bronze bearings are worn such that the shafts have excessive play, new bearings may be pressed in using a drift with a shoulder fitted to the bearing. The bronze bearing for the screw gear shaft is retained by a straight dowel pin which must be removed with a 3/32" punch if the bearing is to be replaced. Drive out the pin via the access hole indicated. If the ball bearing for the lead screw is being replaced, drive the old one out of the recess with a steel rod and press the new one into the housing. Press on the outer race only when installing. Gearbox disassembly is complete.

Double Tumbler Gearbox - Assembly

Oil Distribution Gallery   **Right Side Oil Passages**

26. Clean all components with a suitable solvent making sure to thoroughly clean all the oil passages that supply the bearings. If you are painting the gearbox refer to the appendix for tips and suggestions. Remove the old felt oil retention plugs or felt strips. Some lathe vintages used keyways with Type 3 felt strips, while or models used replaceable bronze bushings. The oil retentions plugs were typically 3/16" diameter Type 7 felt. Flush out the oil gallery especially well since it is enclosed.

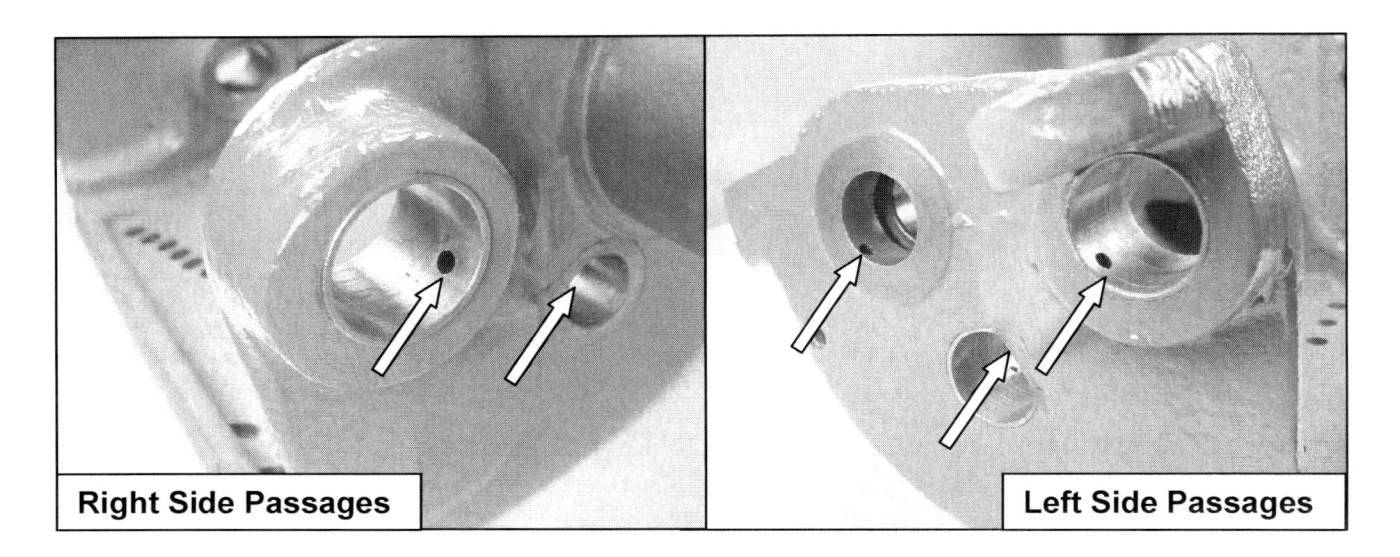

Right Side Passages   **Left Side Passages**

27. It is suggested that you clean all of the oil passages with a brass rifle bore cleaning brush and a strong solvent. Push cotton pipe cleaners or cloth patches soaked in solvent though the passages to do the final cleaning.

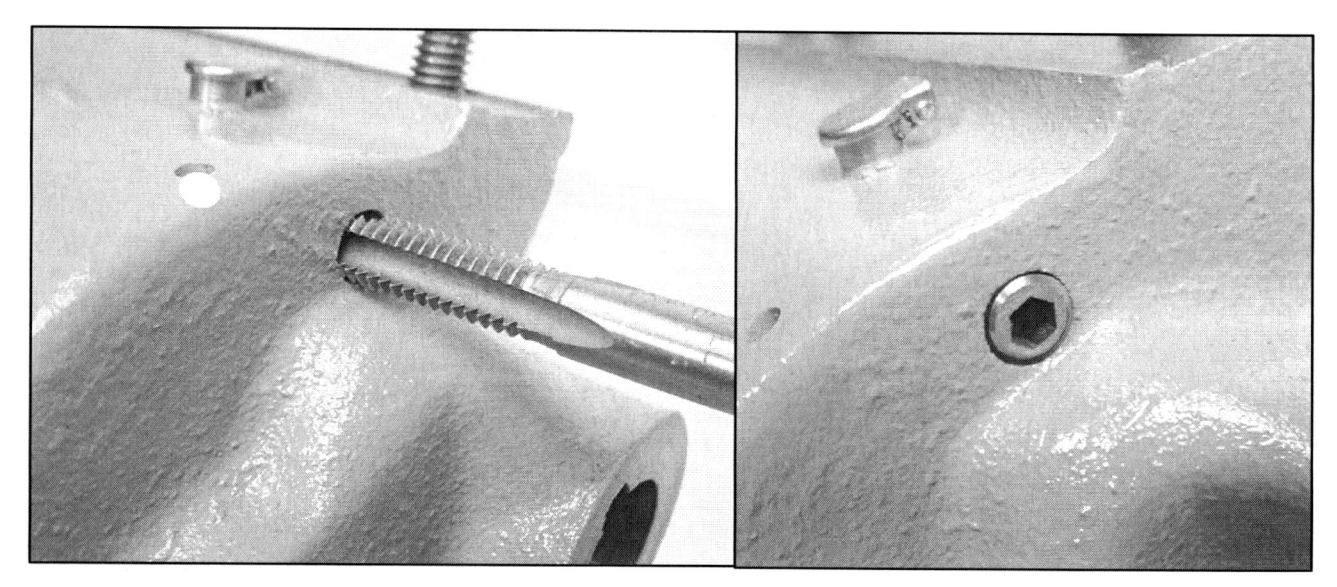

28. The Oil Gallery has a pressed-in plug on each end of the casting. To thoroughly clean the gallery and to provide future access, it is easy to drill out these plugs, thread the holes with a 5/16"-18 or 7/16"-14 hand tap (depending on the gearbox size) and then install a ¼" long socket set screw as a plug. Make sure that the set screw does not cover any oil passages located on the each end of the oil gallery. Grind the length of the set screw to fit if necessary & use Teflon tape on the threads to prevent leaks.

29. Install ¼" lengths of Type 7 felt in the LOWER end of the oil passages flush with the surface. The plug controls oil flow from the gallery. Oil tends to leak out of the gearbox more quickly without these plugs. It will not stop all oil seepage, just slow it down. If the felt is a bit too large, stretch the cord along its length to reduce the diameter prior to installing.

Check Oil Hole Alignment During Insertion !

30.   To fit new bronze bearing on any shaft, measure the oil hole location on the top side of the bronze bearing and drill the new bearing to match. Use a C-clamp or a press to seat the bearing in the casting making sure the oil hole is aligned with the passage above.

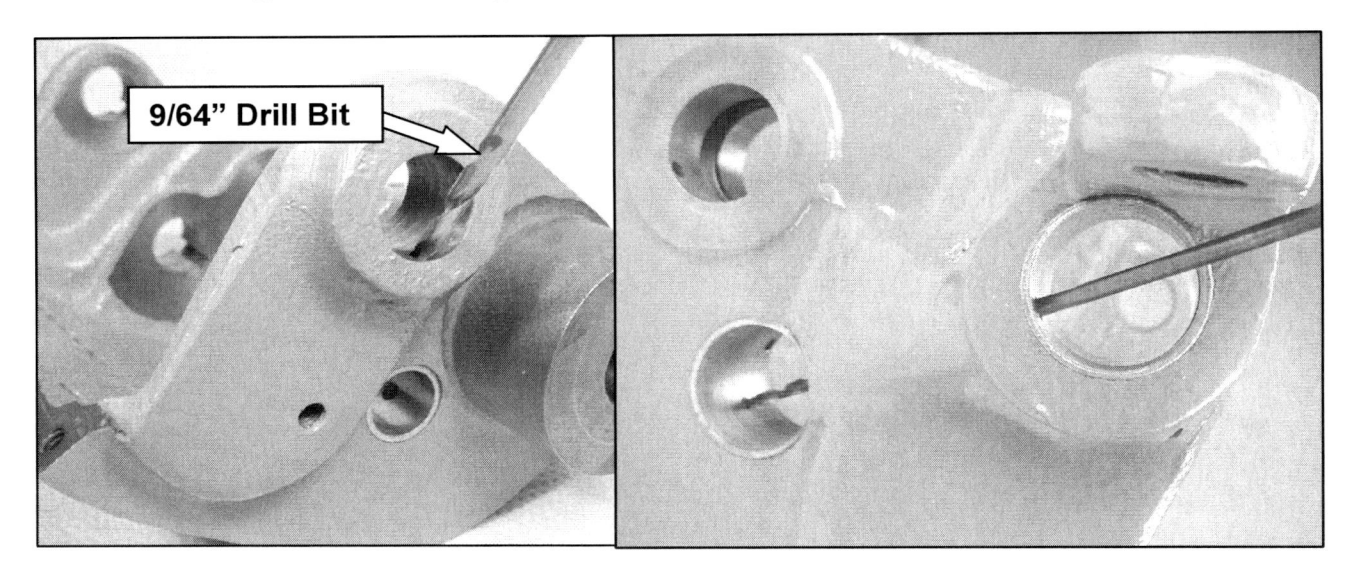

9/64" Drill Bit

31.   It is easiest to drill some of the oil holes in the bearing after it is in place using the oil passage as a drill guide for the adjacent bearing (usually the hole is 9/64" or 3/16" diameter). Be careful not to damage the opposite side of the bearing when the drill bit punches through. If the shaft that mates with the bearing is heavily damaged from abuse (rather common), measure the shaft carefully and use the lathe to make a new shaft later. You can install the shaft the next time you clean the gearbox. The lathe is one of the few machine tools can repair itself.

Oil Control Felt Plug (Hidden)

Felt Wick

Keyed compound gear (press fit)

Insert Shaft

Free-Spinning Compound Gear

32. Replace the felt wick in the screw gear shaft with Type 1 Felt. Stretch the felt slightly along its length if it does not seat easily or if it stands above the shaft diameter. Insert a Type 7 oil control plug into the top oil passage. Lubricate the wicks with Type B machine oil. Make sure the woodruff key is seated properly in the shaft and push the screw gear shaft in from the left and assemble the gears onto the shaft as shown.

33. It may be necessary to tap the threaded end carefully with a plastic mallet to seat the shaft in the keyed gear. Once the shaft protrudes through the bearing install the collar, align the taper pin hole properly (large hole on collar aligns with big hole on shaft). Drop the taper pin in place and drive it into position with a pin punch.

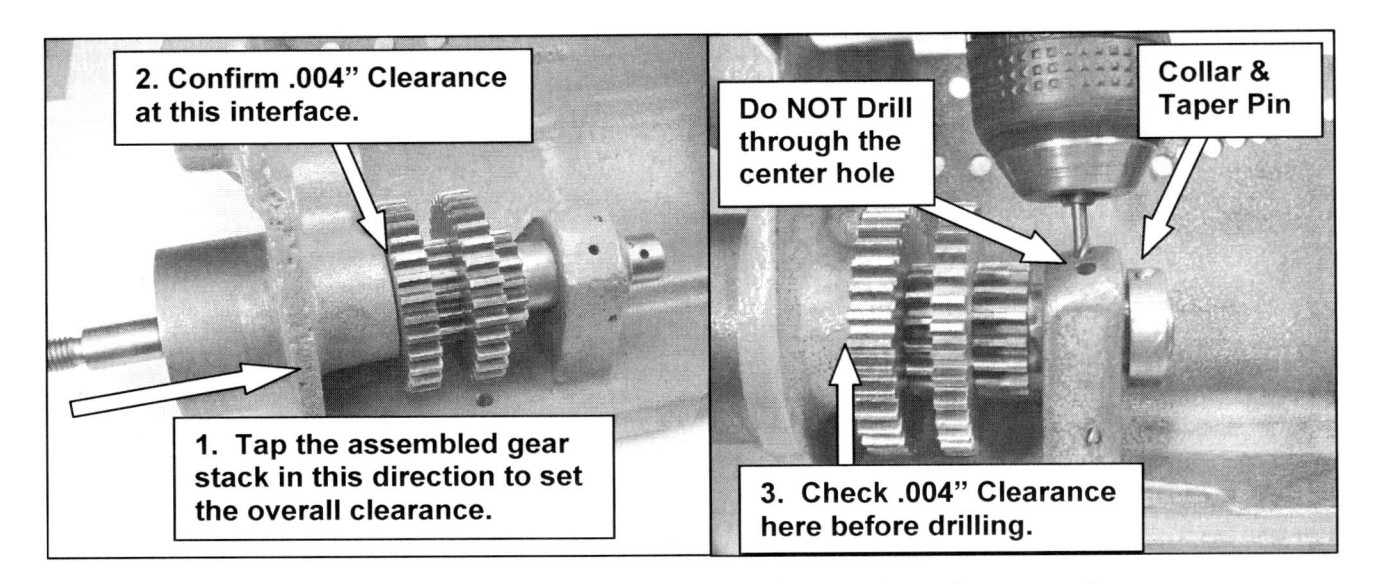

2. Confirm .004" Clearance at this interface.

1. Tap the assembled gear stack in this direction to set the overall clearance.

Do NOT Drill through the center hole

Collar & Taper Pin

3. Check .004" Clearance here before drilling.

34. If you are not replacing the bronze sleeve bearing on the screw gear, skip this step as it is not necessary. When replacing this bearing, the axial position of the gears plus the clearance between the gears and the cast housing is determined by the position of the bronze bearing so position is important to prevent the gears from binding after installation. Since the position of this bearing is determined solely by the dowel pin, the slot for this dowel pin must be drilled in place once the bearing is seated in the correct position. First, match the length of the new bearing to the old bearing exactly, check clearance of the free spinning gear and assemble as before. Make sure that the keyed compound gear is seated tightly against the shoulder on the screw gear shaft. With a brass hammer, tap the screw gear shaft from the threaded end until a .004" feeler gage just fits between the keyed compound gear and the face of the boss on the casting. The feeler gage should not be pinched tightly between the surfaces. Remove the feeler gage and slide the shaft to the left by hand and check for .004" clearance between the free spinning compound gear and the bearing. If everything turns freely, fix the position of the bearing by drilling tangentially through the edge using the existing holes in the casting as a guide. Lock the bearing in position by driving in the dowel pin through the hole. Do not drill through the center hole shown above as it was only used during the lathe manufacturing process to connect the oil gallery to this bearing. If you drill through this hole, then the oil will run out as this is the path of least resistance.

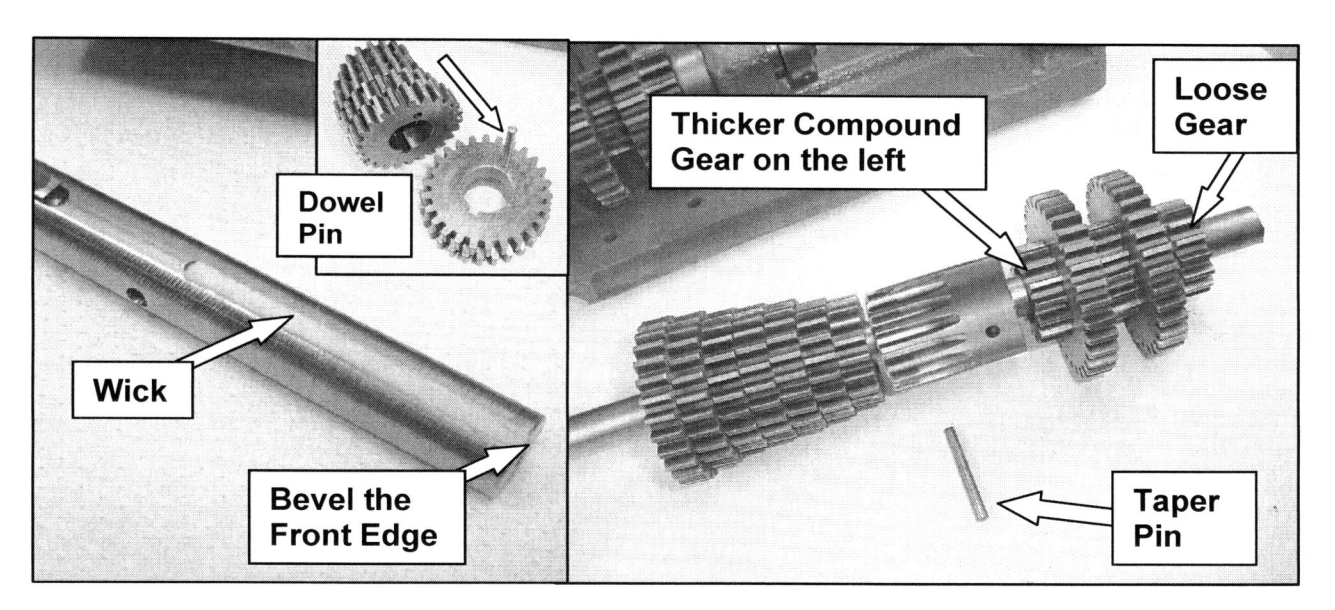

35. Press a new Type 1 felt wick into the slot on then central shaft. Lubricate the wick with Type B oil. Insert the long dowel pin into the gear stack and make sure the keyways line up correctly. Mark the gear keyway positions on the edge of each gear with a felt tip marker for reference and insert the central shaft. Note the position of the loose gear and the two different compound gears above. The shaft insertion takes some patience because of the number of shoulders, gears & keyways so start slowly on the left side work to the right and making sure each gear slides over the key correctly and that the shaft shoulders are not getting stuck on the housing.

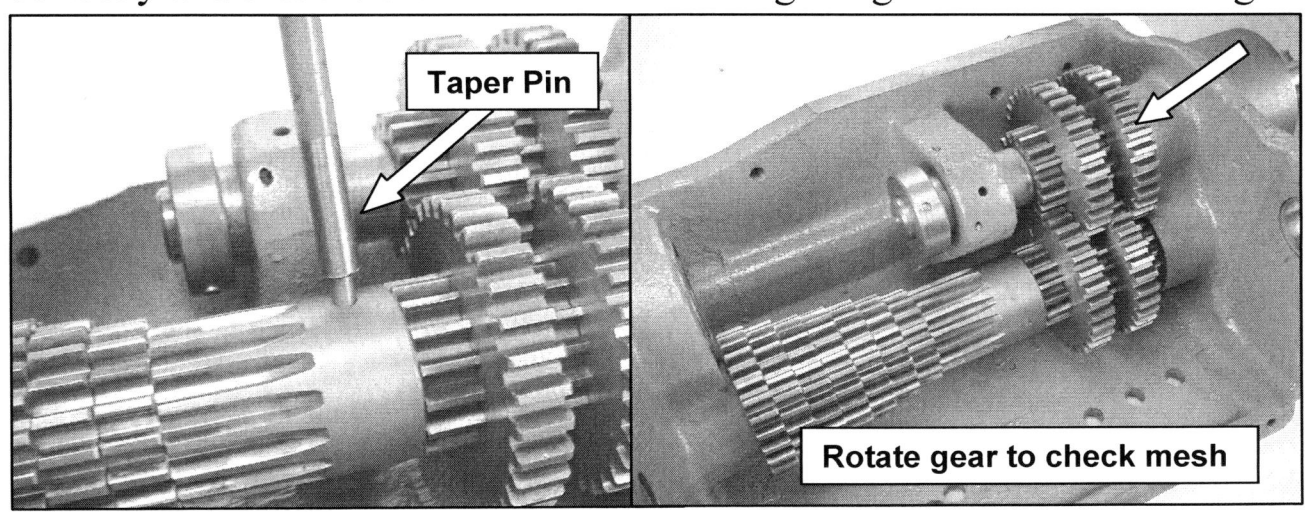

36. After all gears are aligned properly, install the taper pin. Check the rotation and meshing of the gears by turning the large keyed gear on the screw gear shaft nearest the casting. This gear should turn easily by hand so if it does not, check for misalignment or burrs on the gear teeth.

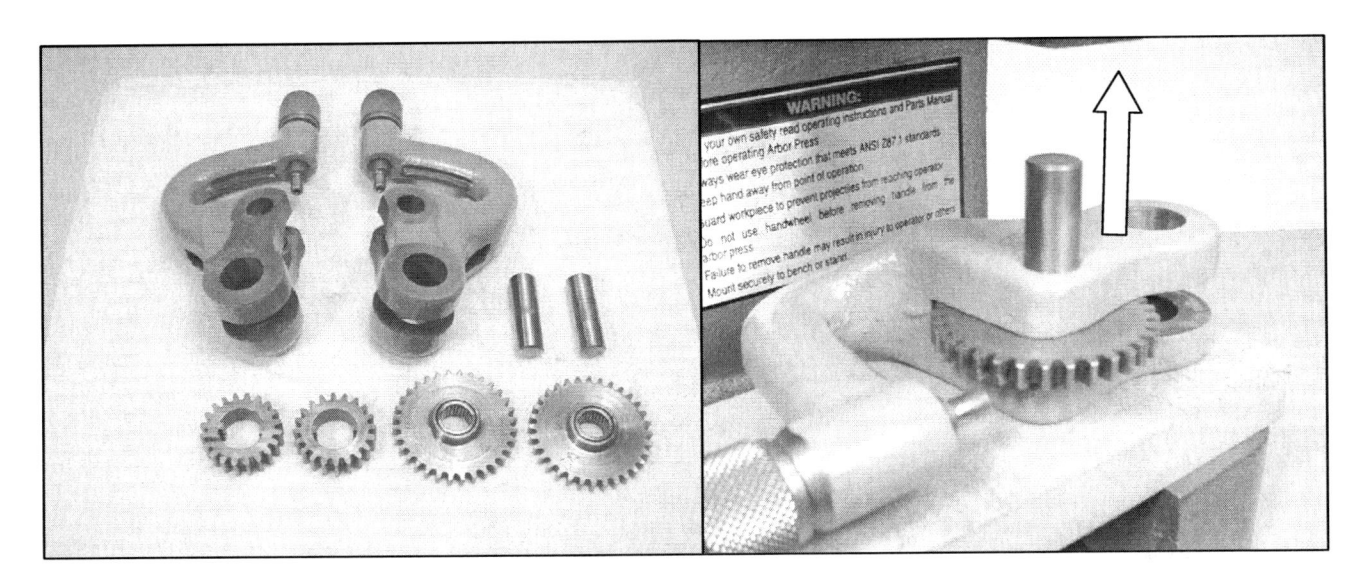

37. Remove the tumbler gears by pressing out the solid steel pin with an arbor press or a brass pin punch. The tumbler gears rides on precision ground needle bearings which need to be cleaned and greased prior to re-assembly. We do not recommend disassembling the knurled plunger handle since locating the dowel pin on the knob and removing it without damage is very tricky and there is very little to clean inside. Soaking in solvent and lubricating it usually sufficient.

38. If the needle bearings are damaged or do not turn freely and need to be replaced, press out the old bearing with an arbor press. Clean and lubricate the new bearings with Super-Lube® Teflon® grease and then press the new bearing into place. Make sure that the end of the bearing is flush with or slightly below the gear faces after insertion.

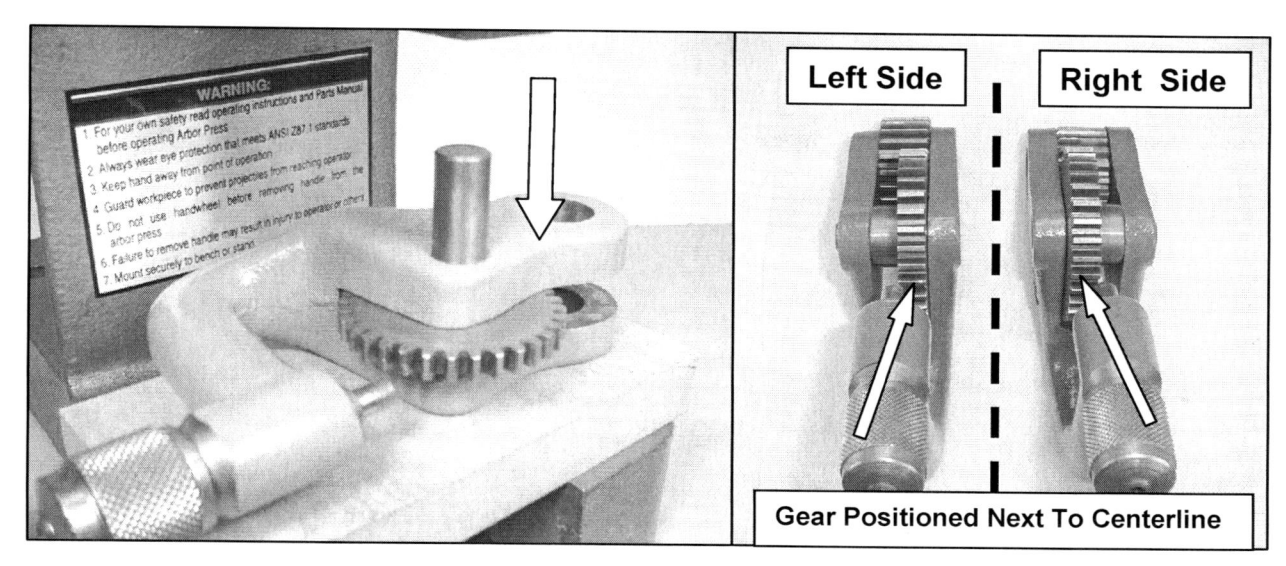

Left Side | Right Side

Gear Positioned Next To Centerline

39. Align the gear inside the tumbler housing and carefully press in the steel axle pin through the needle bearing. Make sure the pin is seated slightly below the surface of the lever boss. (Note the position of the left and right tumbler gear inside each lever relative to the centerline of the gearbox. The big gear goes on the inside as viewed from the front.

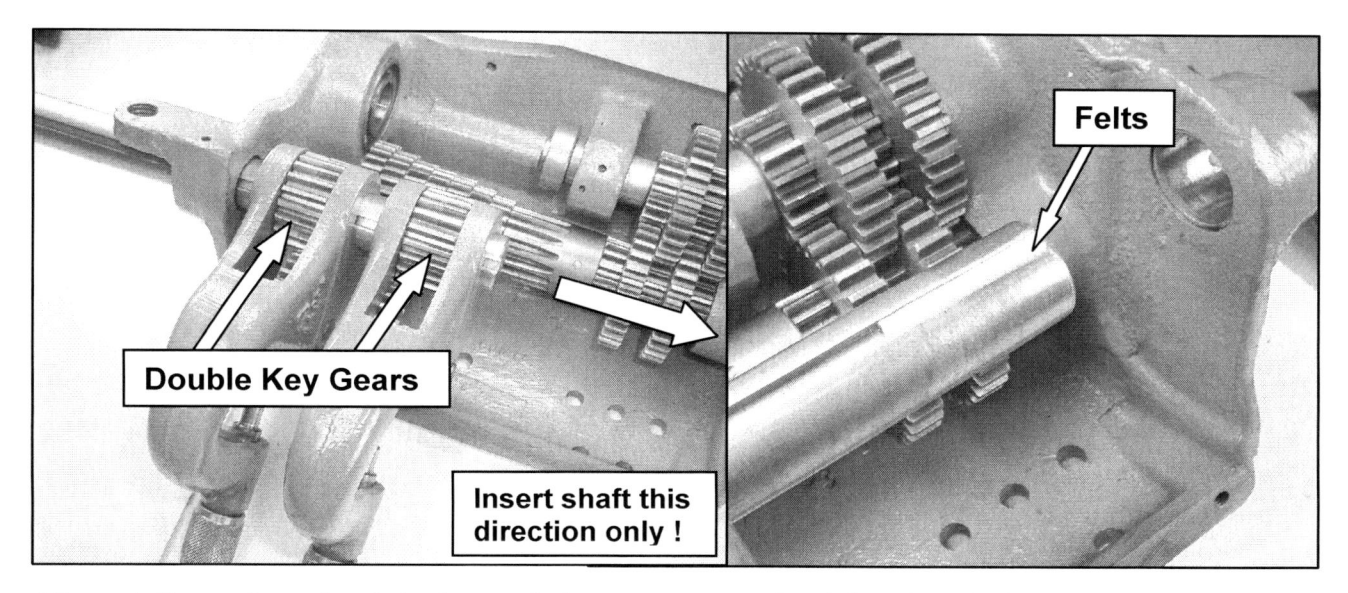

Double Key Gears

Insert shaft this direction only !

Felts

40. Align the double-keyed loose gears inside the left & right tumbler levers and slide the lower shaft through both tumblers from the left. Insert 1" long pieces of new Type 1 felt (with the ends beveled) into the grooves on both sides of the shaft and lubricate with Type B machine oil. These two pieces of felt help retain oil in the lower right bearing and keep it from dripping out via the open keyway.

Install Dowel Pin

41.   With the tumbler shaft in position, run a pin punch through the dowel pin hole to make sure the groove in the tumbler shaft is aligned and then drive in the dowel retaining pin. Check to make sure the shaft and tumbler gears rotate freely. Oil the shaft lightly along its length. Rotate both tumbler levers into position with the plungers in one of the indexing holes on the front of the gearbox and install the lower tumbler lever guide plate; tighten the 2 cap screws. Lubricate the gearbox thoroughly with Type B machine oil and test the gearbox for free rotation. Clean and reinstall the index plate on the front of the gearbox. Gear Train Complete.

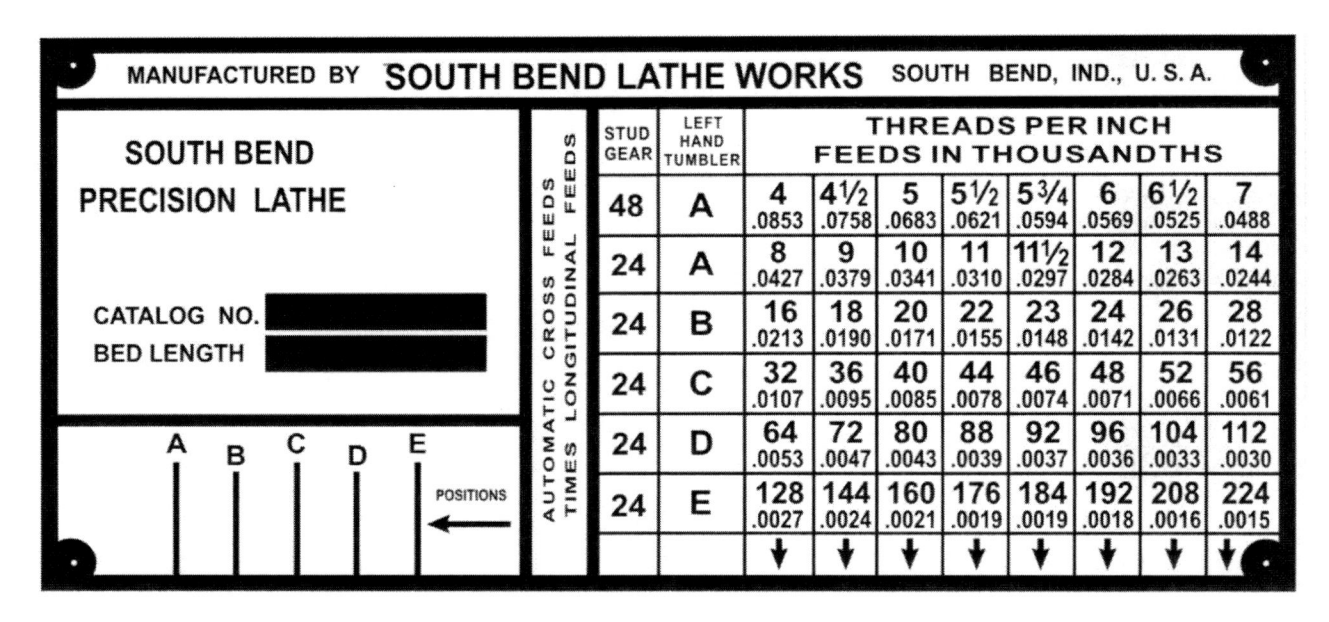

MANUFACTURED BY **SOUTH BEND LATHE WORKS** SOUTH BEND, IND., U. S. A.

SOUTH BEND PRECISION LATHE

CATALOG NO.
BED LENGTH

A   B   C   D   E   POSITIONS ←

AUTOMATIC CROSS FEEDS
TIMES LONGITUDINAL FEEDS

STUD GEAR	LEFT HAND TUMBLER	THREADS PER INCH / FEEDS IN THOUSANDTHS							
48	A	4 .0853	4½ .0758	5 .0683	5½ .0621	5¾ .0594	6 .0569	6½ .0525	7 .0488
24	A	8 .0427	9 .0379	10 .0341	11 .0310	11½ .0297	12 .0284	13 .0263	14 .0244
24	B	16 .0213	18 .0190	20 .0171	22 .0155	23 .0148	24 .0142	26 .0131	28 .0122
24	C	32 .0107	36 .0095	40 .0085	44 .0078	46 .0074	48 .0071	52 .0066	56 .0061
24	D	64 .0053	72 .0047	80 .0043	88 .0039	92 .0037	96 .0036	104 .0033	112 .0030
24	E	128 .0027	144 .0024	160 .0021	176 .0019	184 .0019	192 .0018	208 .0016	224 .0015
		↓	↓	↓	↓	↓	↓	↓	↓

Generic Threading Plate For The Quick Change Gearbox

Single Tumbler Gearbox - Disassembly

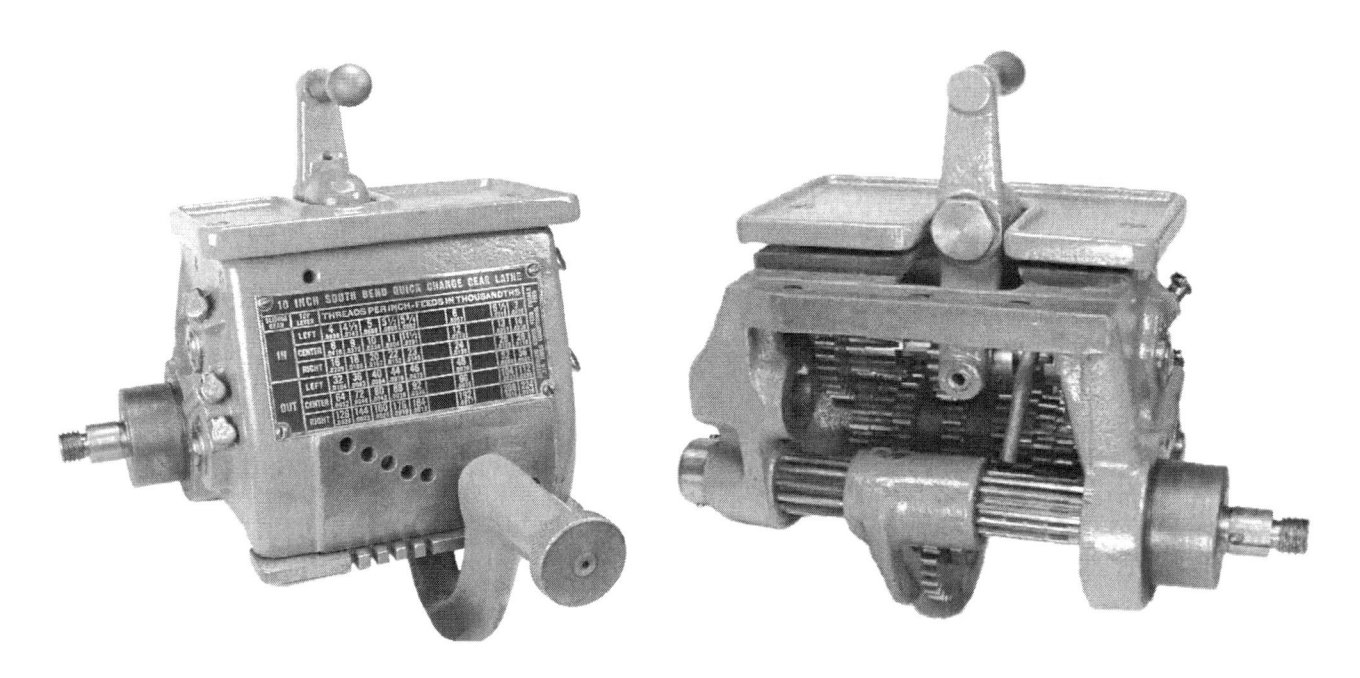

42.   The single tumbler quick change (QC) gear box.   Remove the gearbox as shown in step 18.

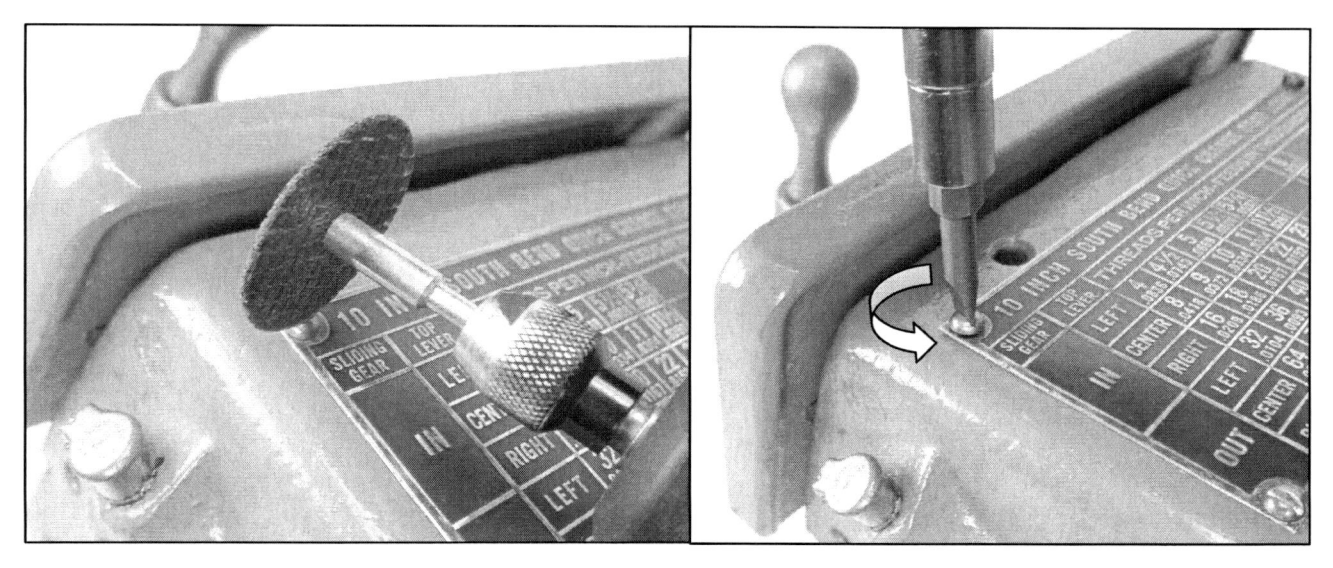

43.   Remove the drive screws holding the index plate. The best way to avoid damaging the plate or breaking a drive screw is to carefully grind a slot in the head with a Dremel® tool, tap the head lightly from the side with a pin punch and then unscrew it counter-clockwise with a screwdriver.

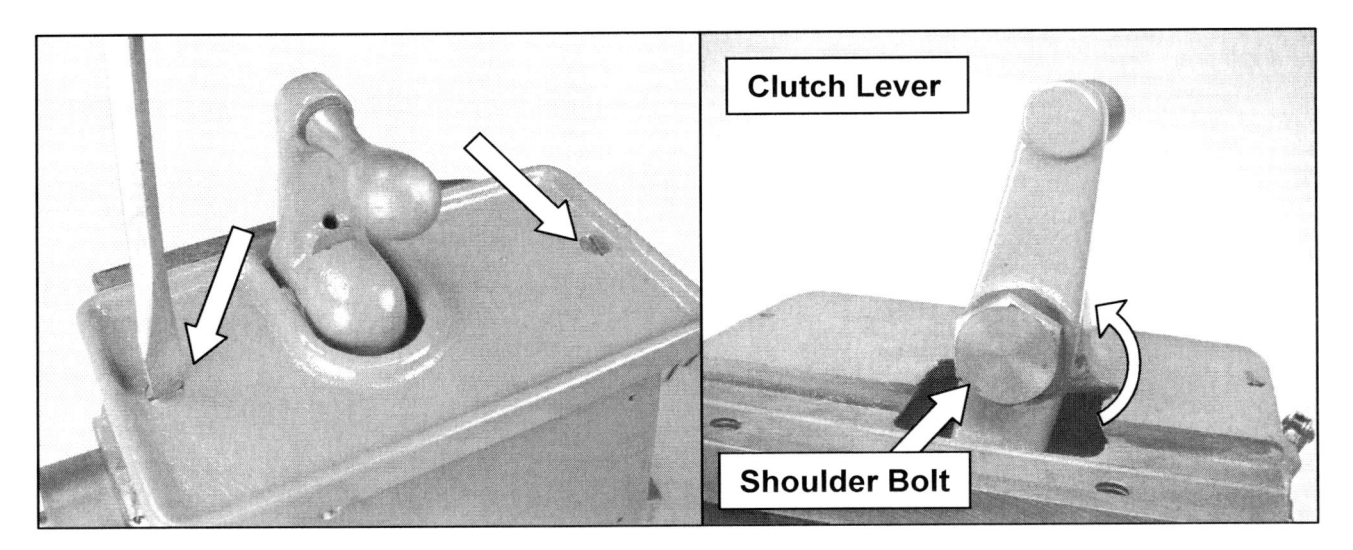

44.   Remove the two slotted machine screws that secure the tray to the top of the gearbox. Remove the shoulder bolt that acts as the pivot for the clutch lever. Disengage the shifter plug from the sliding dog clutch below and lift the lever out of the gearbox through the hole on top of the casting.

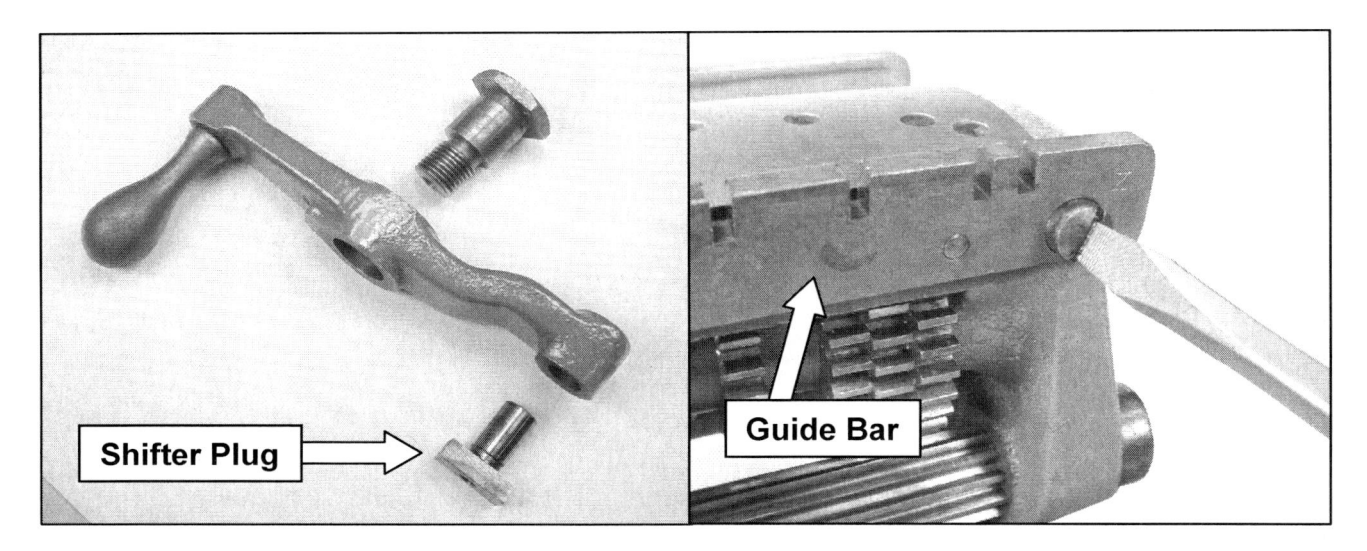

45.   Slide the gear shifting plug out of the clutch lever body. Lay the gearbox on its back and remove the two slotted fillister head machine screws that mount the slotted guide bar to the body. There are two dowel pins that align the bar to the body and they are usually a press fit. Using a brass pin punch, alternately tap the top lip on each end of the guide bar to gradually remove it from the gearbox body.

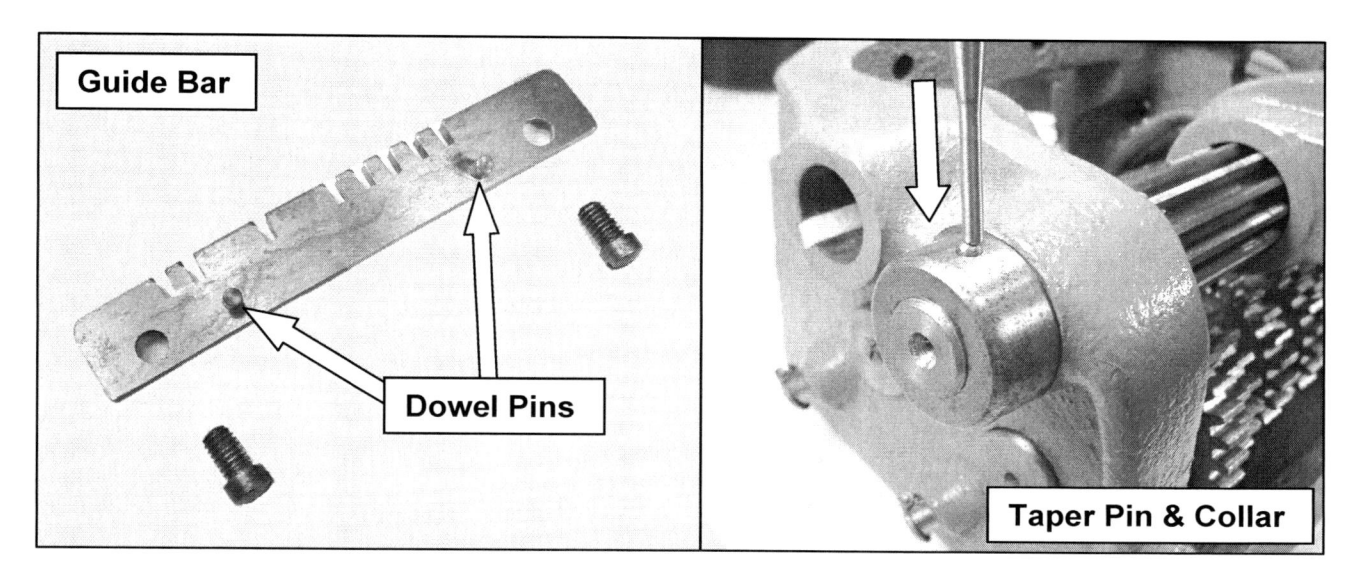

Guide Bar

Dowel Pins

Taper Pin & Collar

46.   To remove the main drive pinion and tumbler lever, first pull back the spring plunger collar on the tumbler lever and swing the lever down and away from the gearbox to simplify access. Next, drive out the taper pin that secures the collar on the end of the drive pinion shaft. Please refer to the taper pin section of the appendix when removing these pins. Strike the pin from the small end only. Slide the collar off of the shaft.

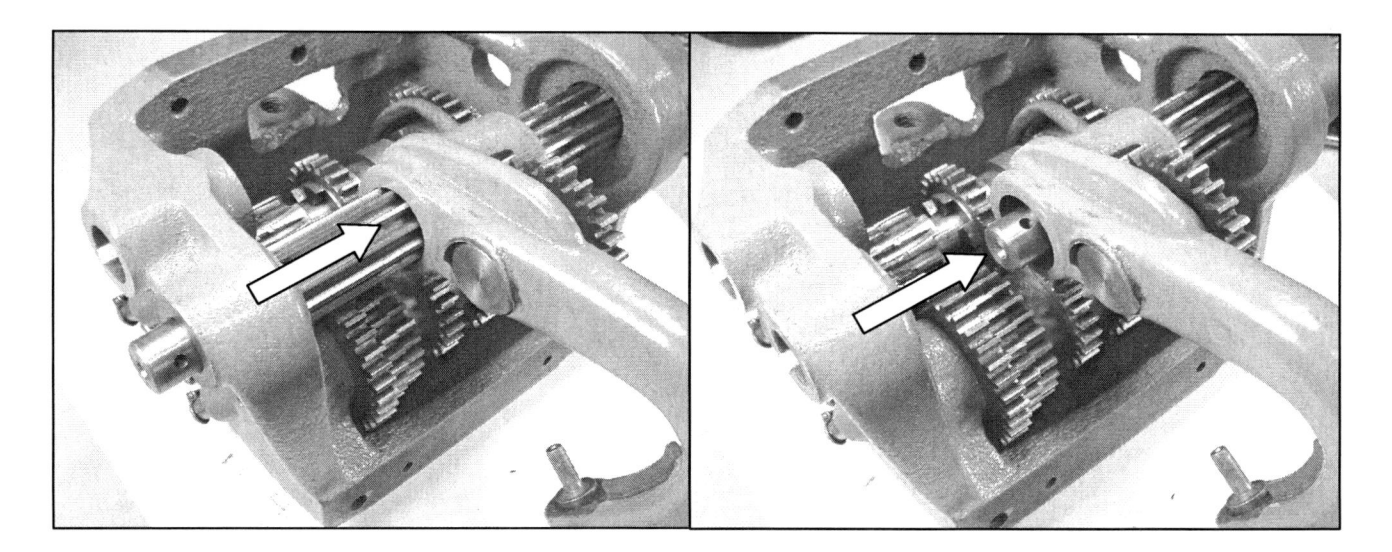

47.   Use a brass face hammer to tap the pinion shaft from the collar end. It can only be removed in one direction so do not strike the pinion from the other threaded end of the shaft. Hold the tumbler lever carefully and withdraw the pinion shaft from the gearbox body.

Plain Bearing Tumbler

48. The typical tumbler gear is held in position on a short shaft that rotates in a plain bearing. Place the pinion shaft you just removed in the soft jaws of a bench vise. Slide the tumbler over the pinion to secure the gear. Hold the lever with one hand & loosen the nut with a box wrench. If it is tight, you can heat the nut gently with a propane torch to loosen it up.

Needle bearing used on later tumbler

Install new wick and trim flush

49. Note that some later versions of the single tumbler lever used a pressed-in shaft with a needle bearing. If your tumbler is this style, press the shaft out from the small end being careful not to damage the needle bearing. Disassembly of the knurled plunger handle is not recommended. Thoroughly soak the tumbler components in solvent and then lubricate the plunger. Replace the felt oil retaining wick with a length of Type 3 felt and trim flush with the casting. Remount the gear and tighten the nut in place

50. Remove the two slotted locking screws that secure the upper and lower gear shaft bushings in left side of the gearbox housing. Leave the bushings in place for now. Next, move to the central gear shaft or "Cone Gears". Using a pin punch, remove the taper pin from the locking nut which secures the gear tree. Make sure to strike from the small end of the pin only. Rotate the gears to remove the loose pin.

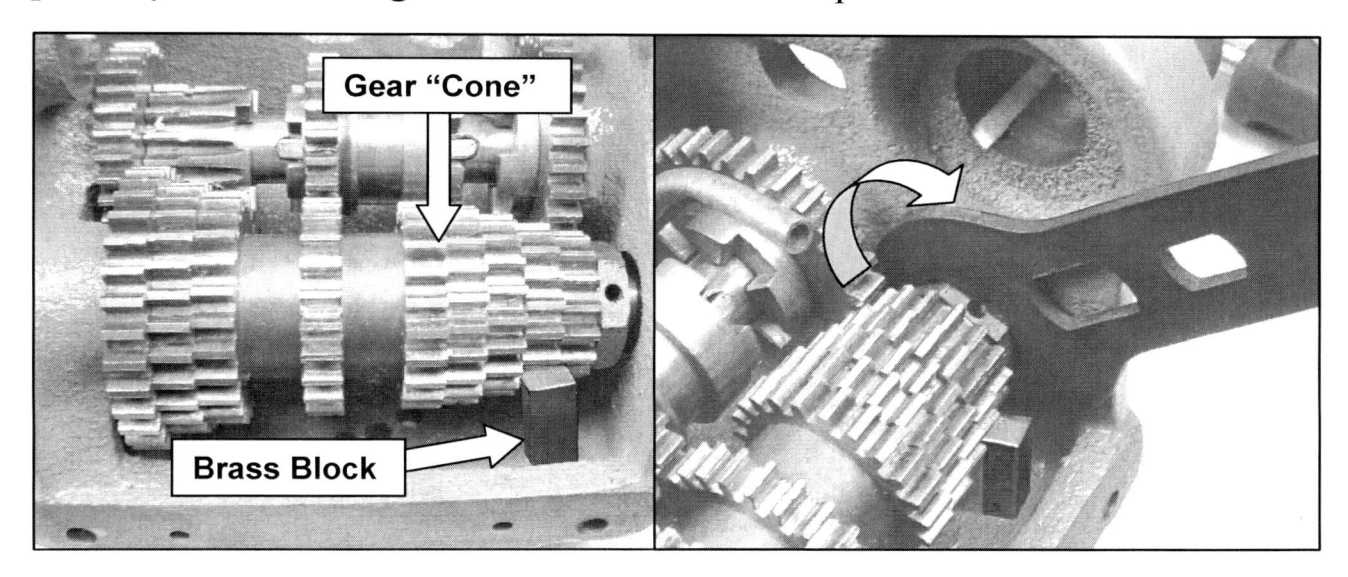

51. To remove the locking nut, clamp the gearbox body to the workbench to hold it steady. Place a small block of brass or hardwood beneath the gear teeth of the tree to keep them from rotating. Using a thin 1" wrench apply pressure to the nut in order to remove it. If it is seized, do not apply excessive pressure or the teeth may snap off. Heat the nut gently with a propane torch and try again. Patience is essential on old machinery.

Pull shaft to the left and remove gears

52. Once the locking nut is free, unscrew it until it is completely disengaged from the gear mounting shaft. Tap the shaft to the left to allow removal of the nut and gears. As the nut, spacers and gears are taken off, place them on a length of wire to keep them in the same order & orientation for assembly. It is easy to drop the entire loop of wire into a solvent bath for cleaning and brushing so the gears do not have to be removed.

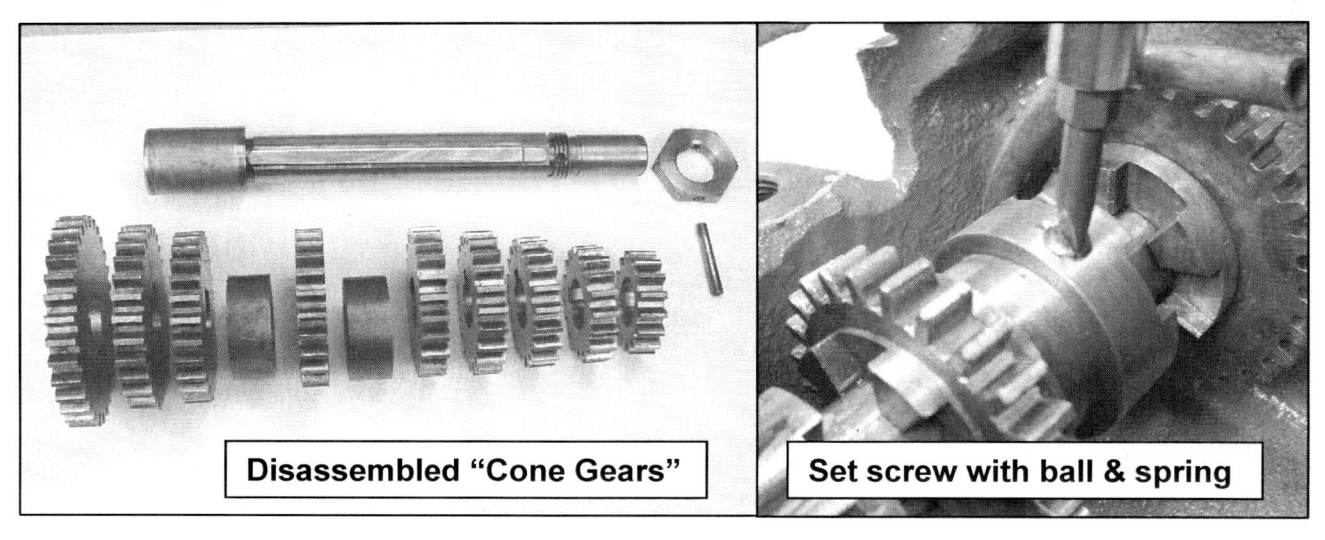

Disassembled "Cone Gears" **Set screw with ball & spring**

53. The components of the central cone gear shaft are shown above for reference. Next move to the clutch gear shaft. There are two dog type clutches on this shaft which are actuated by the clutch lever. First remove the set screw which covers the spring and ball detent. Be careful when removing as the spring may shoot out. Since the set screw is typically "staked" in place it may be slightly difficult to turn the first time.

54.   The ball bearing detent is shown above. Next, block the pinion teeth on the left side dog clutch and use a pin punch to drive out the dowel pin that is staked in place on the gear. Be careful not to damage the gear teeth. This dowel pin is driven in tangentially so that it rides freely in a groove in the clutch shaft.

55.   With the exception of the one pressed-on gear shown above, all gears should now slide back and forth on the clutch shaft.   It is important to first line up the slot in the pinion gear with the key on the shaft so that it can be removed. From the right side of the casting, use a brass punch to drive the clutch shaft to the left. Once the pressed-on gear is clear of the mounting collar, the shaft should slide out easily. It if does not, make sure that the pinion gear has not rotated and blocked the key.

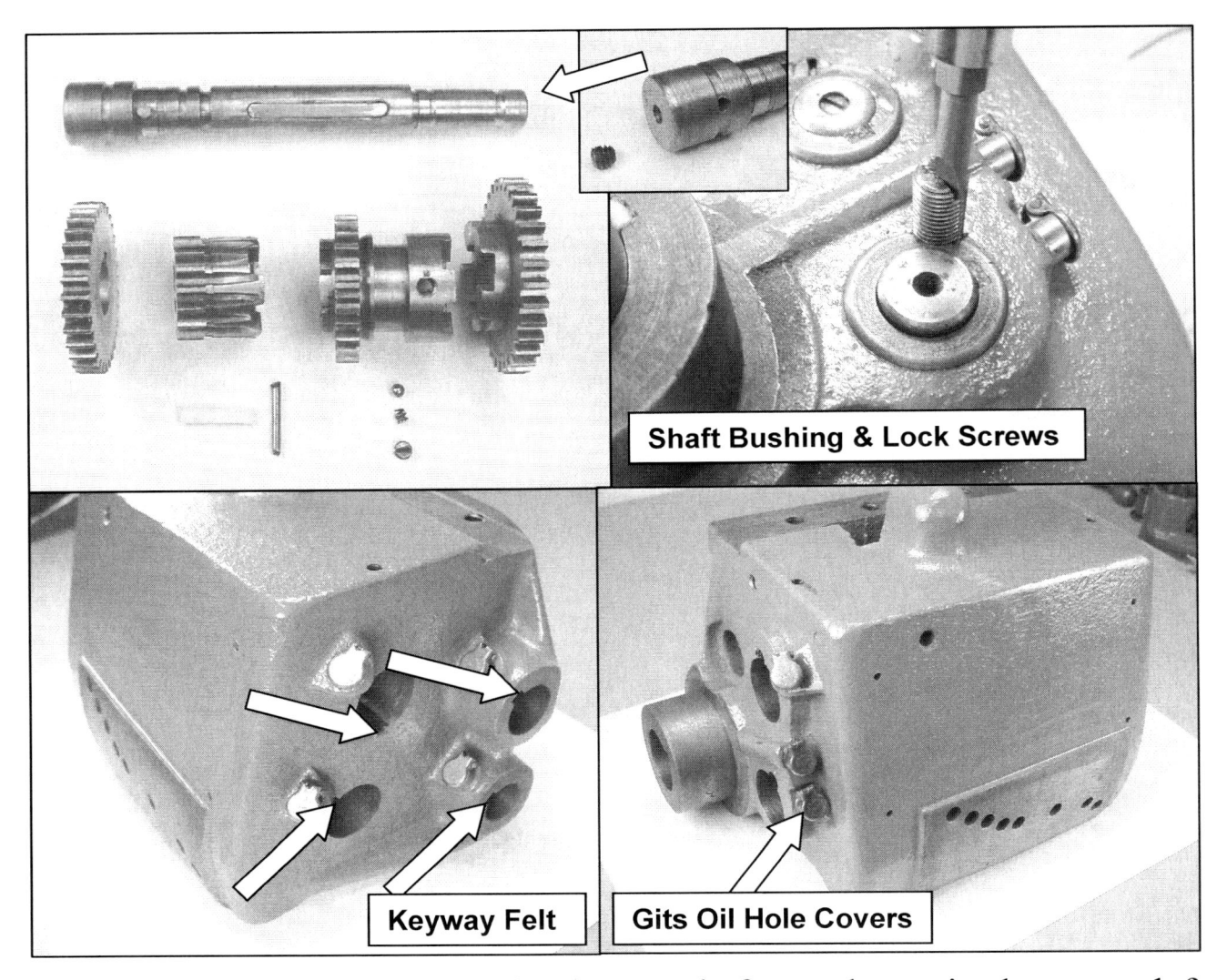

Shaft Bushing & Lock Screws

Keyway Felt

Gits Oil Hole Covers

56.   The components of the clutch gear shaft are shown in the upper left photo. Remove the two lock screws and shaft bushings in the side of the gearbox. Remove the old felt oil retention strips that are found in the keyways of the gearbox and the sliding gears. These felt strips become clogged with residue over time and are difficult to clean so they should be replaced with new felt (see appendix for sources of supply). Do not try to remove the Gits oil hole covers or the copper oil supply tube as they can be easily damaged. If the oil hole covers are broken or missing, new ones can still be purchased (see appendix). Clean all components in a suitable solvent making sure to thoroughly clean all the oil passages that supply the bearings. Remove the two set screws from each end of the Clutch Gear Shaft in order to access the oil supply passages. Cotton pipe-cleaners work very well for cleaning grubby oil passages.   If you are stripping and re-painting the gearbox, refer to the appendix for tips and suggestions.

Single Tumbler Gearbox - Assembly

57. **Assembly Preparation**: Start with the clean gearbox housing. Insert lengths of Type 3 felt strip into the keyways on both sides of the gearbox and then trim the ends flush with the machined face. Repeat felt installation on the two removable shaft bushings that will be installed later.

Oil Retention Felt

Clutch Shaft

58. Make sure that the oil passages inside the clutch shaft are clean and then install the two set screws in the ends of the shaft. Prepare the free spinning dog clutch gear by inserting a short strip of Type 3 oil retention felt into the keyway and then trimming flush with the fact of the gear. Lubricate the gear bearing surface and felt with Type B oil and set it aside.

Pressed-on Gear

Dog Pinion Gear

59. Now assemble the clutch gears onto the clutch shaft keyway one at a time. First install the pressed-on gear and then the dog pinion gear. Note that even though there is a keyway in the pinion gear for the oil retention felt, it cannot be installed until the gear is in position. More on that later.

Free Spinning Dog Clutch Gear

Dog Clutch Gear

Bushing

60. Next align and install the dog clutch gear that contains the spring-loaded ball detent. Finally, insert the free-spinning dog clutch gear into the stack and push the shaft to the right until resistance is felt. Install the loose bushing (with oil retention felt) onto the protruding shaft outside the gearbox to help align the shaft. Now for the fun part.

Pin

Tap Shaft Into Gear

61. First, align the keyway in the pressed-on gear with the round pin in the gear shaft. It is easiest to mark the key position on the gear face with a felt-tip marker to make it easier to see. Place two blocks of brass approximately 5/8" in thickness between the pressed-on gear and the dog pinion gear (one one each side of the shaft). This will support the gear as it is pressed on. Tap the shaft to get the pin started into the keyway.

Press shaft fully into the gear

Bushing and locking screw

62. Move the entire set-up to the arbor press and press the shaft into place. The shoulder on the gear shaft should bottom out on the face of the pressed-on gear if mounted properly. Lubricate and press the shaft bushing fully into the gearbox housing, align the threaded hole and then install the slotted locking screw. The locking screw should be fully seated and the shaft should turn freely upon completion.

Trim felt flush with gear face

63. Slide the dog pinion gear to the right slightly as shown. Tightly twist a short length of flexible wire around the end of a Type 2 strip of felt. Pull the strip of felt through the slot until the trailing end of the felt strip is flush with the clutch side of the gear. Trim the leading end with a razor blade so that it is flush with the gear face and then lubricate it with Type B oil.

64. Place a block of brass beneath the dog pinion gear teeth to keep it from spinning. Look through the hole in the gear to make sure it is aligned with the groove in the clutch shaft. Push the dowel pin into the tangential hole and tap it with a hammer to get it started. Follow with a pin punch to drive the pin fully into position. Stake the end lightly with a center punch to keep the dowel pin in place. The dog pinion gear should spin freely on the shaft.

| Ball | Spring | Screw | Stake Screw |

65. Lubricate and insert the ball detent and the spring into the hole in the sliding dog clutch. Install the slotted set screw and tighten until it bottoms out and then back off one half to one full turn. Align the slot with the old stake. Re-stake the set screw at the screw slot using a center punch. Lubricate the shaft and then slide the gear back and forth on the shaft. It should "snap" cleanly into each of the three detent positions on the shaft.

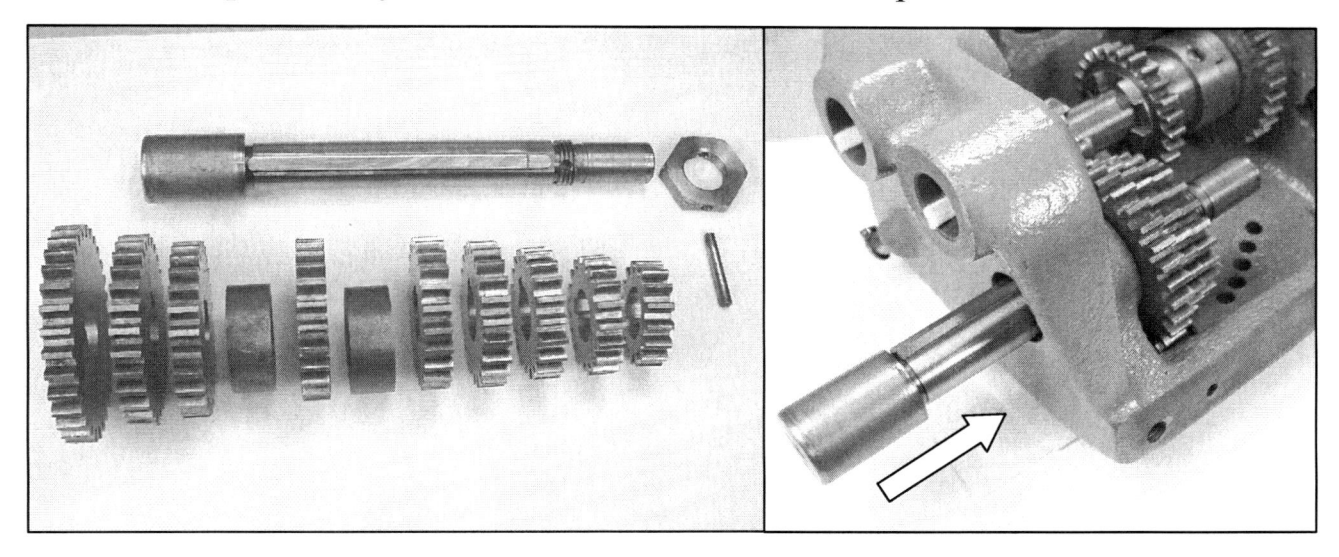

66. The most difficult part of the gearbox assembly… get a cup of coffee and take your time. Line up the gear "cone" in the order of installation as shown above. Mark the face and edge of each gear to show the relative position of the keyway. DO NOT install the shaft bushing in the right side of the gearbox yet. Start the shaft into the gearbox housing and slide the first three gears into position on the shaft. That was easy enough.

67. Install the two spacer collars with the 4th gear sandwiched in-between. Align and install gears 5 through 7 and slide them into position on the key. The 8th and 9th gear, the nut and the last inch of the shaft is the difficult part to get into position. Use a brass bar through the right side of the gearbox to help align the gear and nut on the shaft once in position. Make sure the 8th gear clears the clutch gear on the shaft above before positioning the 9th gear. With the 9th gear in mesh with the clutch gear above, hold the nut and 9th gear with the brass bar and slide the shaft through.

Cone Gear Shaft Bushing

68. Once the gears are all in mesh and properly aligned, start the locking nut onto the treaded portion of the shaft but do not tighten. Fully insert the bushing (with felt) into position on the outside end of the shaft to assist with alignment of the gear faces but do not fully seat it yet. Check that everything turns freely at this point.

Hardwood Block

Wedge gears & tighten nut

Check hole alignment

69.   Wedge a hardwood block into the cone gear teeth to keep the gear from turning and tighten the locking nut with a thin wrench. Look through the taper pin hole to check the alignment and once the hole is aligned, start the taper pin into the hole.

70.   Fully seat the shaft bushing in the right side of the casting, align the set screw hole so that it is concentric and install the slotted set screw. The entire cone gear shaft should turn freely. Rotate the cone gear so that the taper pin is vertical and drive it into the locking nut.

71.   Align the pre-assembled tumbler lever in the gearbox and insert the pinion shaft through the tumbler lever and into the bearing on the left side. Assemble the collar onto the shaft, align the taper pin holes properly and insert the taper pin. Seat the taper pin with a pin punch and make sure the pinion shaft turns freely.

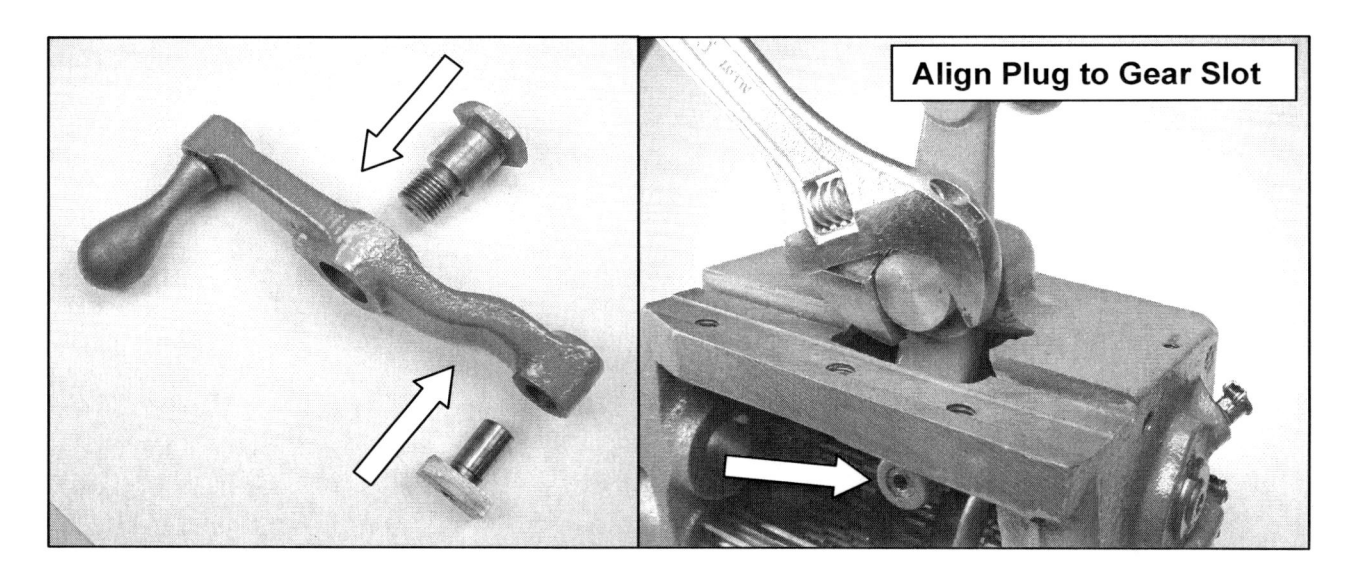

Align Plug to Gear Slot

72.   Lubricate the shoulder bolt and insert it into the clutch lever casting. Lubricate the shifter plug and insert it into the lever. Align the shifter plug with the slot in the dog clutch below. Thread the shoulder bolt into the casting and tighten. Move the lever back and forth to make sure the ball detent snaps smoothly into all three positions. Rotating the gears may be necessary in order to mesh them properly.

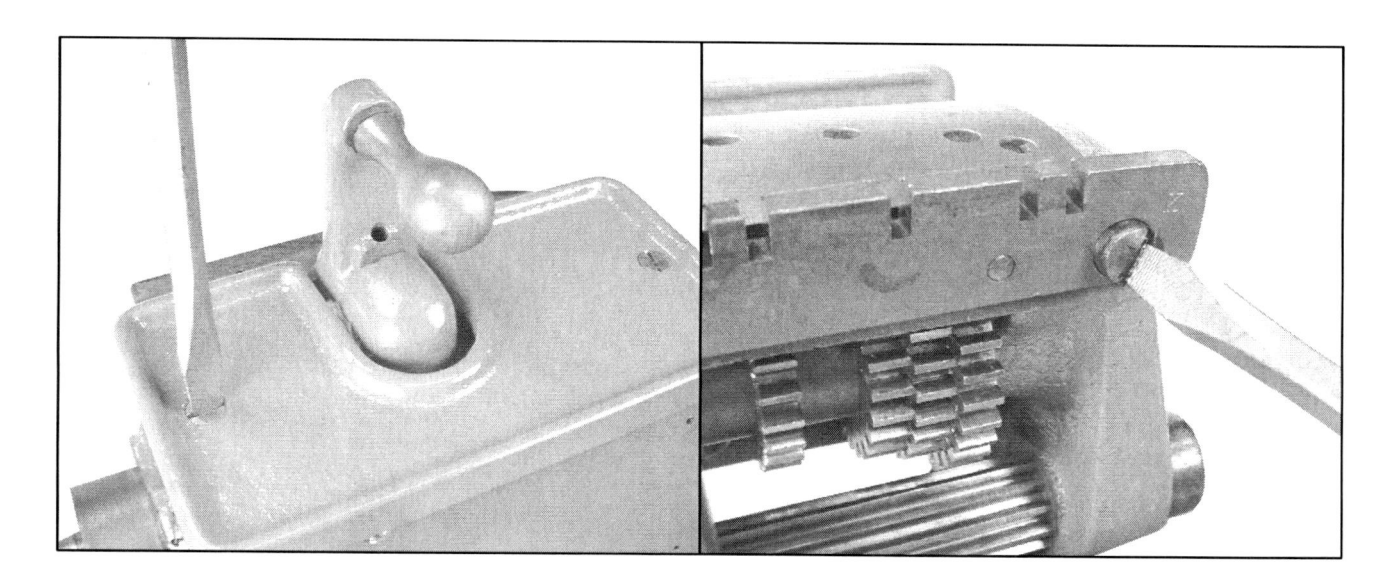

73.   Place the gearbox tray in position and secure it to the body with the two slotted machine screws. Swing the tumbler lever up and into position in one of the holes in the front of the gearbox. Position the guide bar on the gearbox and alternately tap the two dowel pins until the guide bars is tight against the gearbox. Install the two slotted fillister head screws and tighten.

74.   Clean the threading index plate carefully (WD-40 works well to remove dirt and grease without damaging the painted background) and remount it on the gearbox.   To reinstall the drive screws, place the screwdriver bit in the slot that you ground and then tap them back into position by striking the screwdriver handle with a wooden mallet. Lubricate thoroughly with Type B oil at all lubrication points. Gearbox complete.

Section 2: Saddle & Apron

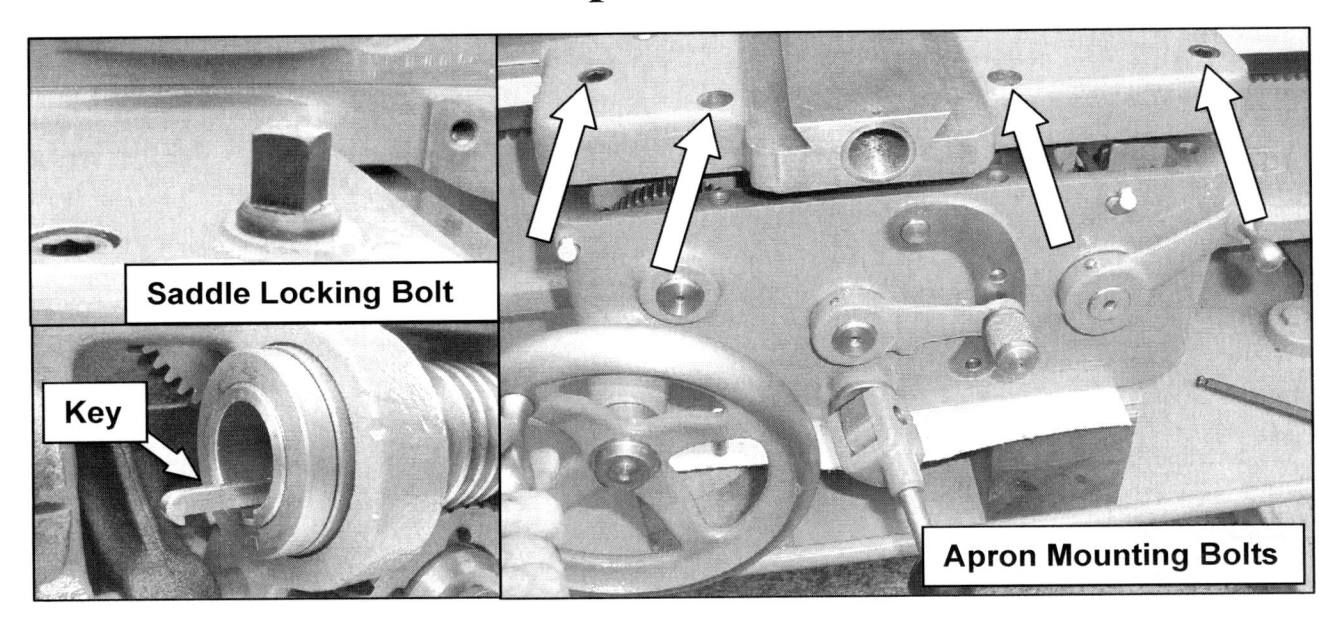

Saddle Locking Bolt

Key

Apron Mounting Bolts

75. Unscrew and remove the square Saddle Locking Bolt from the saddle. Support the apron with two 4x4 blocks of wood in the chip pan. Remove the large slotted or socket hex screws in the top of the saddle. The 10L used 2 screws, the larger lathes used 4. Gradually lower the apron until it is completely disengaged from the saddle and set it aside. Remove the lead screw key from inside the worm gear as it can fall out easily.

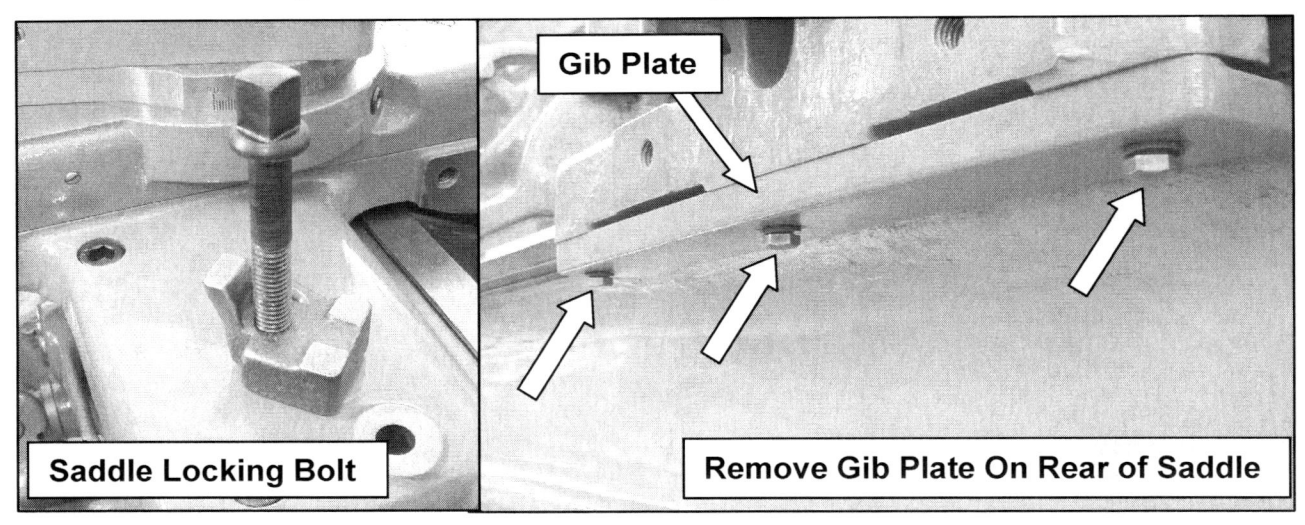

Gib Plate

Saddle Locking Bolt

Remove Gib Plate On Rear of Saddle

76. Remove the saddle locking shoe from inside the apron. The photo above shows how the saddle lock looks when mounted inside the apron. The shoe clamps to the underside of the lathe way to lock the carriage in place. Remove the long gib plate from the rear of the saddle by removing the hex-head bolts and lock-washers. Leave the saddle in place for now.

Apron Disassembly

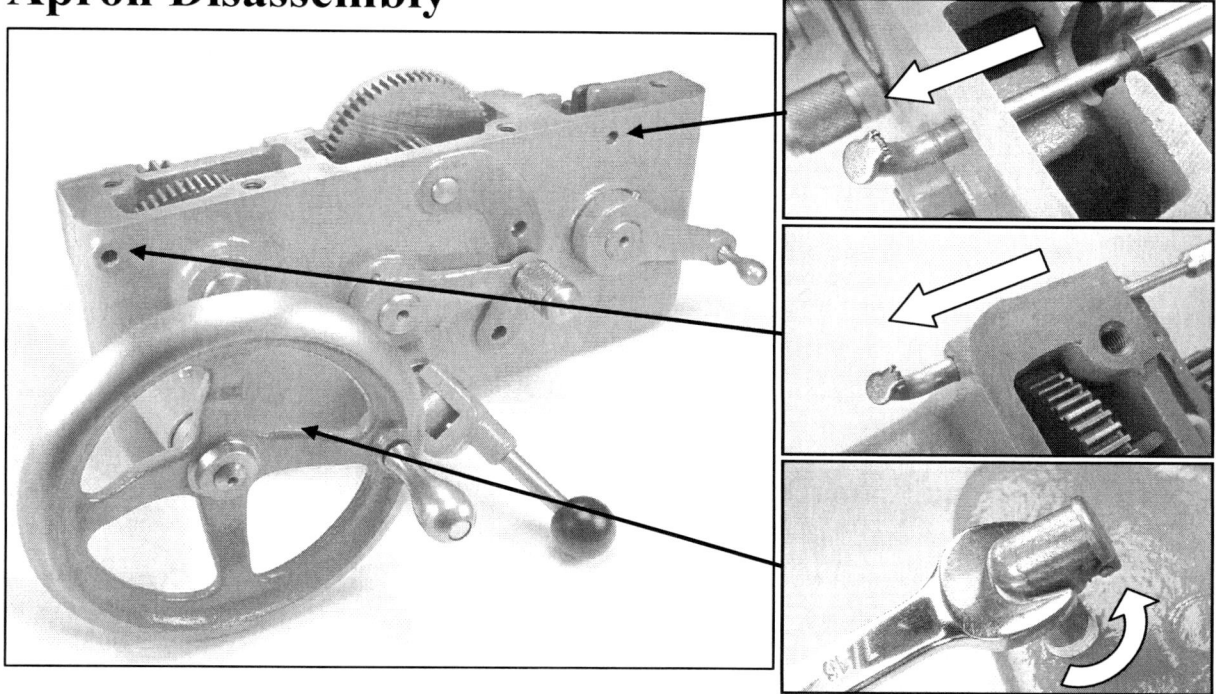

77. Lay the apron on a soft surface. To avoid damage to the oil hole covers, remove them first. On the top two oilers, use a brass punch to carefully drive them out from the back side of the apron. Remove the lower oiler on the front of the apron by unscrewing (counterclockwise).

Pinion Shaft

78. Remove the large carriage hand wheel from its shaft by first driving out the **Taper Pin** with a hammer and 3/32" round punch. Make sure to strike the pin from the small end only. (See appendix for tips) Tap the shaft through the hand wheel from the front with a brass punch. Extract the pinion shaft through the rear of the apron as shown.

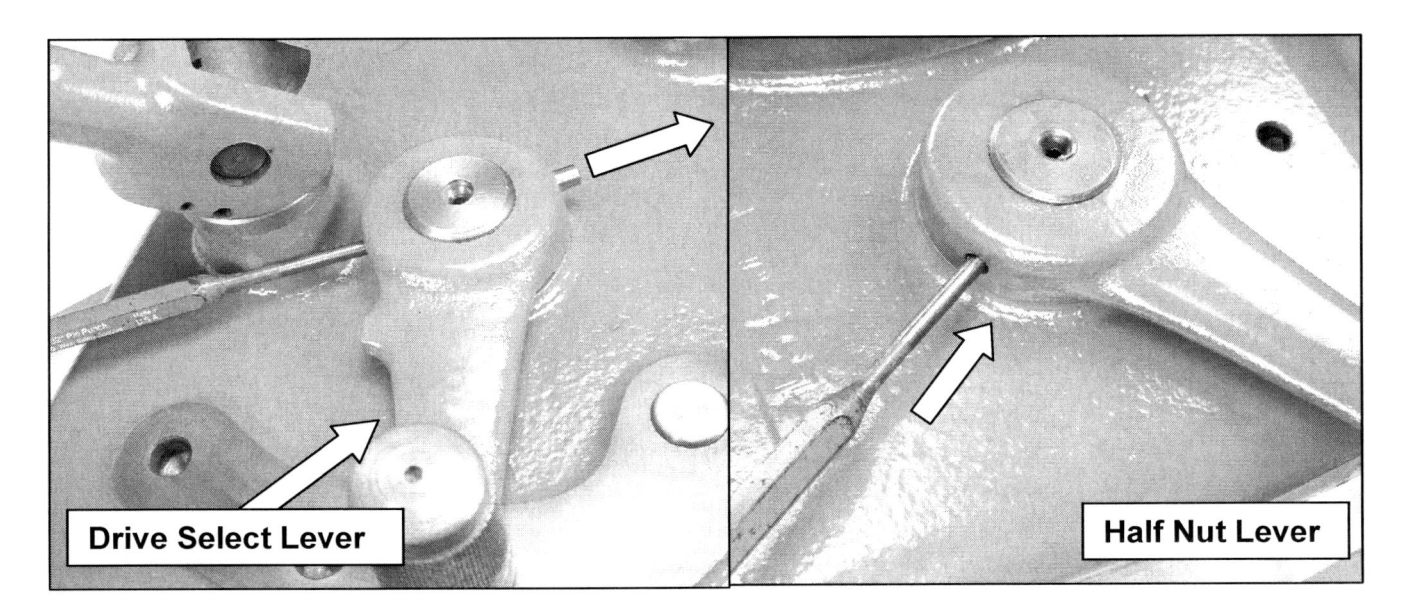

Drive Select Lever

Half Nut Lever

79. Position the drive select lever in the top hole to allow access to the taper pin from below. Using a 1/8" punch and hammer, drive the taper pin out of the lever & shaft. Place the half nut lever in the "up" position and repeat the taper pin removal for this lever.

80. To remove the shift lever and half nut lever from their respective shafts, use an old wood chisel (bevel side up). Gently tap the chisel into the seam between the lever and the apron housing. If the lever does not come off the shaft easily, go slowly and alternate from one side of the collar to the other until the lever is free. DO NOT pry or bang on the levers from beneath. They are cast iron and will break before they bend.

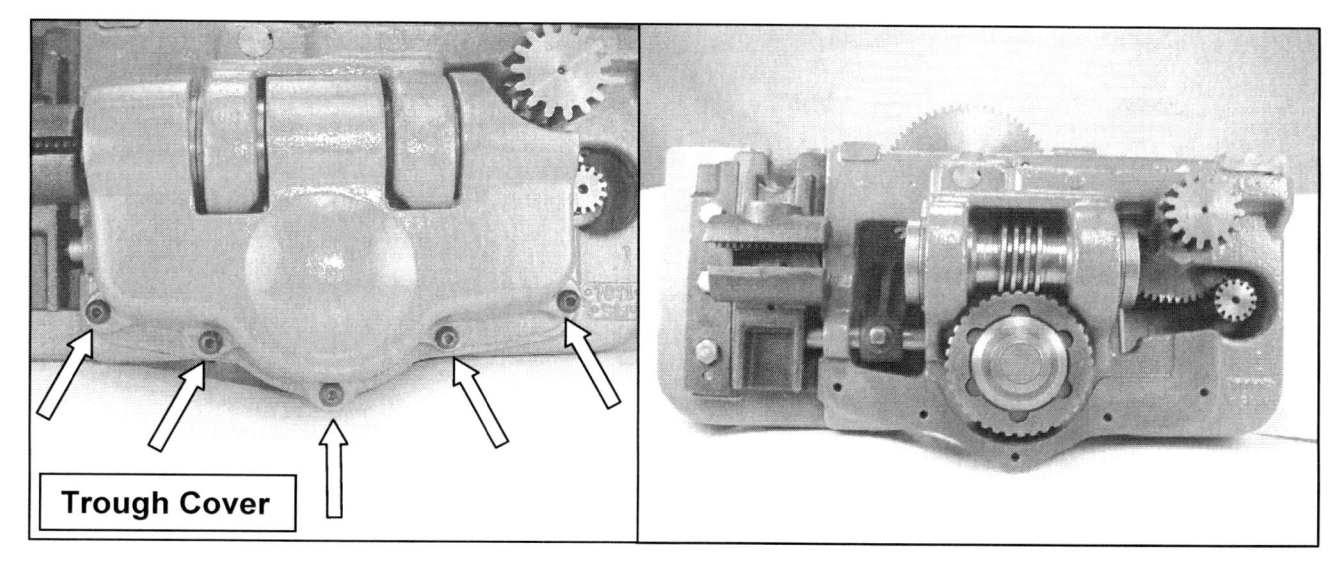

Trough Cover

81. Remove the rear apron oil trough cover by removing the 5 cap screws securing it to the apron. The center screw is usually longer than the other four. Gently insert the wood chisel to pry the cover from the apron. The old gasket may have permanently adhered to the cover or apron, so do not worry about gasket damage. It is often unavoidable and the gasket should be replaced with a new one anyway. (See appendix)

Remove Set Screw

Dowel Pin

Wooden Wedge

82. Remove the set screw securing the cross-feed gear shaft in the apron. Block the large gear with a wooden wedge to hold it in place firmly and drive out the dowel pin from the gear collar with a pin punch. The pin is typically crimped in place on both ends so work the pin out gradually. If the pin is difficult to remove in one direction, rotate the gear 180° and try from the opposite side.

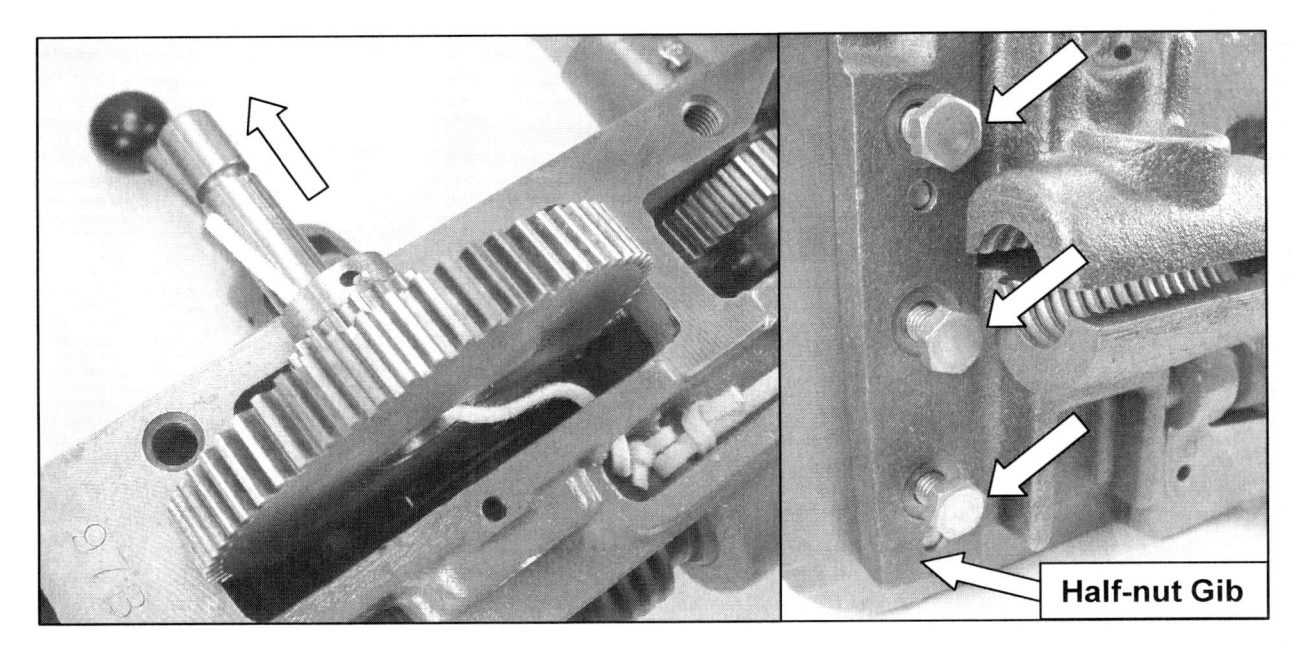

Half-nut Gib

83. Drive the cross-feed gear shaft out of the apron from the rear of the housing using a 3/8" brass punch. Remove the felt wicking from the shaft by pulling it out of the slot and through the gear. Remove the gear from the apron. Next, disassemble the threading half-nuts by first removing the 3 hex cap screws securing the half-nut gib on the left side of the apron.

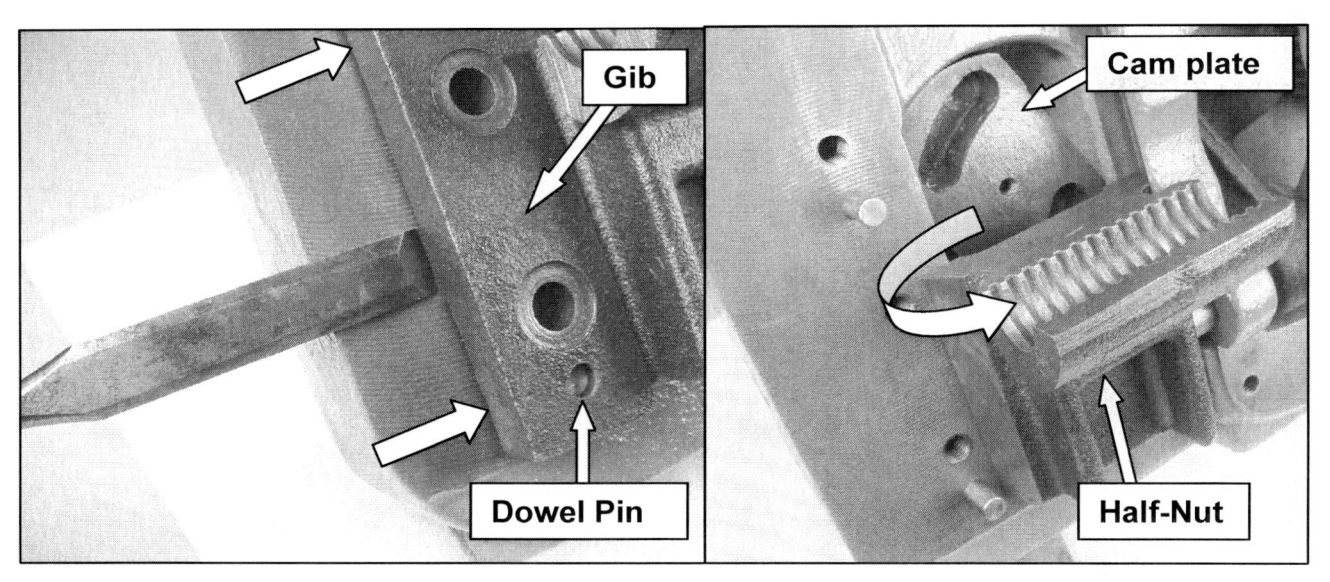

Gib

Dowel Pin

Cam plate

Half-Nut

84. The half-nut gib is mounted on two fixed dowel pins. Gently tap the wood chisel into the interface between the gib and apron, alternating between the top and bottom of the gib. Once the gib is free of the dowel pins, remove it from the apron. The upper and lower half nuts can now be removed easily by rotating them out of the dovetail and cam plate.

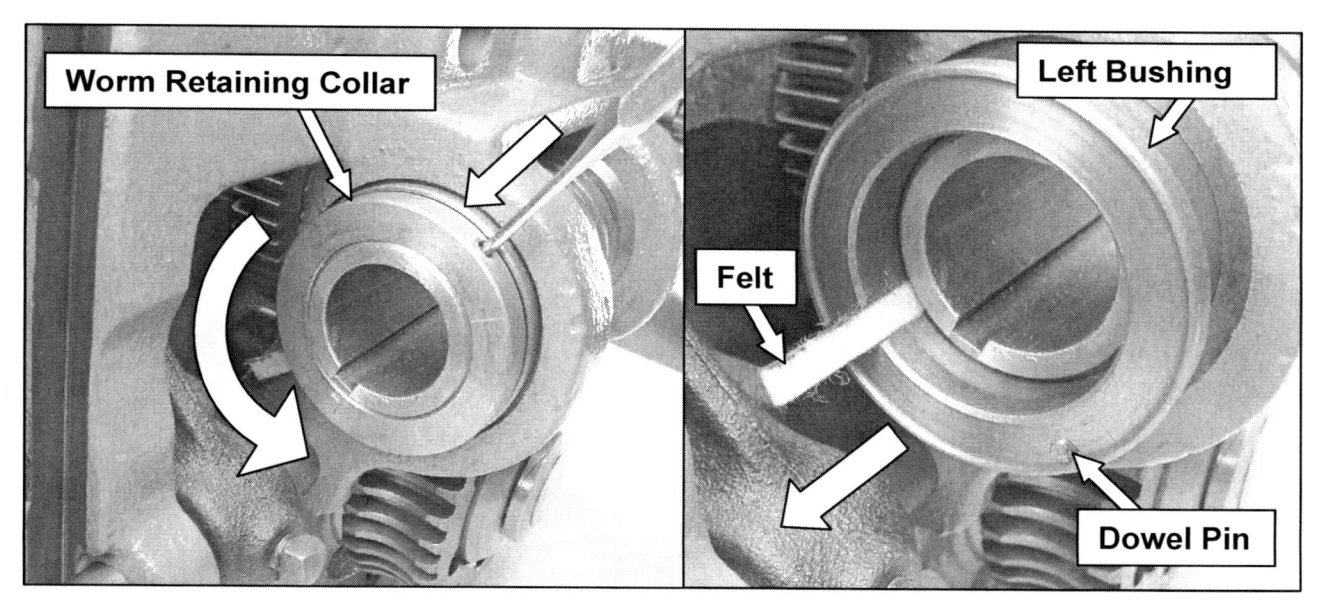

85. The two worm retaining collars are pinned to the worm on each end with a small dowel pin. Use a 3/32" pin punch to drive the dowel pin out of the left collar and then unscrew the collar from the worm gear. Remove the left worm bushing from the worm by tapping from the back side with a brass pin punch. The old felt wick will be pulled through the bushing upon removal. Note the dowel pin that locates the bushing in the apron housing.

86. Mark the worm, collar and bushing faces with a metal stamp showing left and right side to ensure they are returned to their original location later. "L" for left and "R" for right is appropriate when viewed from the rear of the apron. Remove the right side collar. Unscrew the worm so that it exits from the left side of the housing. It may be necessary to rotate the worm and gear back and forth to free it up if it is excessively dirty.

87. After the worm is removed, use a soft brass pin punch to tap the remaining right side bushing from the housing. Note the dowel pin position in this bushing as well.

88. Now move to the upper rack pinion gear. The gear is affixed to the shaft with a *Taper Pin*. Locate the small end of the pin and use a pin punch to drive the taper pin out. It will probably fall into the oil sump so just fish it out if it does. If not, rotate the gear 180° and pull the pin out.

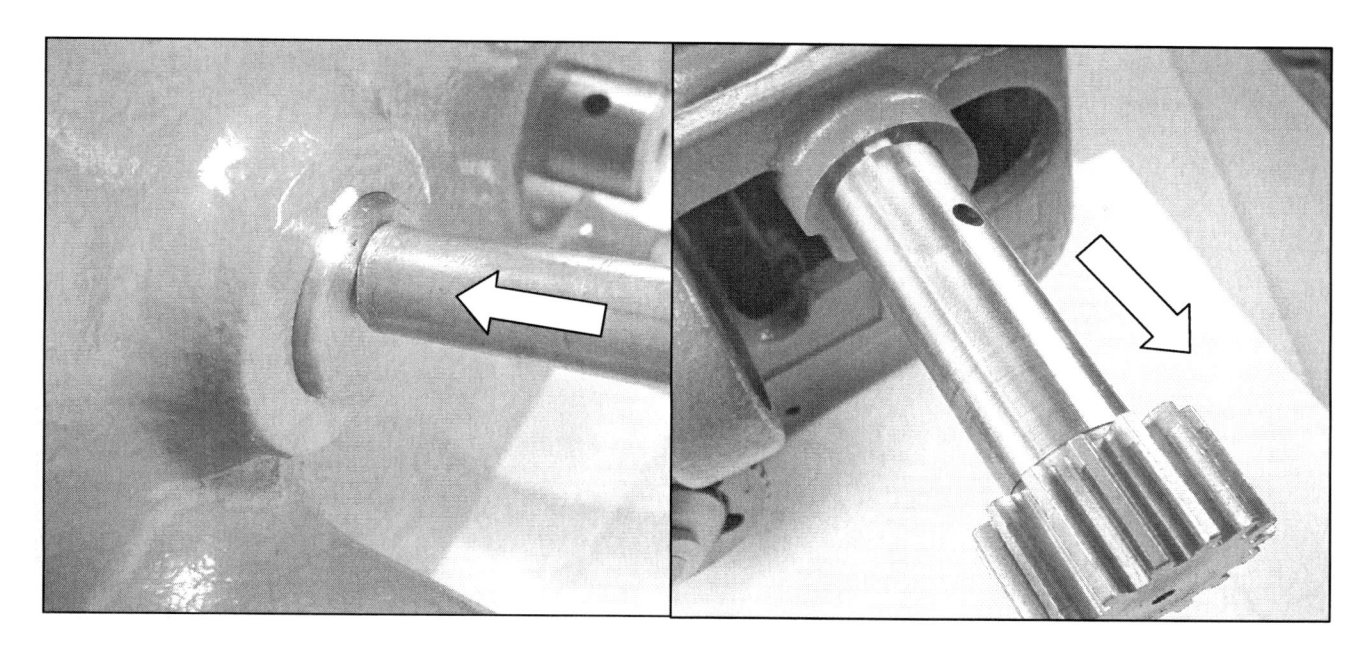

89. From the front side of the apron, use a brass rod and hammer to drive the rack pinion out of the pinion gear and the housing.

Front Wick Secured in Sump

Rear Wick Secured in Trough

90. Remove the old felt wicking strips from both bearing surfaces on the rack pinion. The rear felt wick is typically secured to a cast pin in the upper oil delivery trough and the front felt wick is secured to a cast pin in the lower right oil sump just beside the hole for the gravity feed oil cup.

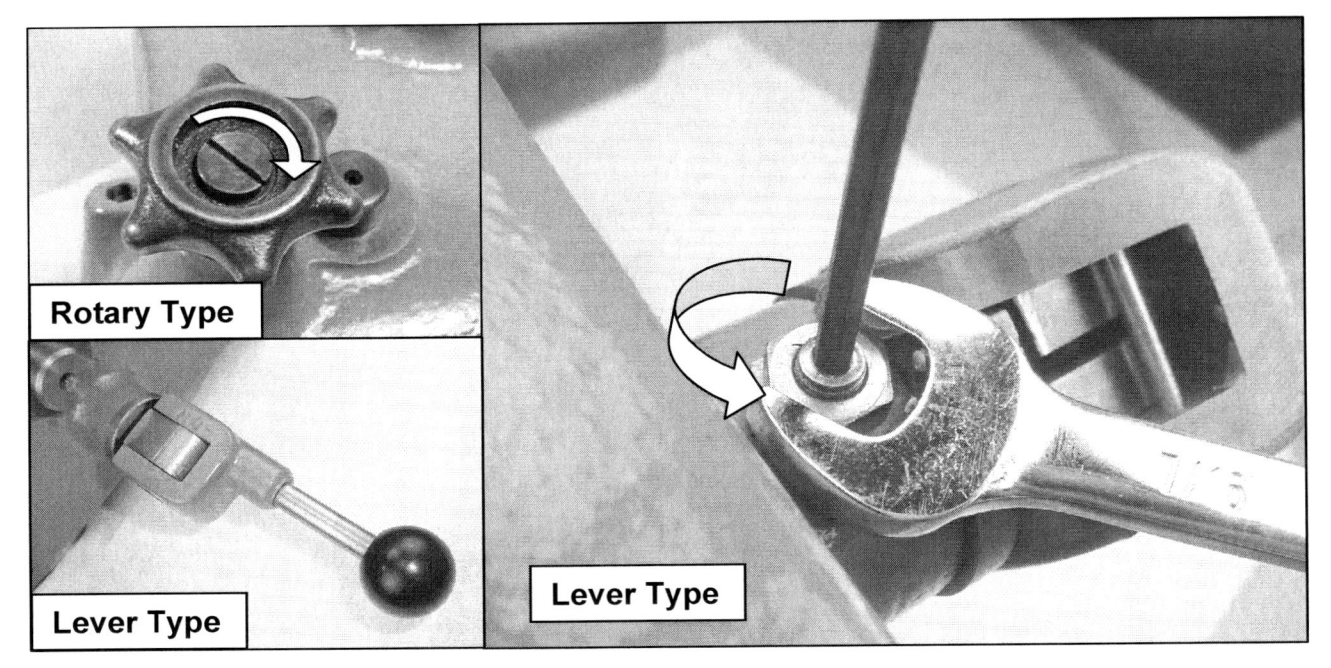

Rotary Type

Lever Type

Lever Type

91.   Remove the clutch actuator mechanism. South Bend used two types of actuator. The older type was the rotary "star " knob which engaged the clutch by rotating it clockwise. The later type was a toggle actuated cam which engaged when the lever was raised. To remove the star knob type, remove the slotted screw in the center of the wheel. ***This is typically a "Left Hand" thread so turn it clockwise to loosen!*** For the lever type, first remove the set screw and lock nut from the bottom of the housing.

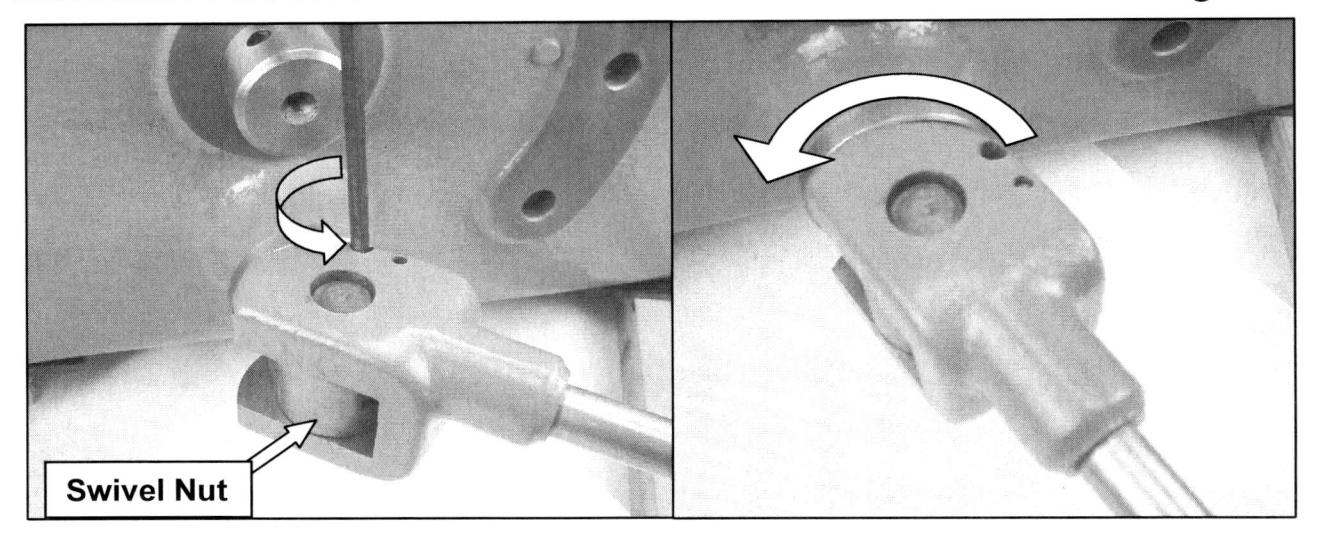

Swivel Nut

92.   Remove the cam lever by aligning the access hole in the lever with the socket cap screw beneath it that locks the swivel nut to the clutch shaft. Loosen the lock screw but ***Do Not*** try to remove it. Hold the clutch drawbar from the rear of the apron and unscrew the swivel nut from the drawbar.

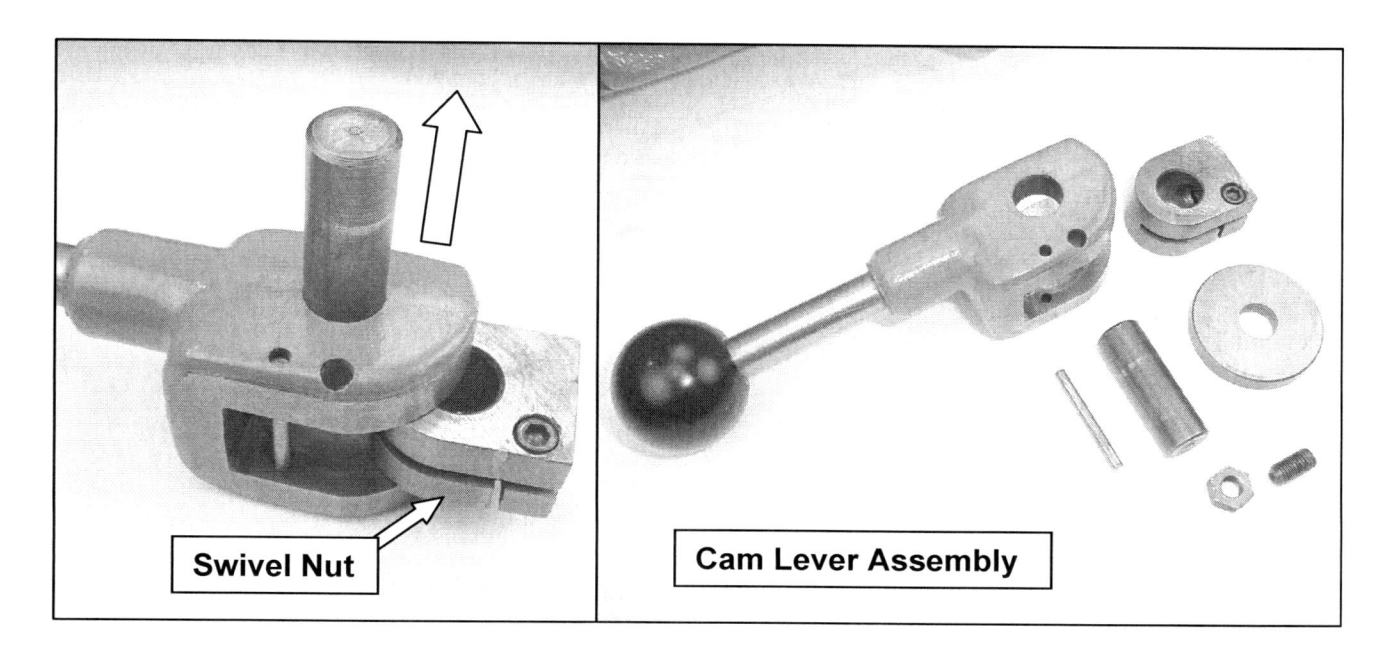

Swivel Nut

Cam Lever Assembly

93. The swivel nut can be removed from the cam lever by pressing out the center pivot pin with an arbor press. The components of the cam lever are show in the photo above right.

Cam Washer

94. After removing the cam lever, remove the hardened washer beneath it. On models with the star knob, there will be a hex nut beneath the knob. Grip the clutch gear from the rear and remove the hex nut. The clutch drawbar and worm gear assembly can now be removed from the rear of the apron. If dirty, it may be necessary to rotate it back and forth to free it up.

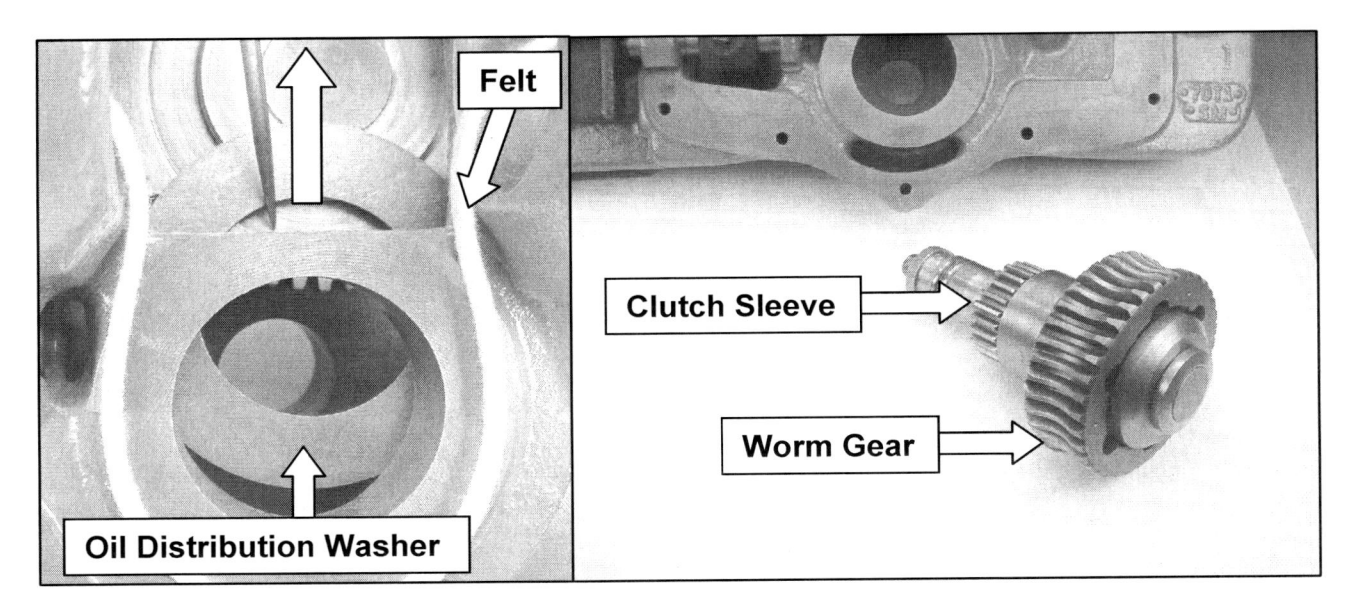

95. When removing the clutch assembly a large oil distribution washer will remain behind inside the apron. Remove it from the top of the apron using a wire with a hook on the end. The washer just "hangs" in a slot on the clutch. Remove the old felt "horseshoe" from the apron.

96. Slide the retaining bushing off of the end of the drawbar and remove the 3-part thrust bearing. Depending on the vintage, there is an alignment pin or a woodruff key that mates with the retaining bushing. Remove the pin or key from the drawbar shaft. Extract the drawbar, washers and the 3-part thrust bearing from the clutch assembly.

97. Take out the clutch spring. Remove the alternating lobed and splined clutch plates from the housing. It is important to keep these in order and in the same orientation upon reassembly. It is recommended that you mark these and string them together on a wire loop during cleaning.

98. Using a pair of external lock ring pliers remove the crescent shaped lock ring from the groove in the splined clutch sleeve. Press the sleeve out of the worm gear and use a needle file clean up any burrs on the splines or groove caused by disassembly. A burr here may cause the clutch to stick.

Clutch Assembly

99. All of the clutch components are shown above.

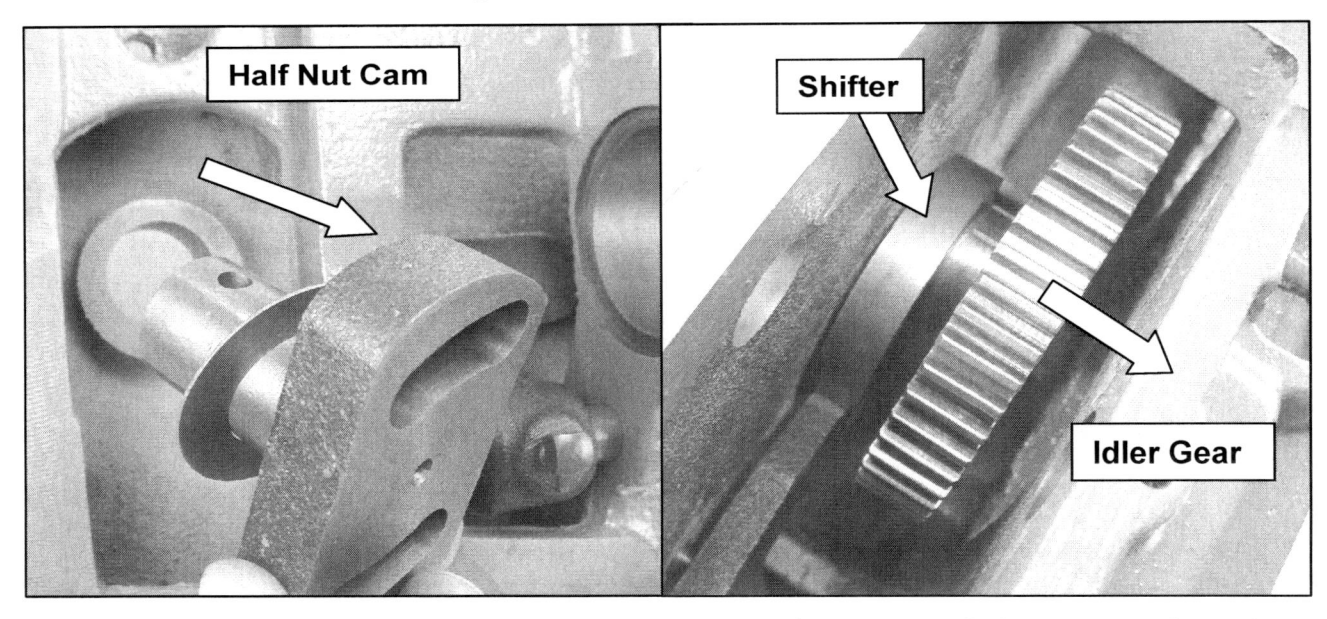

Half Nut Cam

Shifter

Idler Gear

100. Slide the half-nut cam and spring washer out of the apron housing. Mark the "Top" end of the cam so that it can be reinstalled in the same position. From the top opening in the apron, remove the remaining idler gear and shifter by first sliding the idler gear to the rear of the apron and off of the shifter. Lift the gear out of the top of the apron.

Idler Gear Shifter

101. To remove the idler gear shifter, rotate the shaft until the flats on the shifter body align with the opening in the rear of the apron as shown above. Push the shifter straight out the back of the apron.

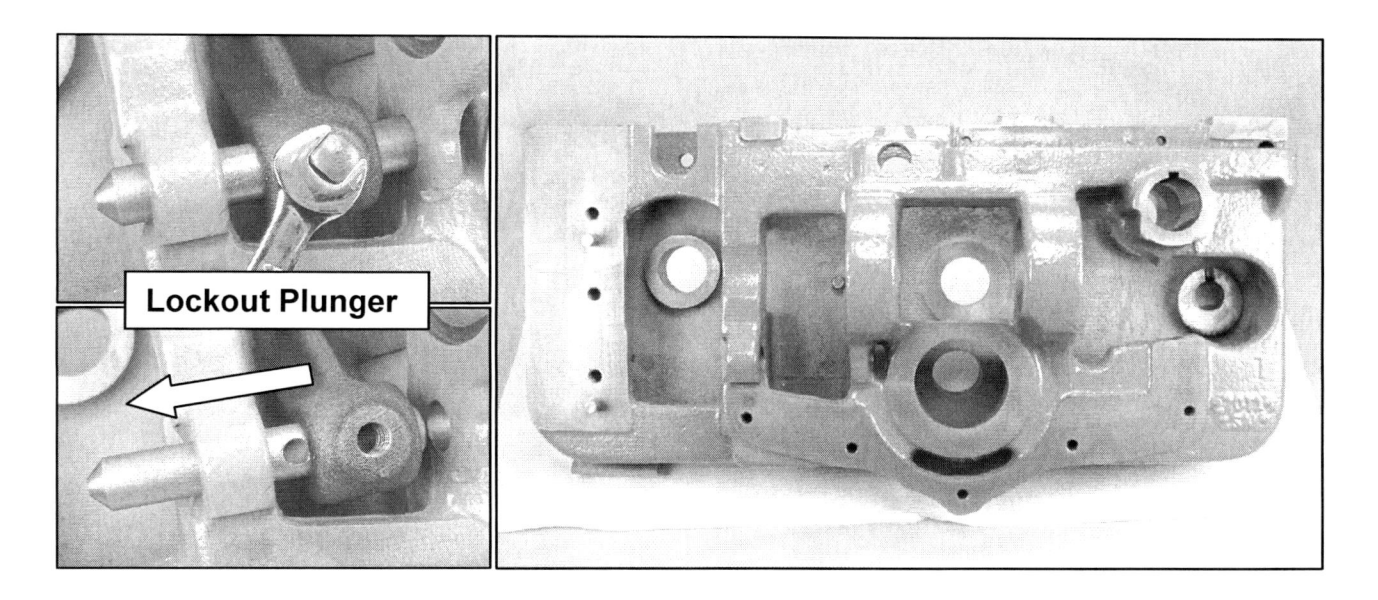

Lockout Plunger

102. The lockout plunger shown above keeps the half-nuts from being engaged at the same time the power feed is engaged. Remove the lockout plunger arm by first removing the square head set screw and then sliding the plunger shaft out the left side of the apron casting. Note the countersink in the plunger that aligns with the set screw. The plunger arm is free-floating on a dowel pin and can now be extracted from the apron. Disassembly of the apron is complete and it is now ready for cleaning.

Apron Assembly

At this point all components have been removed from the apron. All parts should be washed in a suitable cleaning solvent to remove grease, oil, sludge and debris and thoroughly dried. A wire brush is especially helpful in removing heavy deposits. Make sure that all oil passages, blind holes, oil cups, wick passages, and similar features are free of dirt and sludge. The best method for cleaning oil passages and blind screw holes is to use a small-bore rifle cleaning brush or a stiff pipe cleaner. Compressed air is not recommended. Parts should be lubricated with the appropriate oil or Teflon® grease during assembly (see appendix). If you are stripping and painting your lathe, see the appendix for a brief guide on refinishing machinery. Take special care not to paint machined surfaces where parts mate. Painting mating surfaces or threaded holes could present significant problems at assembly so attention to detail here will pay off later.

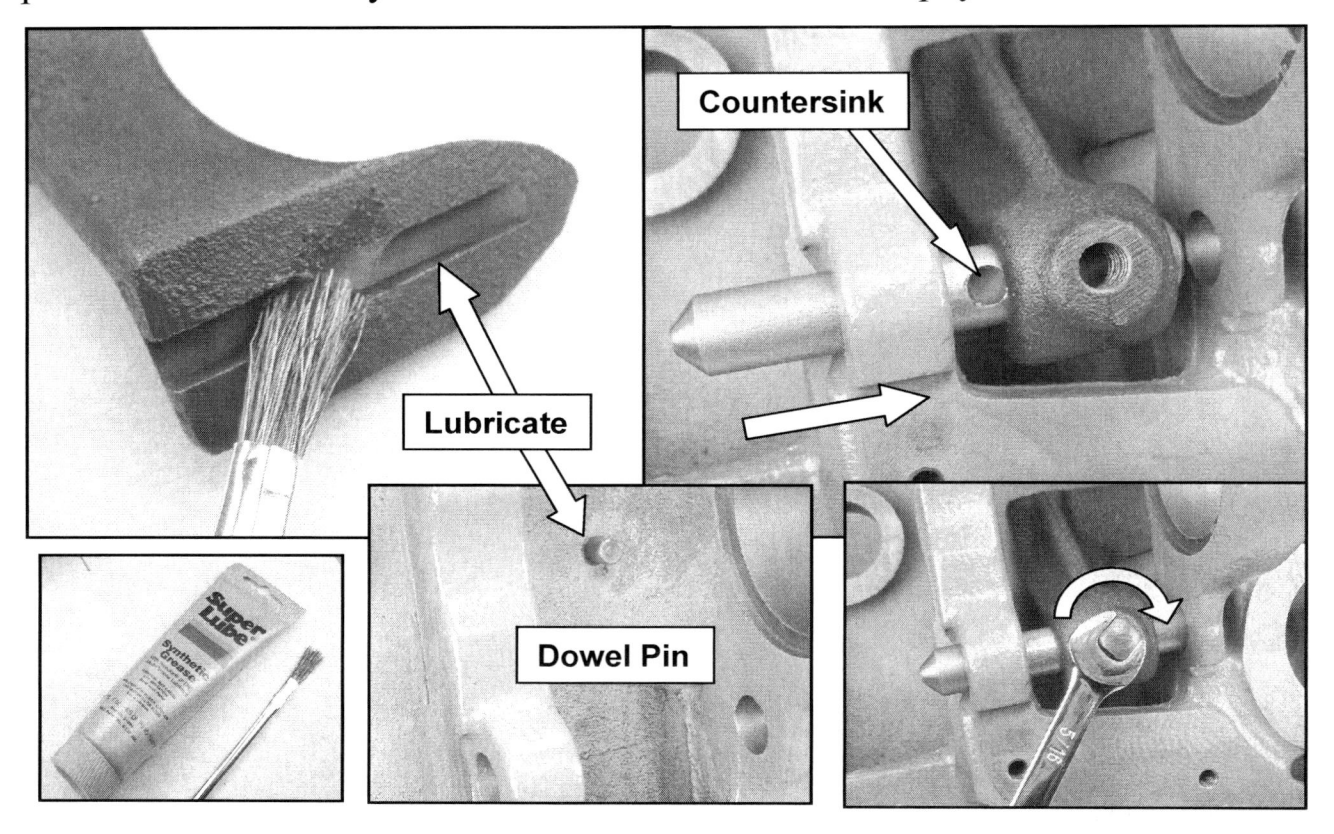

103. First step is to reinstall the lockout plunger. Grease the plunger arm slot and dowel pin with Super Lube® and position it inside the apron. Lubricate and insert the plunger into the apron and position it the arm. Align the countersink in the plunger and tighten the square head set screw.

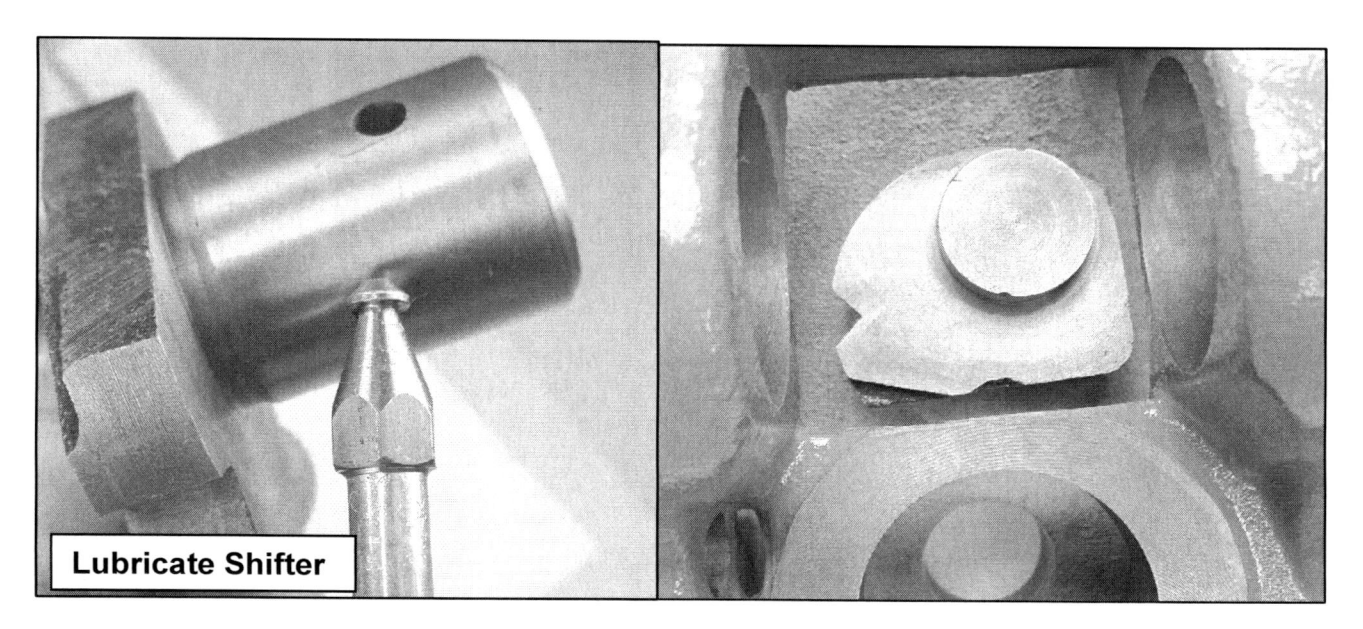

Lubricate Shifter

104. Lubricate the shaft on the idler gear shifter with Type C oil, align the flats with the apron opening and push it into place in the apron housing.

Note that the recess on the idler gear faces to the rear of the apron.

105. Slide the lockout arm back and forth and check that the point engages smoothly with the "V" notch in the shifter. Lubricate the idler gear stud with Type C oil, and then slide the idler gear into the apron from the top and onto the stud. (Note that the recessed side of the idler gear with the small oil passages faces to the rear of the apron)

Apply Grease

106. Lubricate the half-nut cam stud with Super Lube®, position the spring washer on the stud and slide it into the housing making sure that the "TOP" side marked earlier is facing up. Lubricate cam recesses with Super Lube®

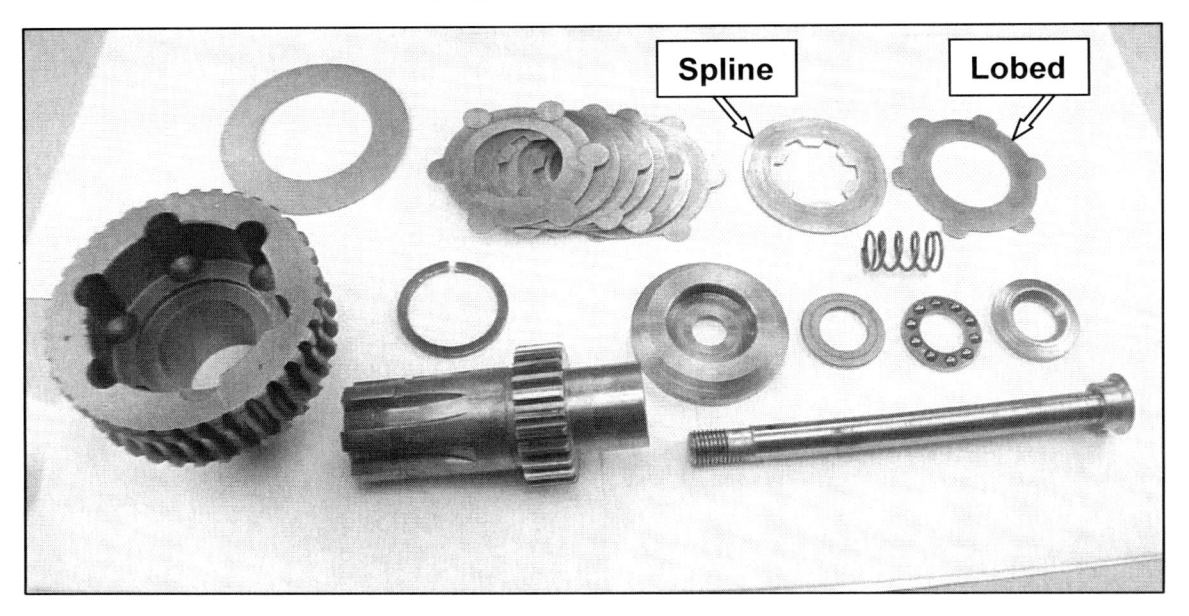

Spline   Lobed

107. **Clutch Assembly**: Collect all of the clutch parts, check the clutch plates, spacers, splines and washers for burs. If any burs are present, carefully remove them with a hard Arkansas stone or a small needle file. Depending on the model of your lathe, there may be more (or fewer) lobed & splined clutch plates than shown above. Model 10L:(4 Lobed / 3 Spline), 13" Lathe: (5/4), 14.5" Lathe: (7/6), 16" Lathe: (5/4)

108. Press the splined clutch sleeve into the worm gear and fasten in place with the external lock ring. Make sure the ring is fully seated in the groove.

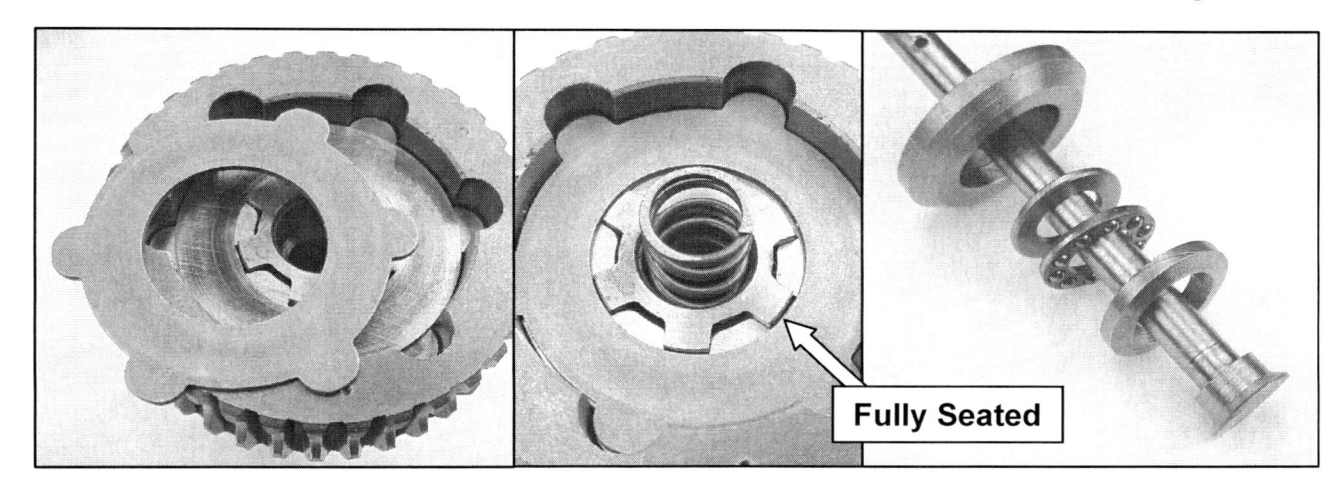

Fully Seated

109. Install the alternating clutch plates in the original order and orientation. Insert the clutch spring. Assemble the thrust bearings and washers onto the drawbar as shown above. Lubricate with Type A oil.

110. Slide the drawbar into the clutch assembly. The topmost clutch plate should be just below the splines and the bevel washer should seat as shown.

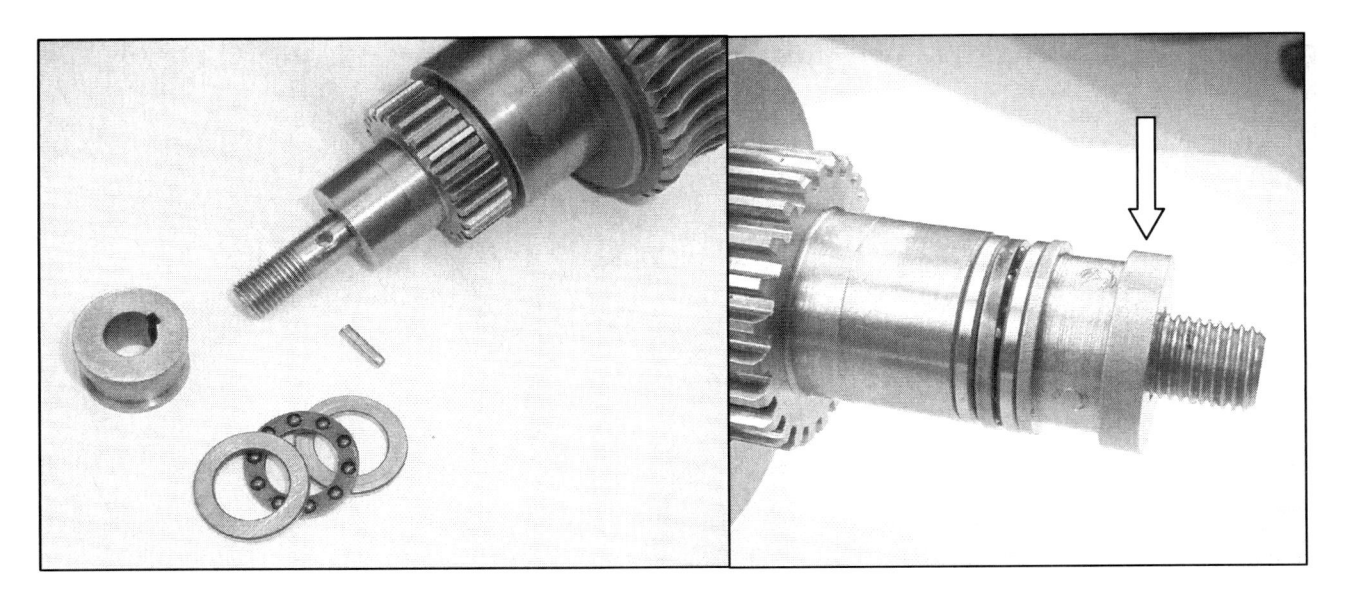

111. Push the drawbar into the clutch assembly and make sure that it moves freely and that none of the clutch plates, spacers or washers are preventing the drawbar from fully extending through the bushing on the opposite end. Install the alignment pin (or woodruff key) in the drawbar shaft and mount the thrust bearing and bushing on the end. The wider collar on the bushing faces to the front of the lathe.

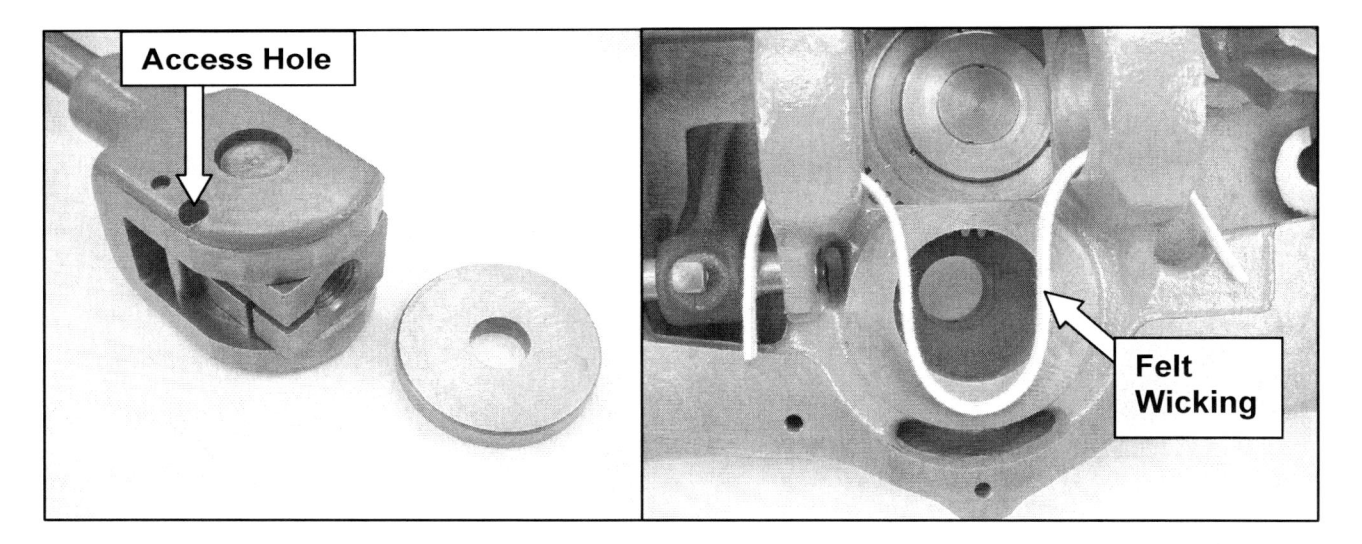

112. Reassemble the cam lever making sure that the locking screw in the swivel nut is on the same side as the access hole. On the rear of the apron, drape a 12" length of Type 3 felt wicking between the openings for the worm gear and pull a loop down below the opening for the clutch. Make sure the length of felt is approximately centered by looking at the ends.

For Demonstration Only. DO NOT Install As Shown !

Oil Distribution Washer

113. Shape the felt loop so that it resembles a "horseshoe". Insert the oil distribution washer through the top of the apron and position it in the oil trough concentric with the opening for the clutch. When the clutch is installed this washer will be suspended loosely in the groove between the worm gear and the clutch sleeve as shown. The purpose of this washer is to pull oil out of the oil trough and distribute it over the gears and clutch.

114. Slide the clutch assembly in from the rear of the housing, passing through the oil distribution washer inside and exiting the front of the apron. Gently work the felt wicking into the groove between the worm gear and the apron housing making sure it is not twisted and does not get caught between the gear and the housing as the clutch is installed. Push the clutch assembly into the apron until the drawbar shows on the other side.

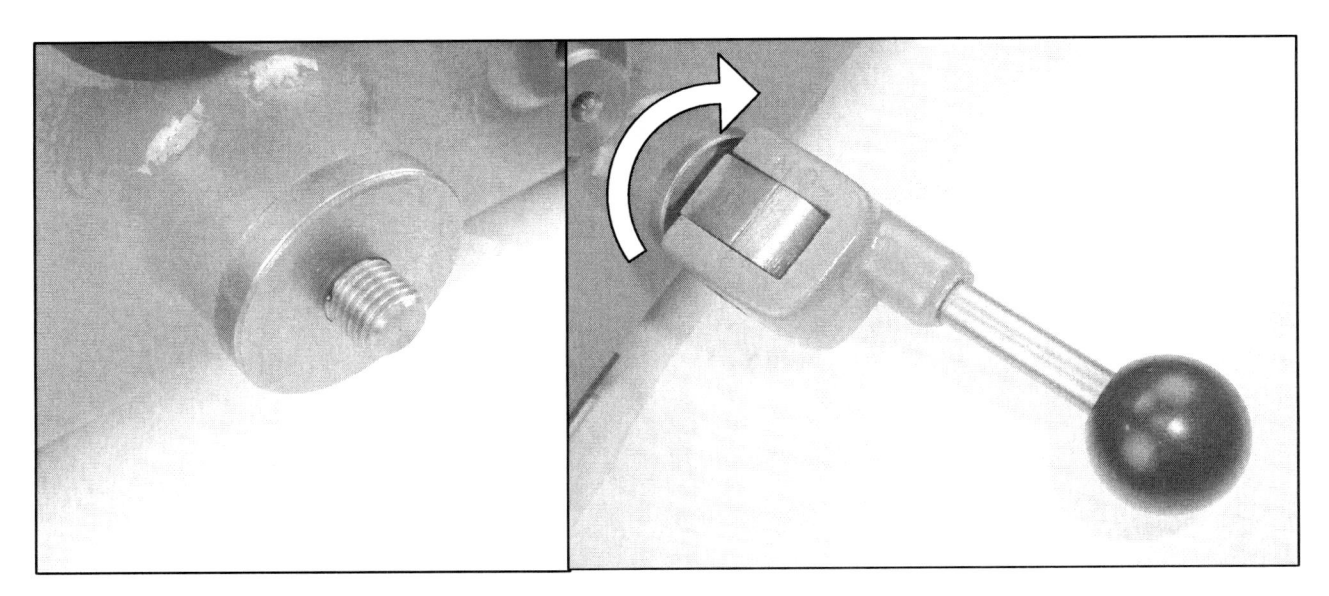

115. From the rear of the apron, compress the clutch drawbar fully against the spring. Mount the hardened cam washer on the end of the drawbar. Thread the swivel nut onto the threaded end of the drawbar just enough to hold the clutch in the apron against the spring tension.

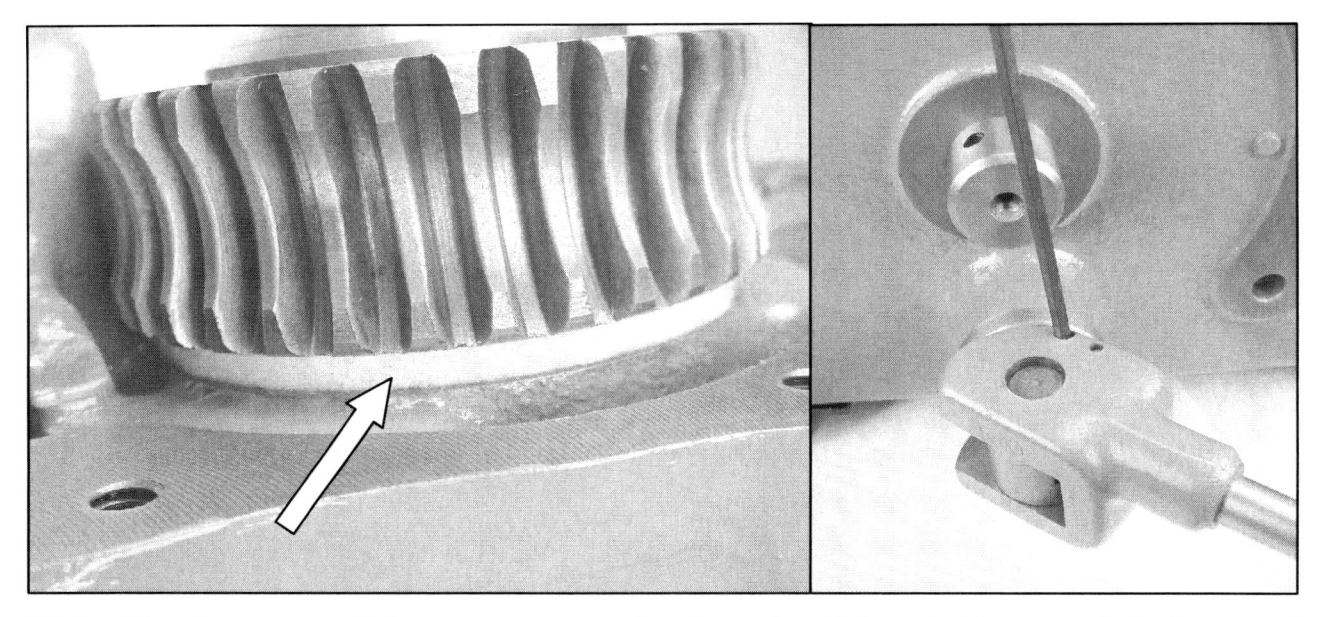

116. On the rear of the apron, manipulate the felt wicking until it is evenly distributed around the worm gear and centered such that the two free ends of the felt are approximately equal in length. Continue rotating the front cam lever to tighten the swivel nut and draw in the clutch assembly. Continue tightening until the lever is almost perpendicular to the front of the apron and tight when the lever is fully extended. Relax the lever, align the access hole in the cam lever body and tighten the swivel locking screw.

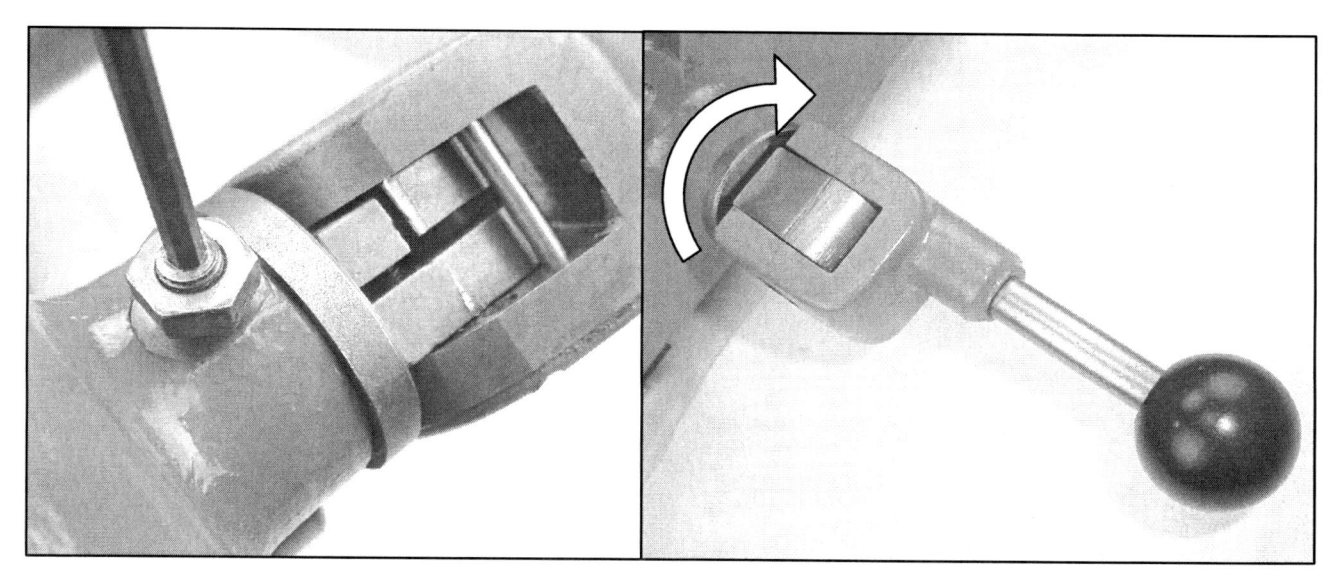

117. The retaining set screw on the underside of the apron only positions the lever so that it can be locked at a comfortable angle for the operator. With the swivel nut unlocked, the cam lever rotates freely about its axis. Rotate the lever until it is in a convenient position and tighten the set screw and lock nut. The lever will still actuate but it no longer rotates.

Oil Sump

118. Flip the apron over to install the felt oil wicks for the remaining shafts. Start with the lower right sump. Down inside the sump you will find a bar that is cast into the apron. Tie off a 12" length of Type 3 felt strip (Type 1 for model 10L) to this bar using a simple slip knot. The knot shown above works well for flat strips. Unless you have surgeon's hemostats, tie the knot outside the sump and then slip it into place.

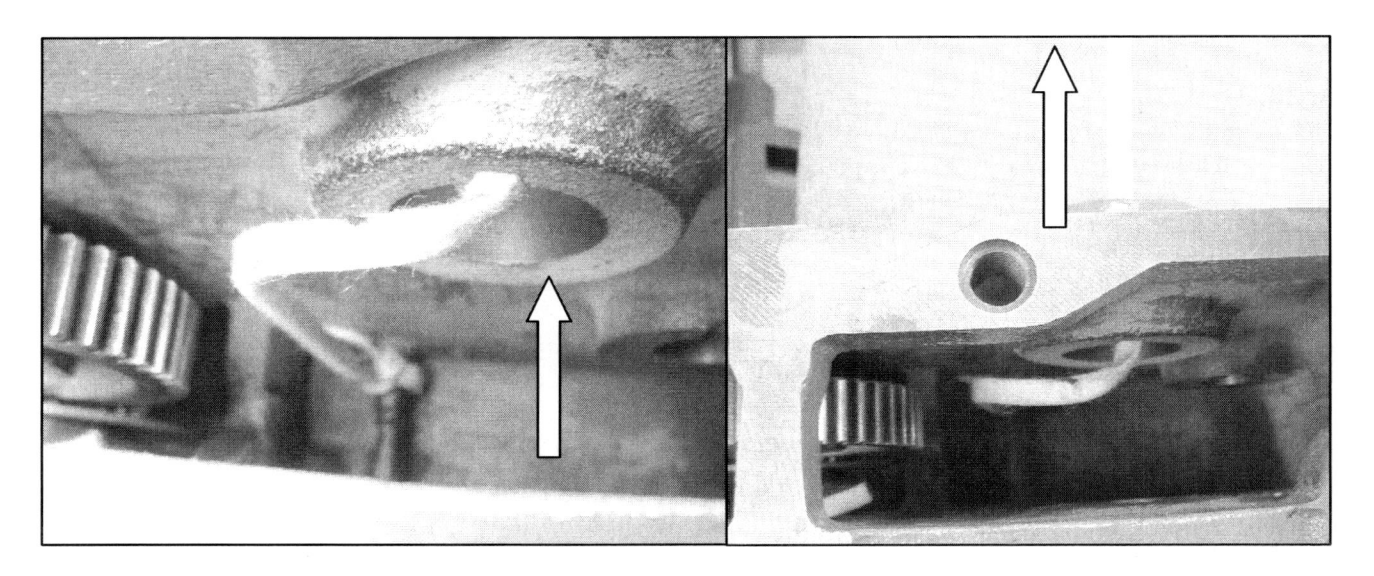

119. The left photo is a view through the top of the apron. Pull the wicking straight up through the apron to the upper front bearing for the rack pinion. Twist the felt strip as shown to help hold the wick out of the way after the rack pinion is installed. Pull through to the front of the apron, seat the wick in the slot but do not trim it off at this time.

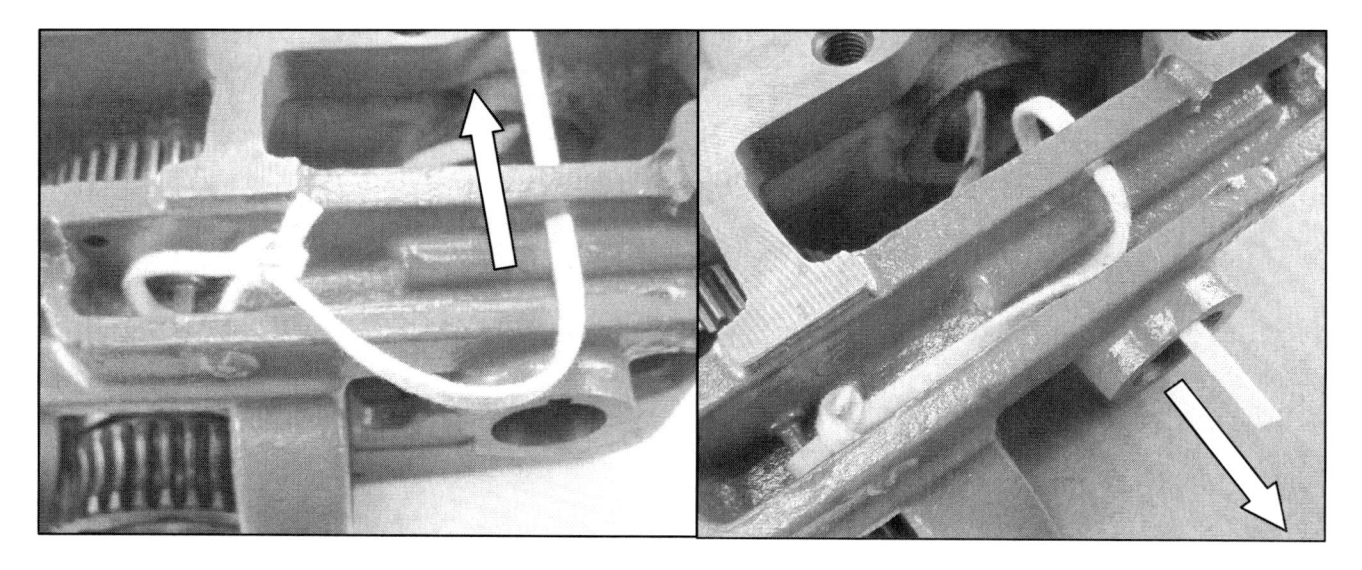

120. Tie off an 8" length of Type 3 Felt strip (Type 1 for model 10L) to the cast-in pin in the upper rear oil trough. Pull the slip knot tight and thread the wick through the hole in the casting as shown. Pass the wick through the rear bearing for the rack pinion, seat it in the slot but do not trim it yet.

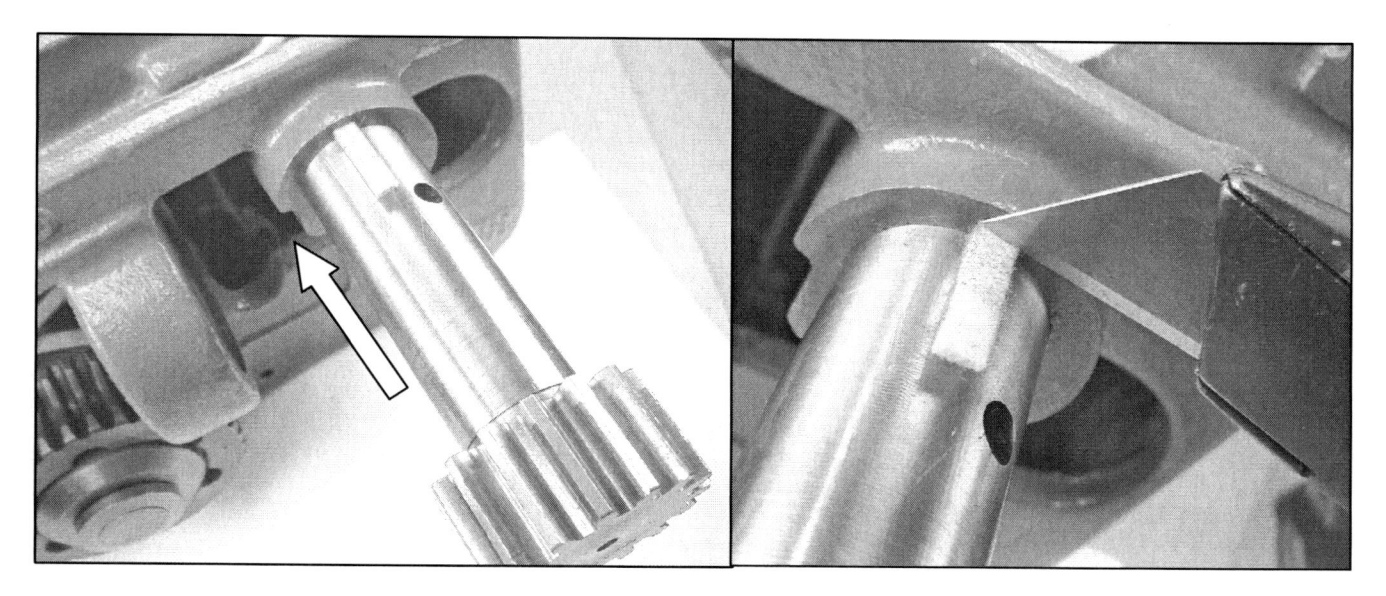

121. Lubricate the rack pinion shaft with Type C oil and insert it into the apron. Hold onto the wicking felt so that the shaft does not pull the wick back into the housing. Once the wick is pulled to the correct length, trim the end flush with the casting.

122. Slip the rack pinion gear into the apron with the collar facing the rear of the apron. Orient the taper pin holes so that they correspond to the hole in the pinion shaft. Slide the pinion shaft through the gear and out the front to the apron. Place the taper pin through the gear & shaft. Check the clearance of the felt wicks on either side to make sure that they are not strained or too loose. If too loose they can get snagged on the gear.

123. Fully seat the taper pin with a pin punch. On the front of the apron, trim the excess wicking flush with the front of the apron. Dribble a small amount of Type C oil on the wicks, just enough to saturate them.

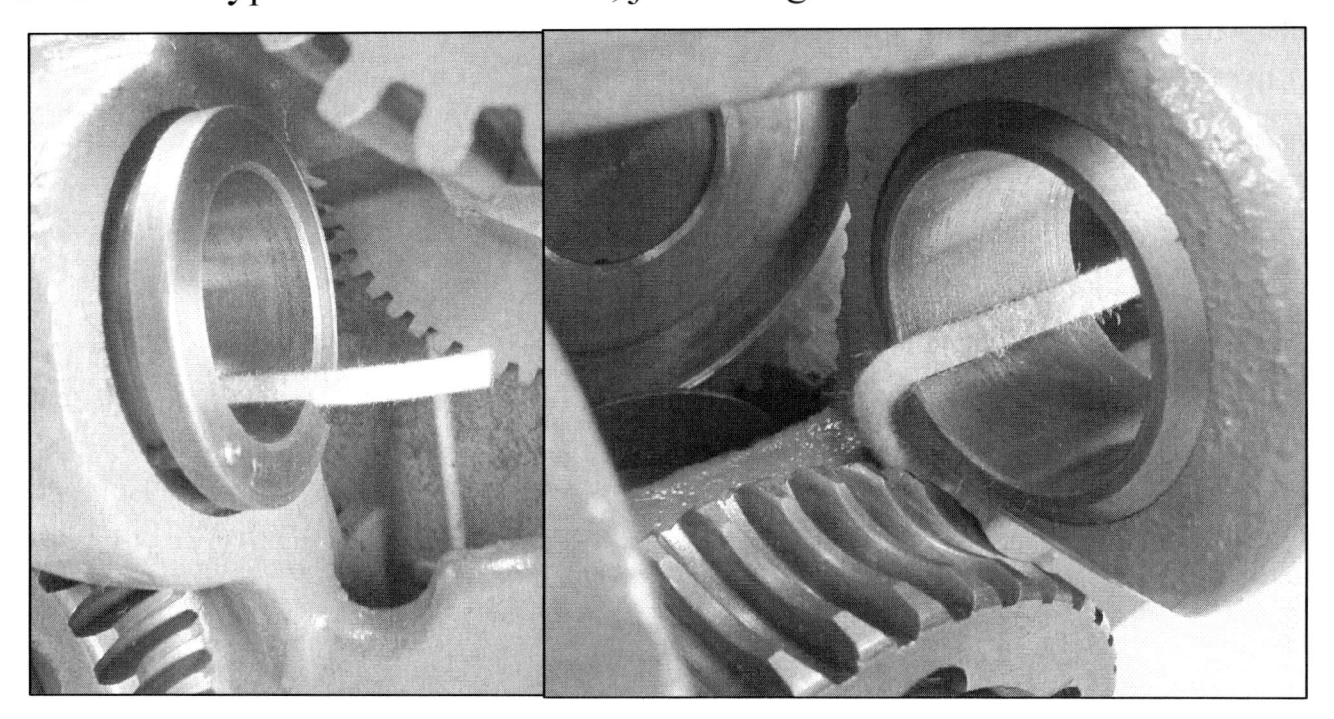

124. Move to the rear of the housing. Install the Right Side worm bushing in the housing. Align the dowel pin in the collar and fully seat it in the housing. Pull the right side of the "horseshoe" felt wick through the bushing and seat it in the slot provided. Check that the felt wick is positioned as shown in the right photo above. The felt tail length is typically about ¾" long. Lubricate the bushing and wick with Type C oil.

125. Push the left ear of the felt "horseshoe" against the idler gear and out of the way. Lubricate the worm with Type C oil. Check the Left / Right side orientation and then feed the worm into the housing from the left side until the threads contact the worm gear.

126. Start rotating the worm counterclockwise to "screw" the worm into the housing and into place on the worm gear. Check the right side felt wick to make sure that it is seated properly in the right bushing groove. Continue feeding the worm in until it is approximately centered as shown above.

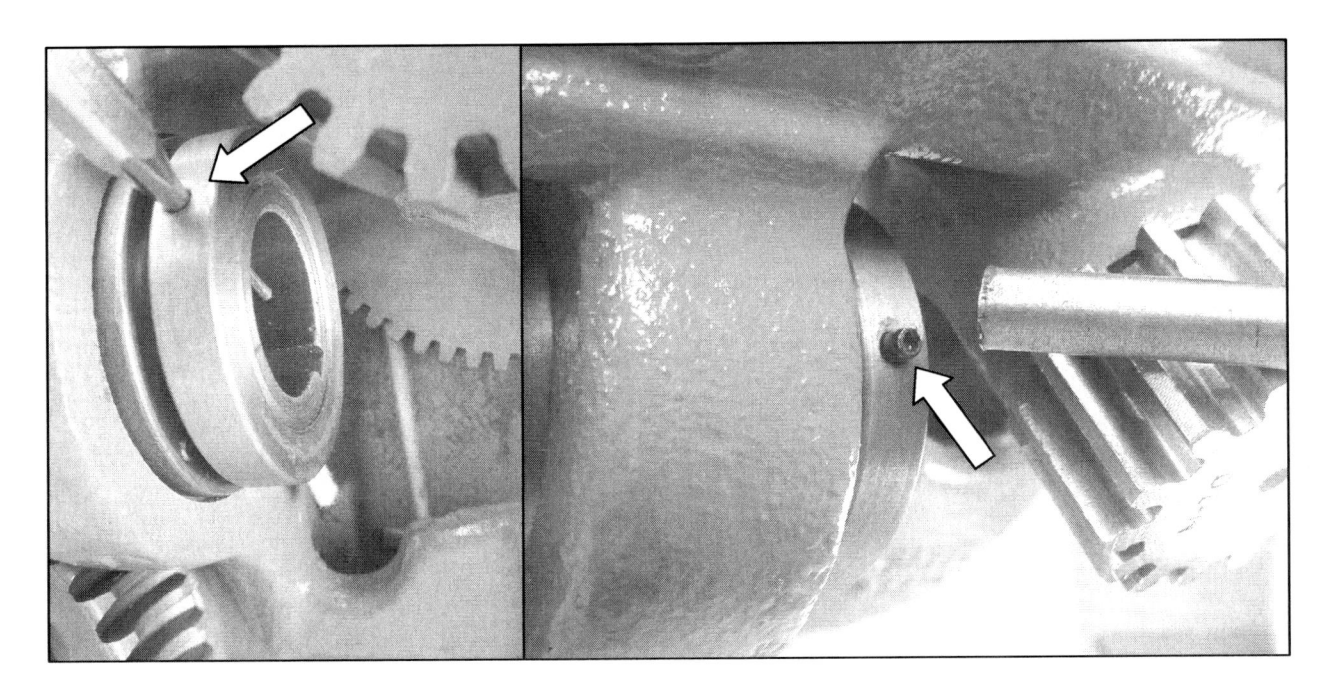

127. Make sure the felt wick aligns to the groove in the bushing next to the collar. Install the right side worm collar and align the hole for the dowel pin. Insert the dowel pin and drive it flush with the outside of the collar.

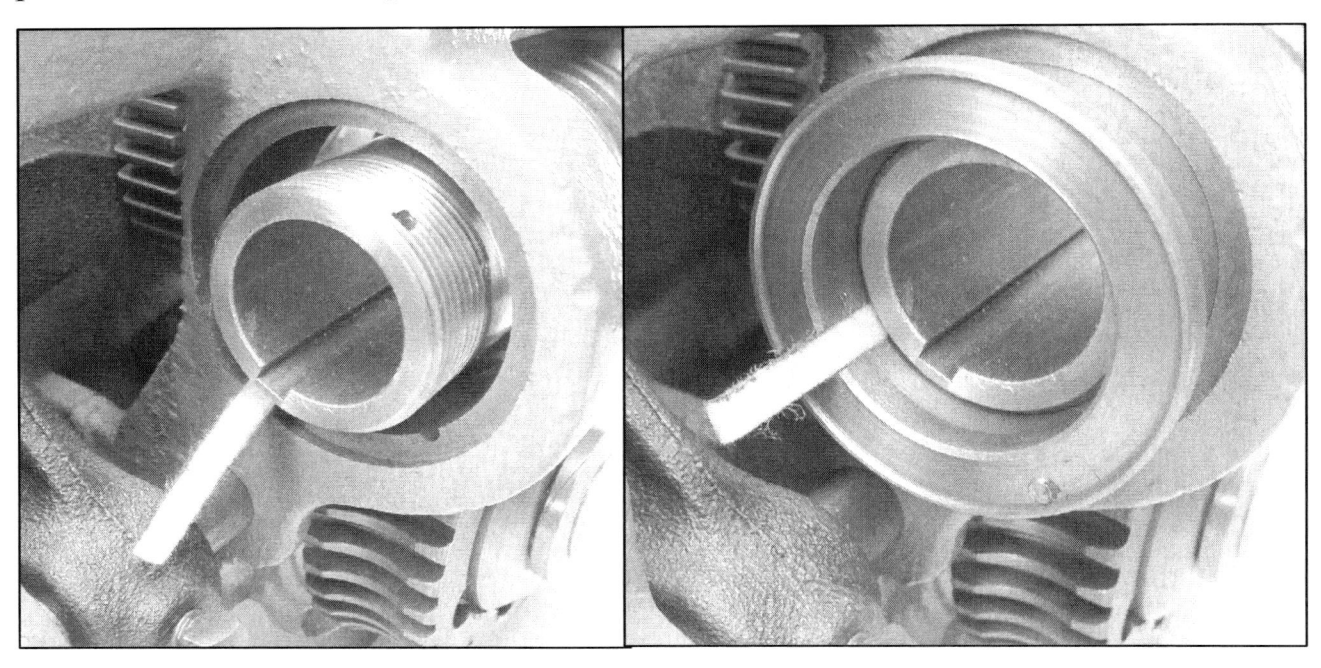

128. Using a length of wire with a hook in the end, fish the left ear of the felt wick through the opening parallel to the worm. Lubricate and slide the left side worm bushing onto the worm while carefully pulling the felt wick through the groove in the bushing. Align the dowel pin in the busing and seat it in the apron housing.

129. Fold the felt wick into the bushing slot next to the collar and then install the collar. Look through the opening just below the worm and make sure the felt wick is not bunched or stretched tight up next to the bushings. If it is, gently pull on the felt wick and manipulate it until it is centered. Align the dowel pin hole with a punch and then drive the dowel pin flush with the collar surface. Install the key in the worm.

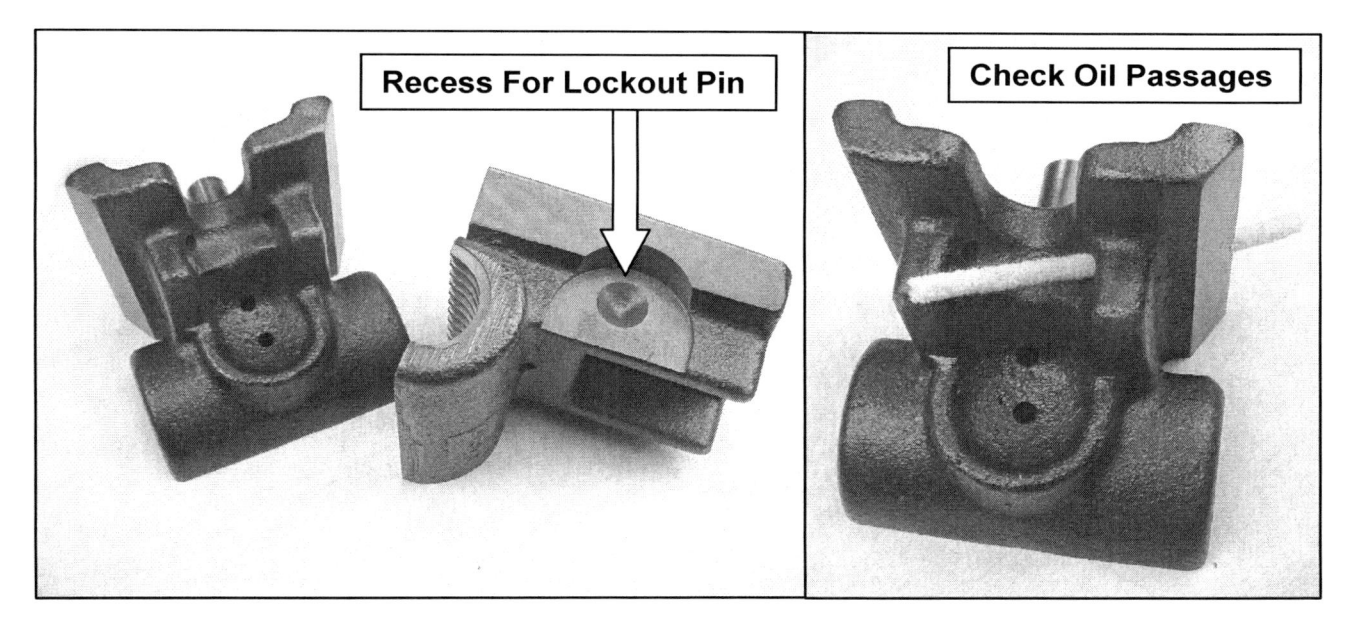

130. Make sure the threading half-nuts are absolutely clean before reinstalling them. Run a pipe cleaner through the oil passages to the lead screw thread and to the dovetail ways. If these holes are clogged, the oil will go everywhere except where it is supposed to.

Lubricate Ways

131. Lubricate the dovetail ways for the half-nuts with Type C oil. Tilt the lower half-nut into the dovetail and cam slot. Check that the lockout pin engages smoothly with the conical recess in the side of the nut (Fig 130).

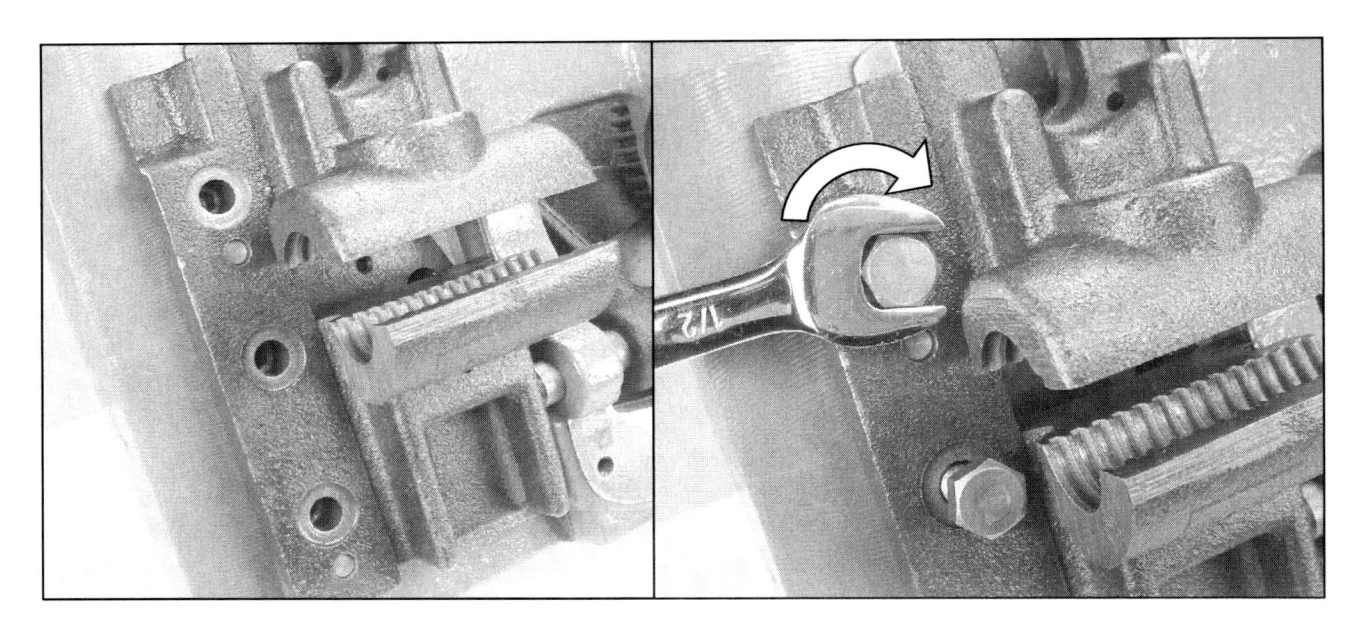

132. Install the upper half-nut in the dovetail ways and cam slot. Lubricate the gib with Type C oil, mount the gib on the two dowel pins and tap into place. Install the 3 hex cap screws and tighten. Even without the half-nut lever installed, you should be able to actuate the half nuts by turning the cam on the other side of the apron and moving the half-nuts up and down. Check the movement to make sure it is smooth but firm.

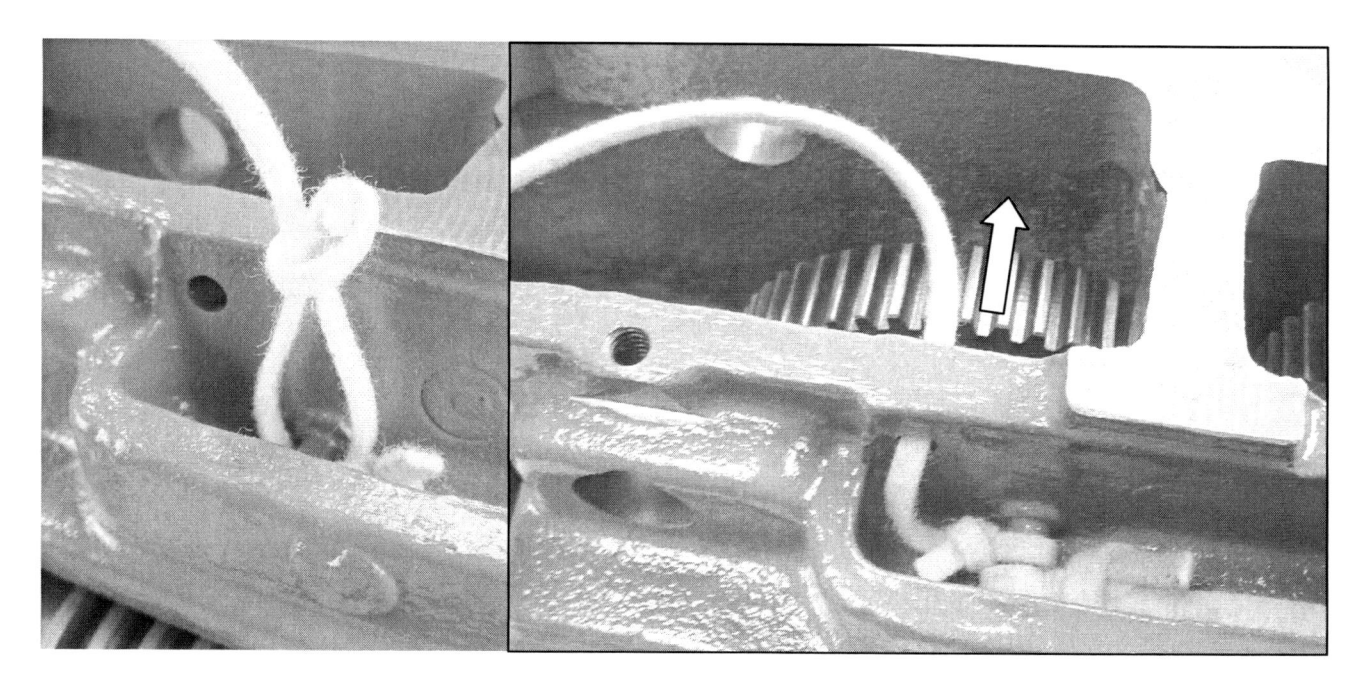

133. Tie off an 8" length of Type 1 felt wicking to the pin in the upper rear oil trough. (Next to the wick that goes to the pinion gear as shown above) Feed the wick through the hole just above the pin.

Pull wick into slot

134. Start the cross-feed gear shaft into the bearing in the front of the apron. Slip the wick through the hole in the gear. Push the shaft into the apron until you can position the wick in the shaft slot. Keep pushing until the shaft enters the gear. Keep tension on the wick and gradually work the shaft into the gear. As the shaft approaches the rear bearing, pull gently on the wick to pull it down into the gap between the gear and the housing.

Trim Wick

135. Just before the retaining groove on the shaft enters the apron, trim the wick flush with the retaining groove and lubricate the wick with Type C oil. Press the shaft into place with the front end just proud of the apron surface. Align the hole in the cross-feed gear with the dowel pin hole. Block the gear with a strip of hardwood to keep it from spinning and drive the dowel pin through the gear. If the dowel pin fit is loose, lock in place by "pinning" it with a center punch. Make sure the gear turns freely.

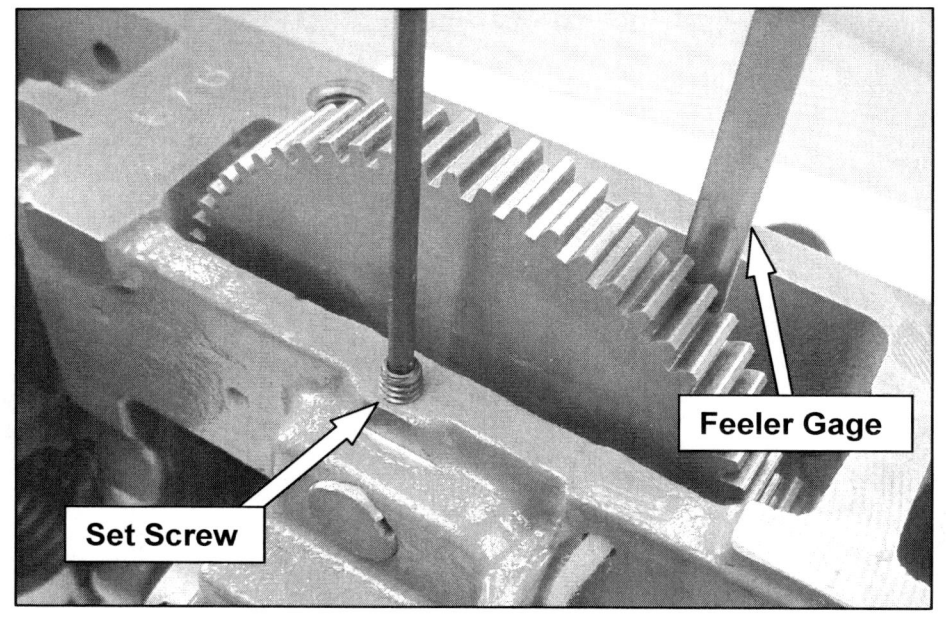

Feeler Gage

Set Screw

136. Now set the gear clearance between the cross-feed gear and the idler gear below. Place a 0.010" feeler gage between the gear faces. Tap the front or rear of the cross-feed shaft to move in or out. Once the clearance is set, lock the set screw onto the shaft as shown above.

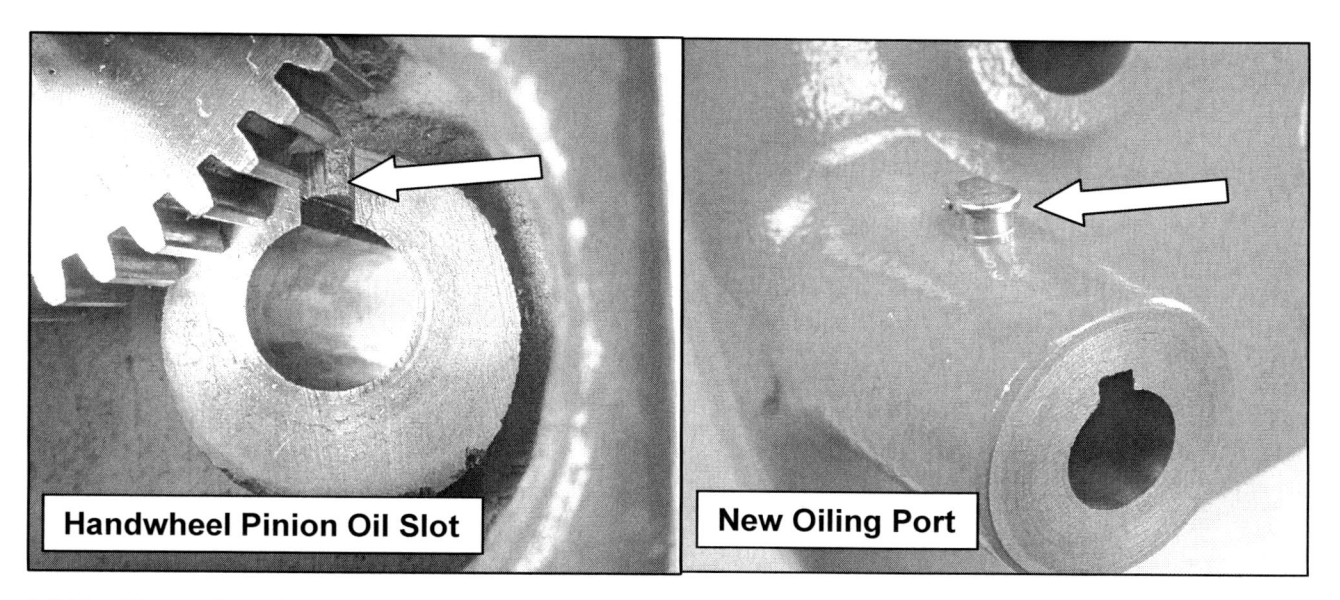

Handwheel Pinion Oil Slot

New Oiling Port

137. For the last wick we typically make a small modification to the lubrication of the handwheel pinion. The handwheel pinion shaft was designed to be lubricated by oil dripping down from the rack pinion shaft and gear above so there was only a small slot to catch the oil and direct it to this wick. We have seen wicks that were tied off in the sump and routed to this same keyway but the pinion teeth usually contact the wick material and it gets chewed up by the teeth over time. You will probably find a frayed end on this wick in most machines. Since the handwheel pinion is the most heavily used component on the apron, direct positive lubrication of this oil retaining wick is preferable... but this is only our opinion.

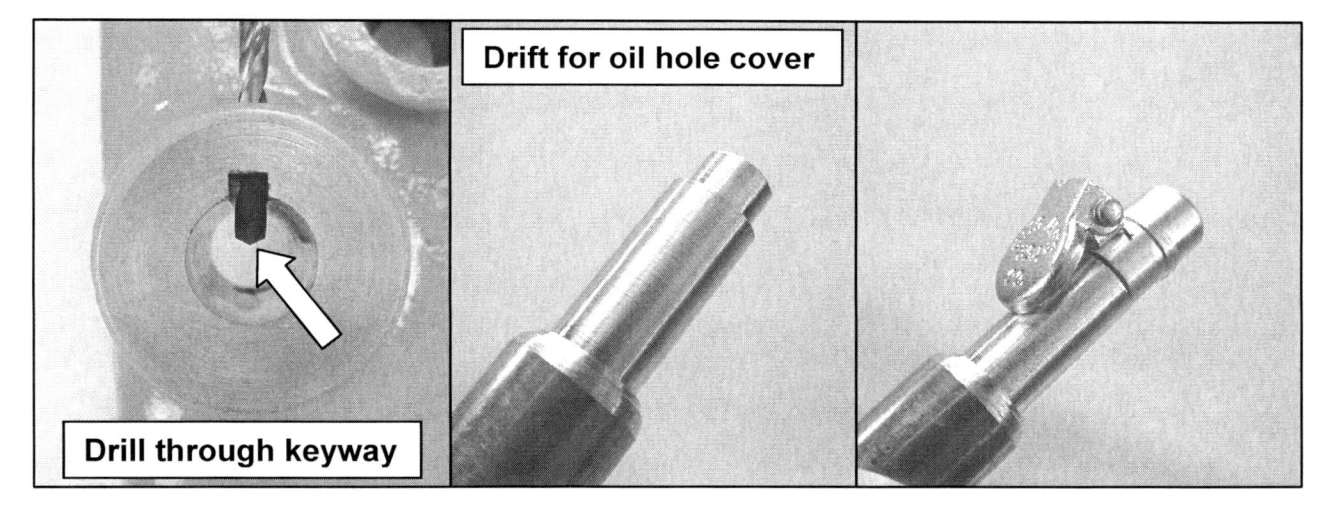

Drift for oil hole cover

Drill through keyway

138. To install a direct oil port, first drill a 3/16" diameter hole in the top of the handwheel boss directly in line with the keyway. Counterbore with a ¼" bit approximately ¼" deep. Make a drift to fit a ¼" oil hole cover.

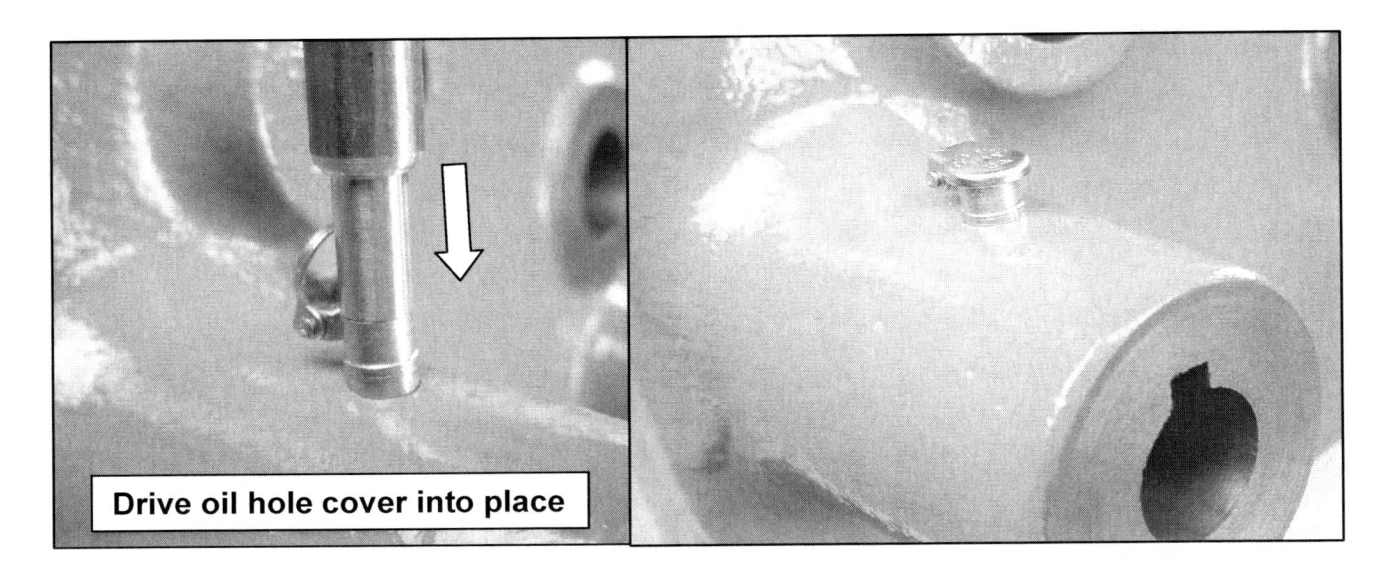

Drive oil hole cover into place

139. Drive the oil hole cover into the hole (hinge facing the rear). The modification is complete. If you decide that you do not want to make this modification to your lathe, skip this step and proceed to the instructions below for installing the pinion shaft wick.

140. Insert a length of Type 3 felt wicking into the slot for the handwheel pinion. Make a small "L" crimp on the end of the wick and turn it up into the oil slot as you install it. Leave the wick long on the front side. Insert the handwheel pinion from the rear making sure not to catch the wick and pull it out of the slot.

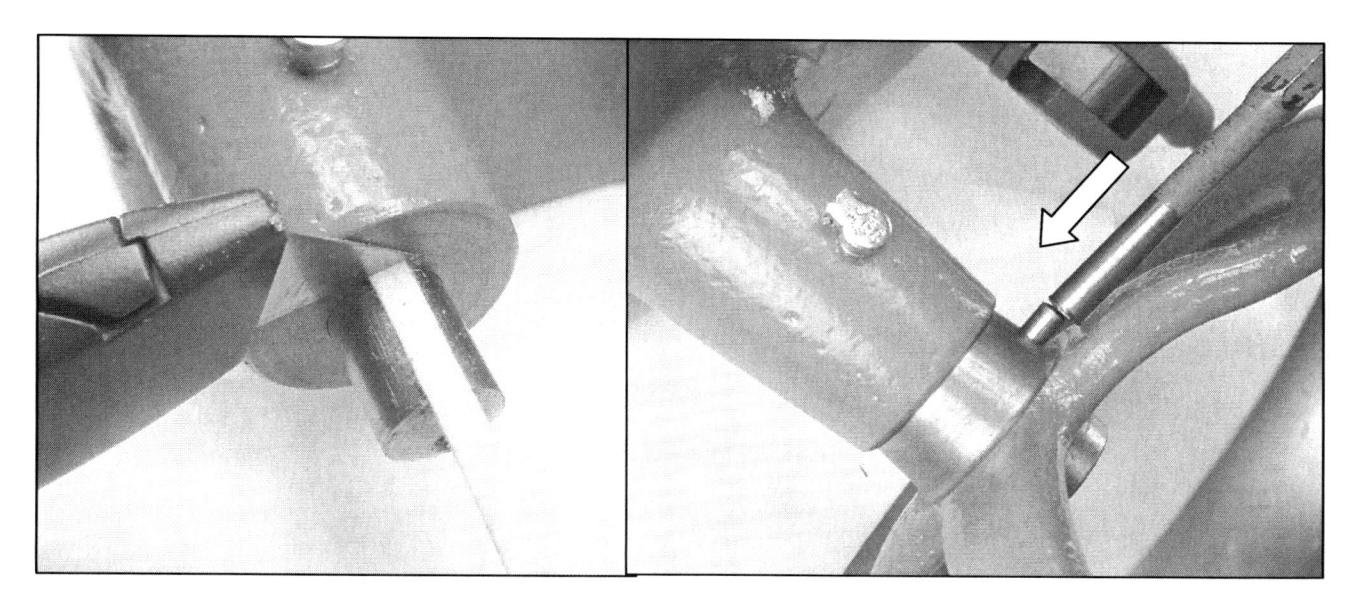

141. Trim the wick flush with the face of the boss. Lubricate with Type C oil via the new oiling port (or the end of the wick) and rotate the shaft a few turns. Hold the pinion from the rear and slide the handwheel onto the shaft. Align the taper pin hole and drive the taper pin into position.

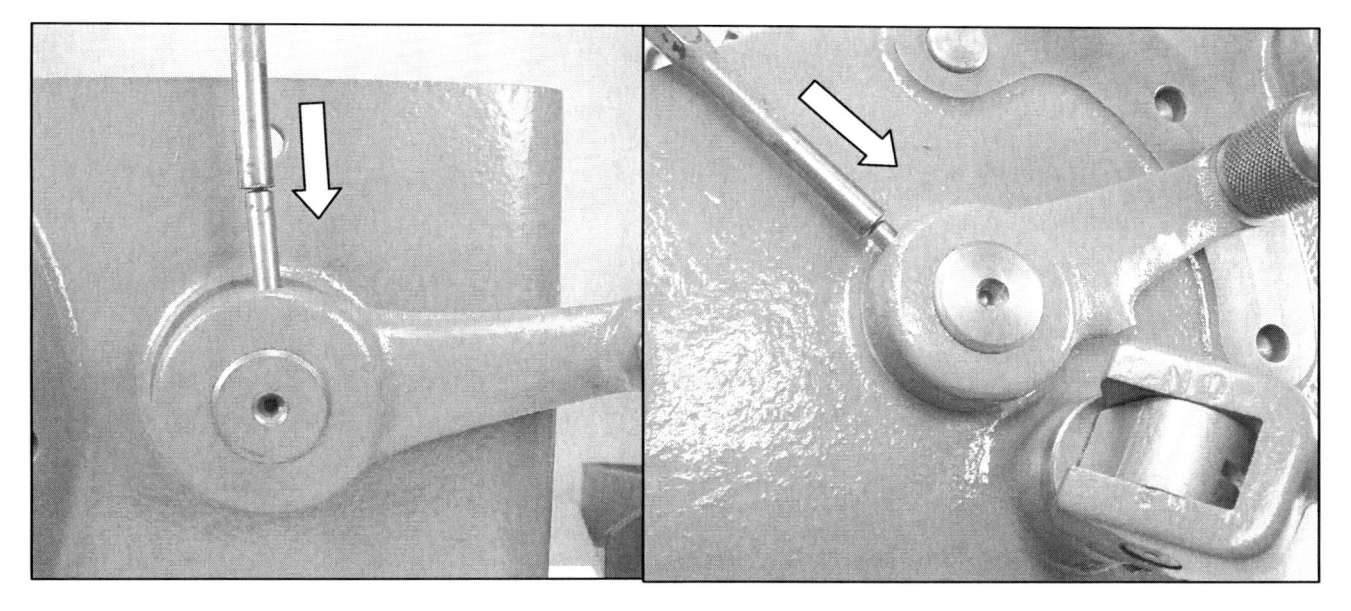

142. Install the half-nut lever on its shaft and drive in the taper pin. Check functionality. Install the power feed shift lever on its shaft and drive in the taper pin. Check functionality by shifting into center "neutral" position and actuating the half-nuts. You many need to rotate the worm gear or idler gear slightly to get the shifter to drop into position. Open the half-nuts and place the shifter in either top or bottom position. The half-nuts should now be "locked out".

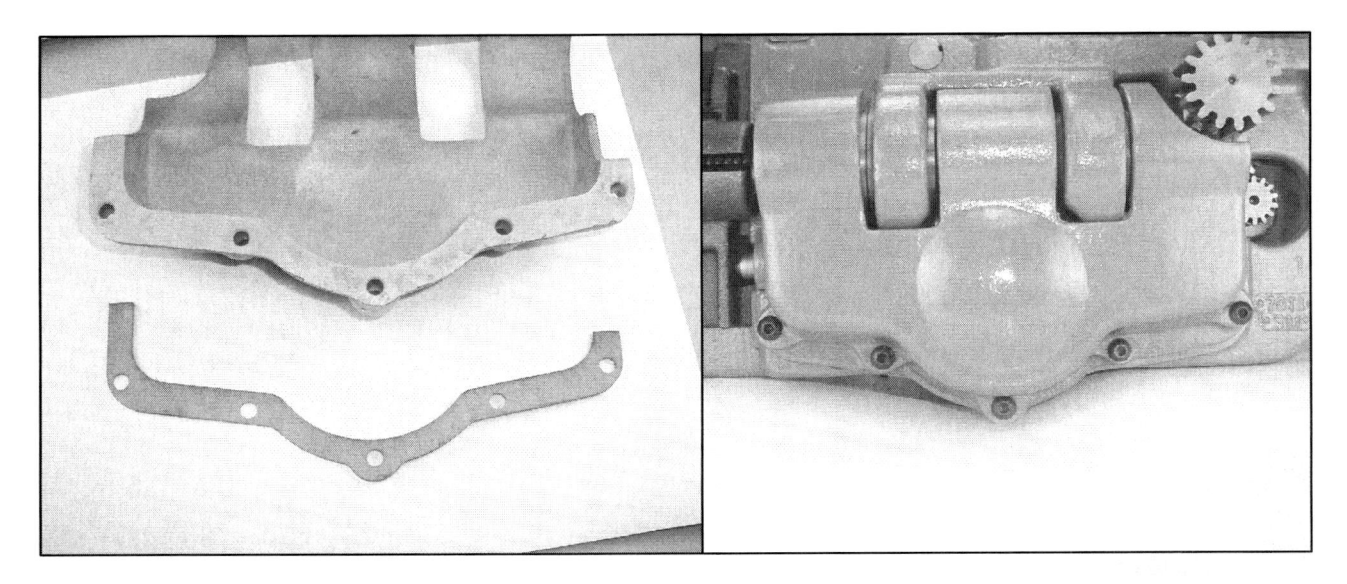

143. To install the trough cover, spread a very thin film of RTV silicone on both sides of the trough gasket. Orient the gasket as shown above with one vertical "tall" leg and one "short" leg. Position the gasket and cover. Install the 5 hex cap screws and tighten gradually to compress the gasket and sealant. The center bottom screw is typically longer than the others.

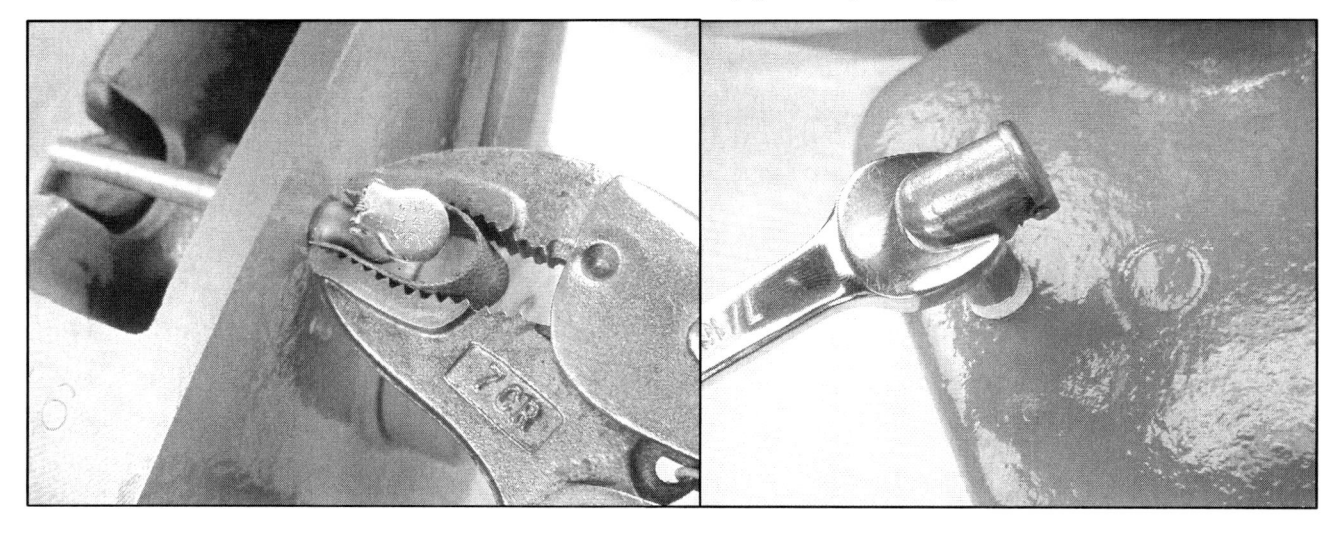

144. To reinstall the press-fit oil hole covers on the front of the apron, wrap a strip of reinforced sheet rubber around the body of the oiler to protect it from damage and grip it with locking pliers. Be careful not to crush the tube. Spread a very thin film of RTV silicone around the neck of the oiler. Place the oiler in the hole and then drive in by taping on the base of the pliers with a hammer. The rubber may slip a bit as you tap so reposition as needed. On the trough oiler, use Teflon® tape to seal the threads before installing. The apron reassembly is now complete.

Disassembly – Saddle & Compound

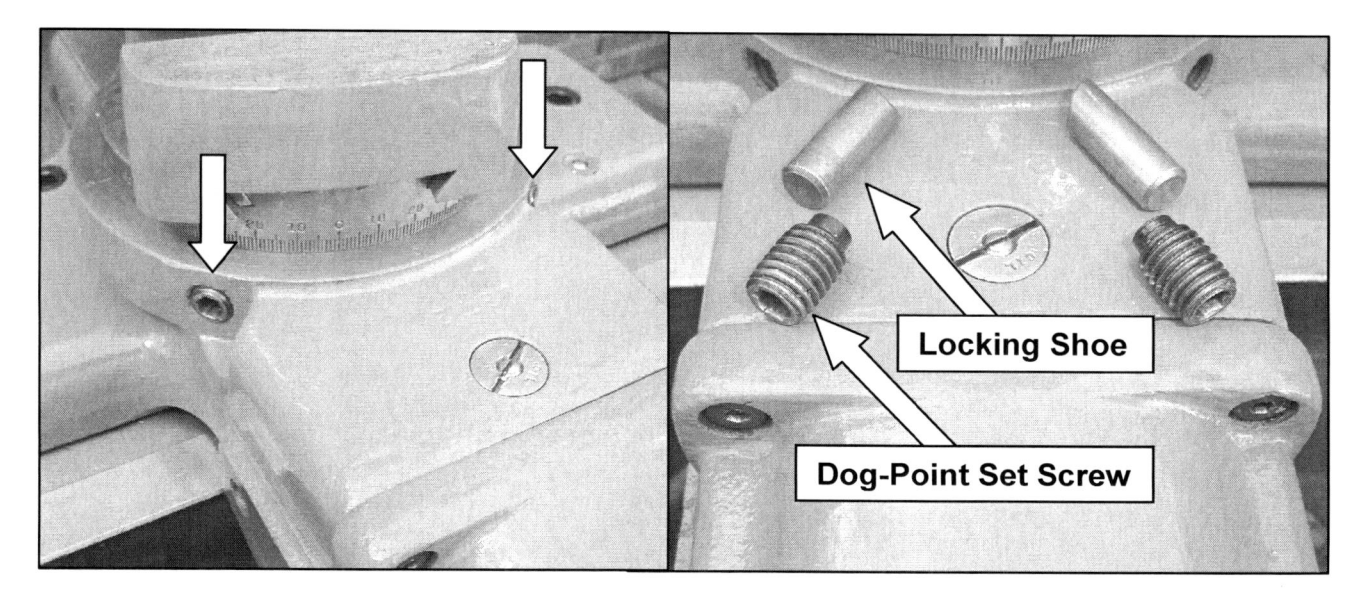

145. Remove the two dog-point set screws on the rear of the cross slide. Lift the compound up while rotating it back and forth to remove it from the cross slide. Push out the locking shoes with a pin punch. The photo above right shows the dog-point set screws and the compound locking shoes.

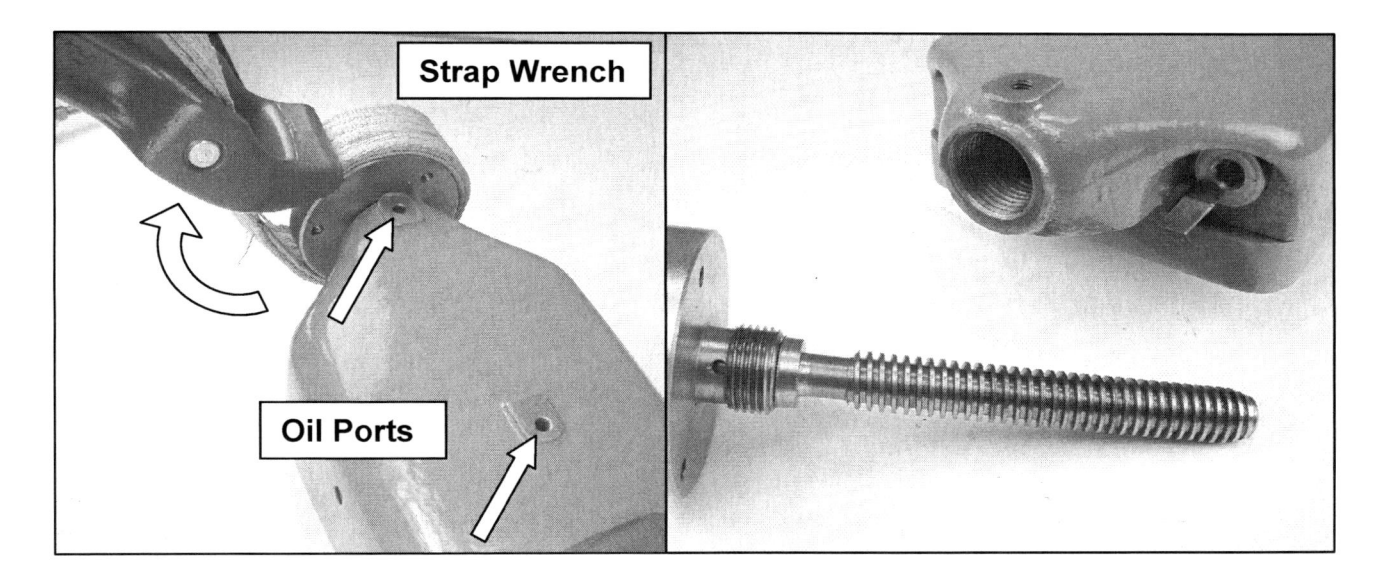

146. To disassemble the compound, first remove the slotted set screws covering the oil ports. Use a strap wrench to grip the dial collar and rotate it counterclockwise to unscrew it. Once the collar is free, unscrew the compound feed screw from the compound (counterclockwise) and set it aside. We'll cover dial disassembly later when we do the cross-feed dial.

147. Loosen the gib screw lock on the right side of the compound. This slotted set screw pushes against a brass shoe to keep the gib screw from loosening once adjusted. Unscrew the gib screw completely from the compound body and lift it out of the slot in the gib strip. The head may bind in the slot periodically as it exits the body, so wiggle the head around as needed as you unscrew it.

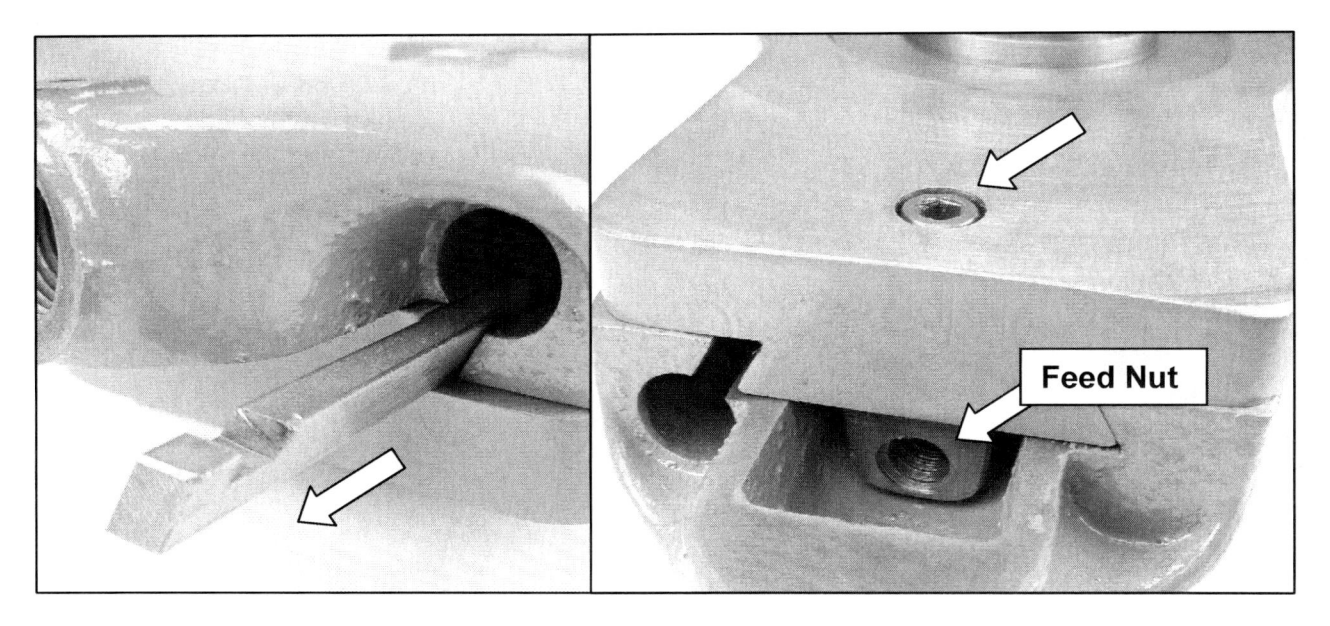

148. Slide the gib strip out of the dovetail way in the compound. Remove the lock screw and small brass shoe from the body so they do not get lost. Flip the compound over. Remove the socket cap screw on the bottom of the compound base that secures the bronze compound feed nut.

Cross Feed Bushing

149. Tap the feed nut down into the cavity in the compound body. Lift the base to clear the feed nut and slide it out of the dovetail ways. Now move to the cross feed. First remove the cross feed screw bushing by using a wrench on the flats.

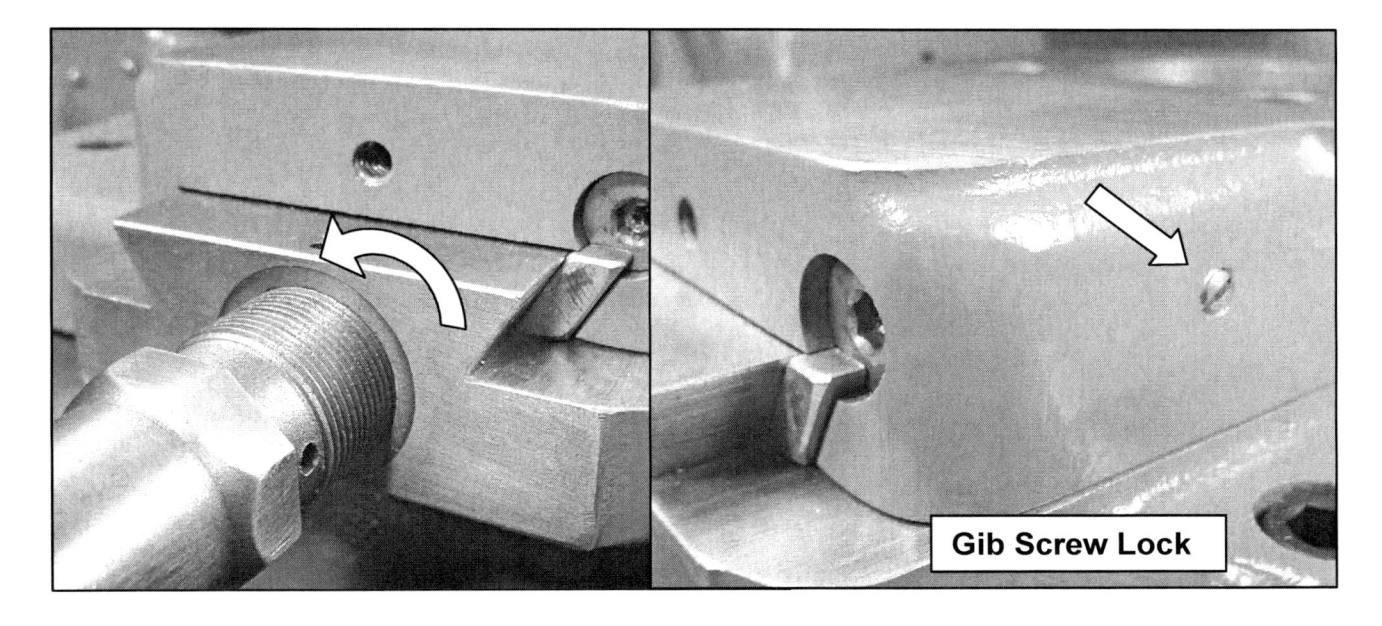

Gib Screw Lock

150. Unscrew the cross feed bushing counterclockwise while rotating the ball crank handle clockwise to unthread the assembly from the cross slide and the internal bronze feed nut simultaneously. As on the compound, loosen the gib screw lock on the side of the cross slide first.

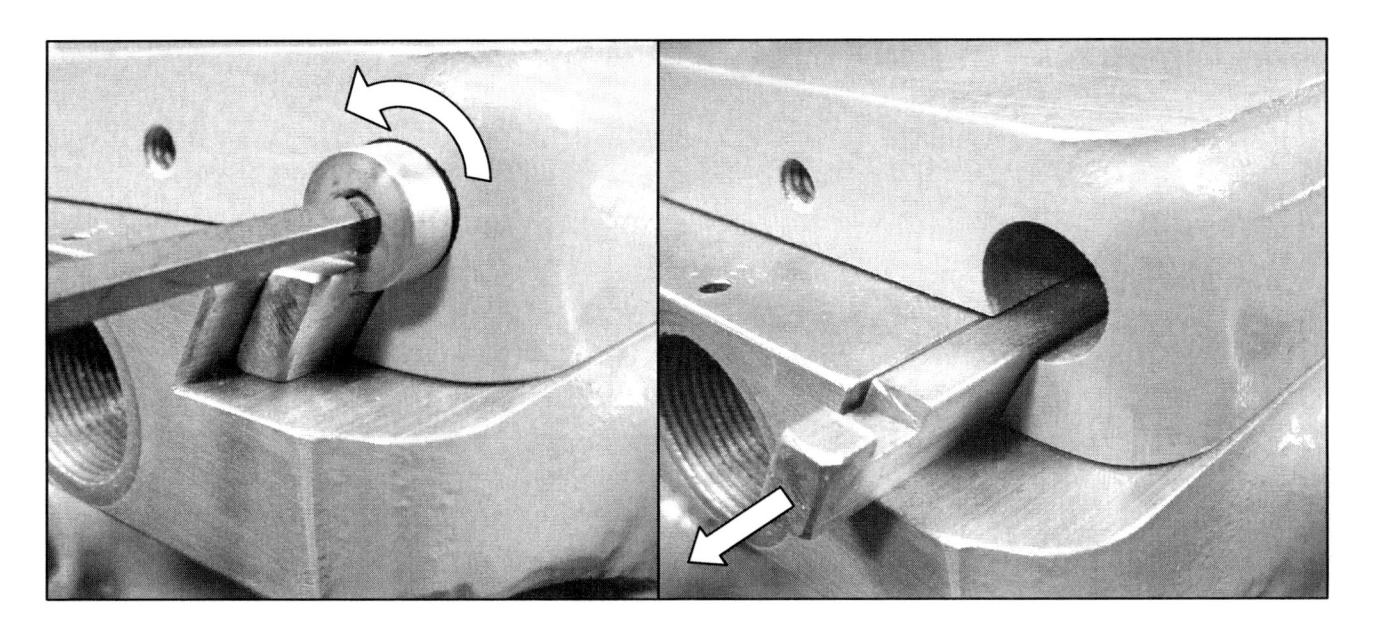

151. Unscrew the gib screw completely from the cross slide body and remove it from the slot in the gib strip. Slide the gib strip out of the cross slide. Remove the lock screw and small brass shoe from the cross slide body so they don't get lost.

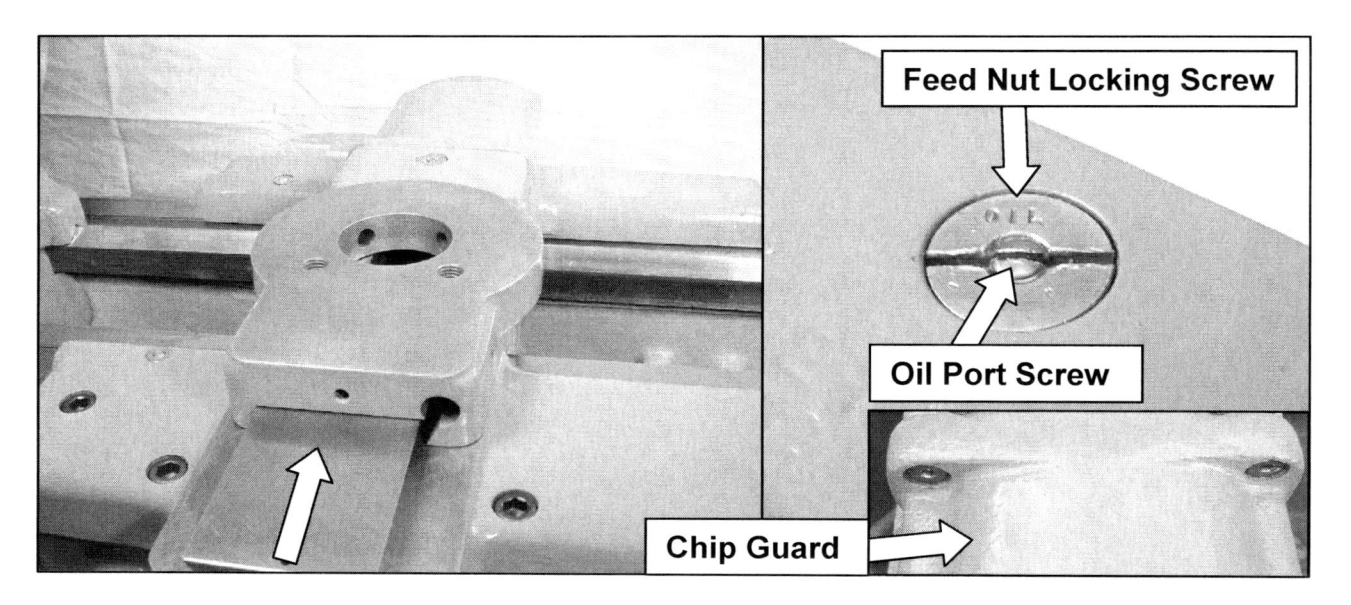

Feed Nut Locking Screw

Oil Port Screw

Chip Guard

152. Remove the cross slide from the saddle by sliding it to the rear of the saddle and off of the dovetail ways. Remove the chip guard on the back of the cross slide by removing the two socket cap screws securing it. On the top of the cross slide, remove the small oil port screw in the center of the feed nut locking screw. Use a large screwdriver or drag link socket to remove the large feed nut locking screw.

Feed Nut

Spanner Bit

153. Flip the cross slide over and remove the feed nut from the base. Move now to the feed screws. The ball crank handles are removed first by using an appropriate spanner bit to remove the retaining nut (see photo). A spanner is needed as the tip of the feed screw blocks the center of the slot.

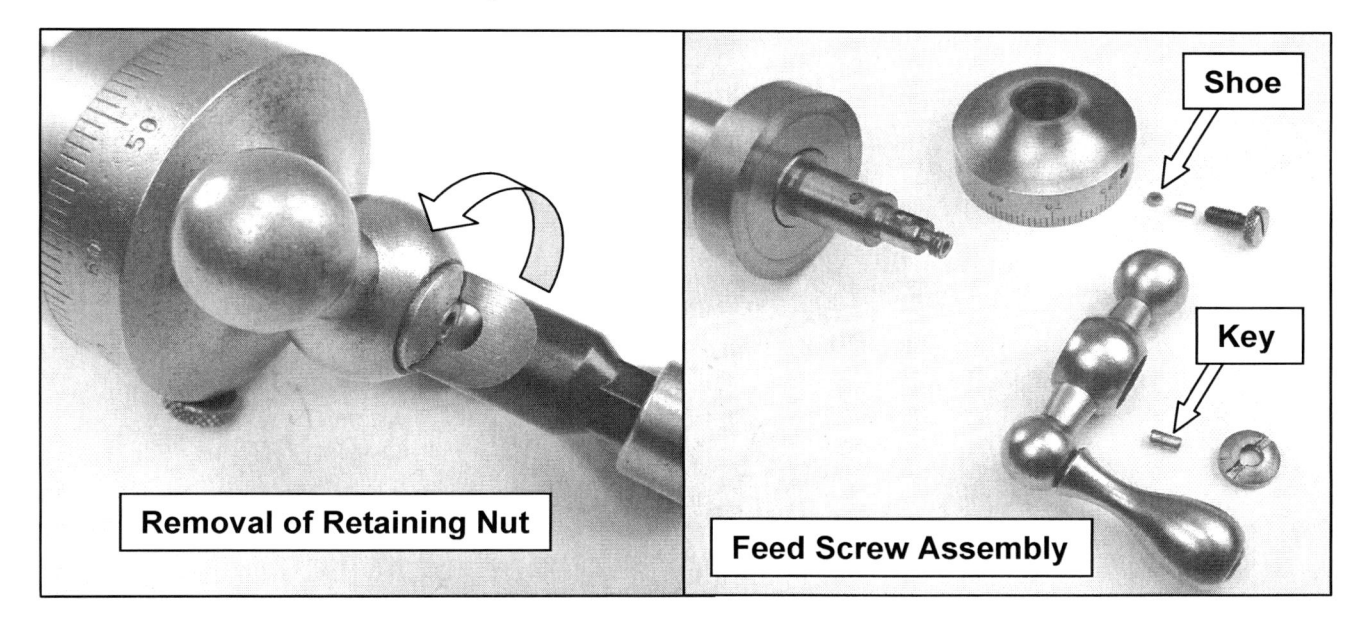

Removal of Retaining Nut

Shoe

Key

Feed Screw Assembly

154. The ball crank handle is keyed to the shaft with a small round key. Tap the ball crank handle from the rear evenly to remove it from the shaft but make sure not to shoot the small key across the room in doing so. Loosen the knurled lock screw on the graduated dial and slide the dial off of the feed screw. Remove the brass shoe and dowel from inside the dial.

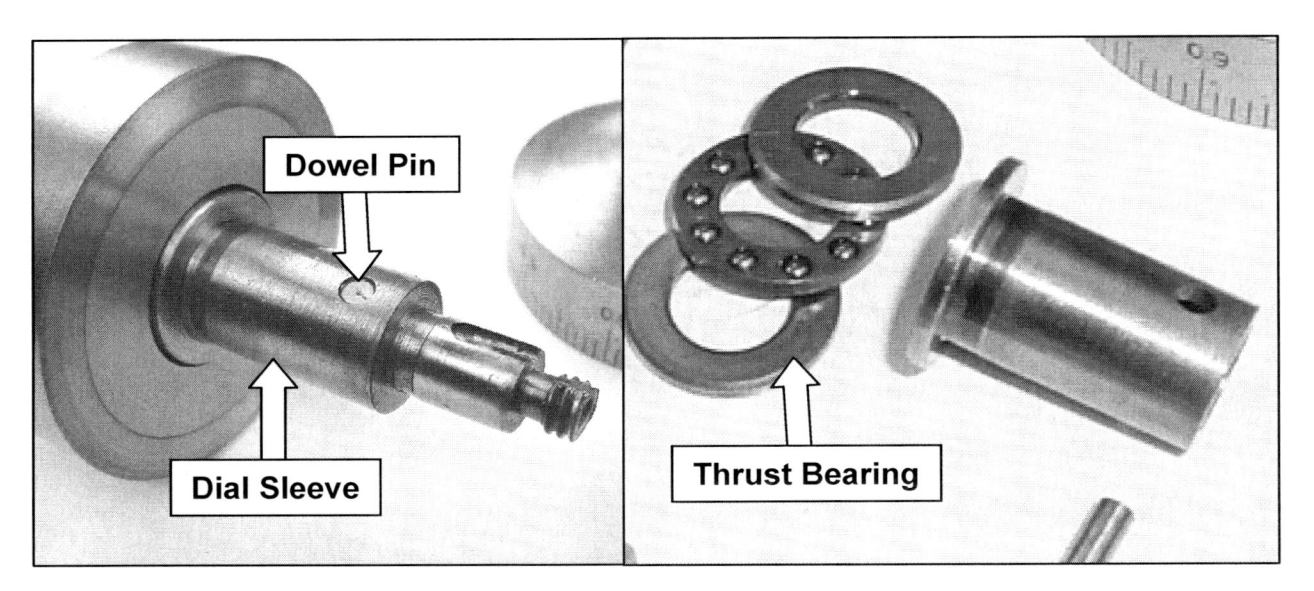

Dowel Pin

Dial Sleeve

Thrust Bearing

155. The dial sleeve is held to the feed screw with a dowel pin. Using a pin punch, tap the dowel pin out of the dial sleeve and shaft. The feed screw can now be removed from the large bushing. Be careful to remove the small 3-part thrust bearings found beneath the dial sleeve.

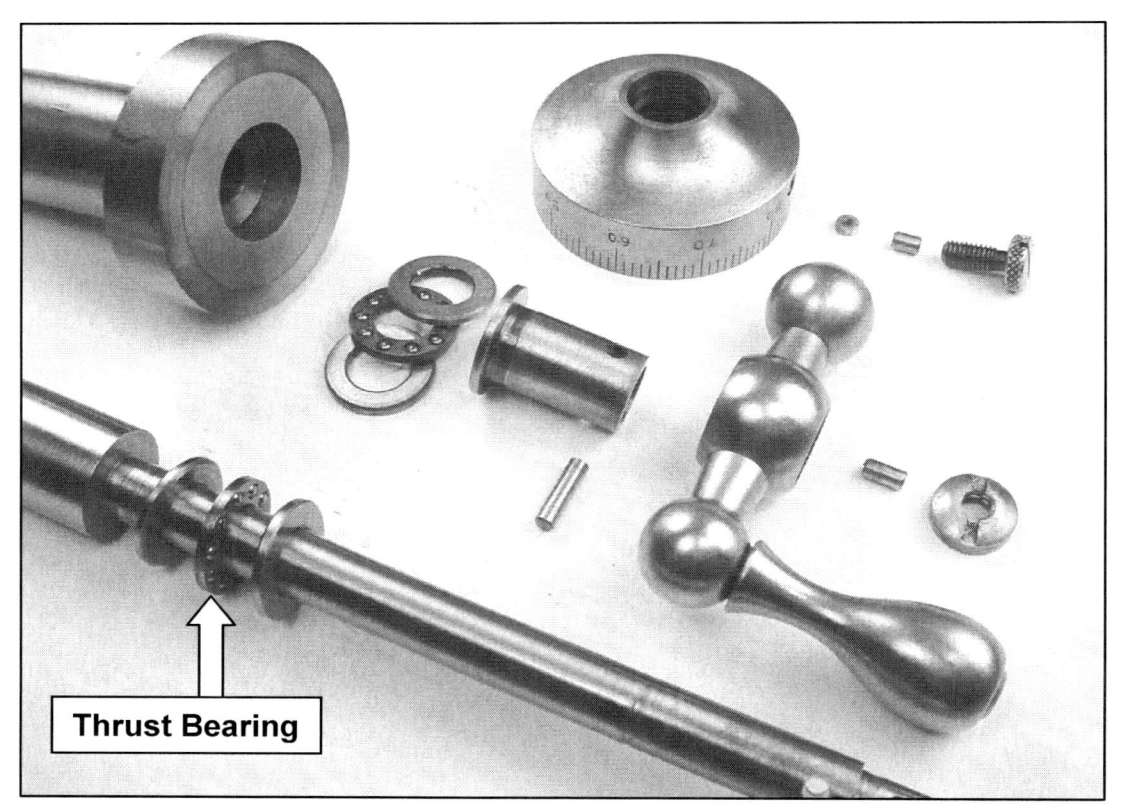

Thrust Bearing

156. The components of the feed screw are shown above. Repeat the disassembly process for the compound feed screw. Note that there are no thrust bearings, sleeve or retaining pin in the compound screw.

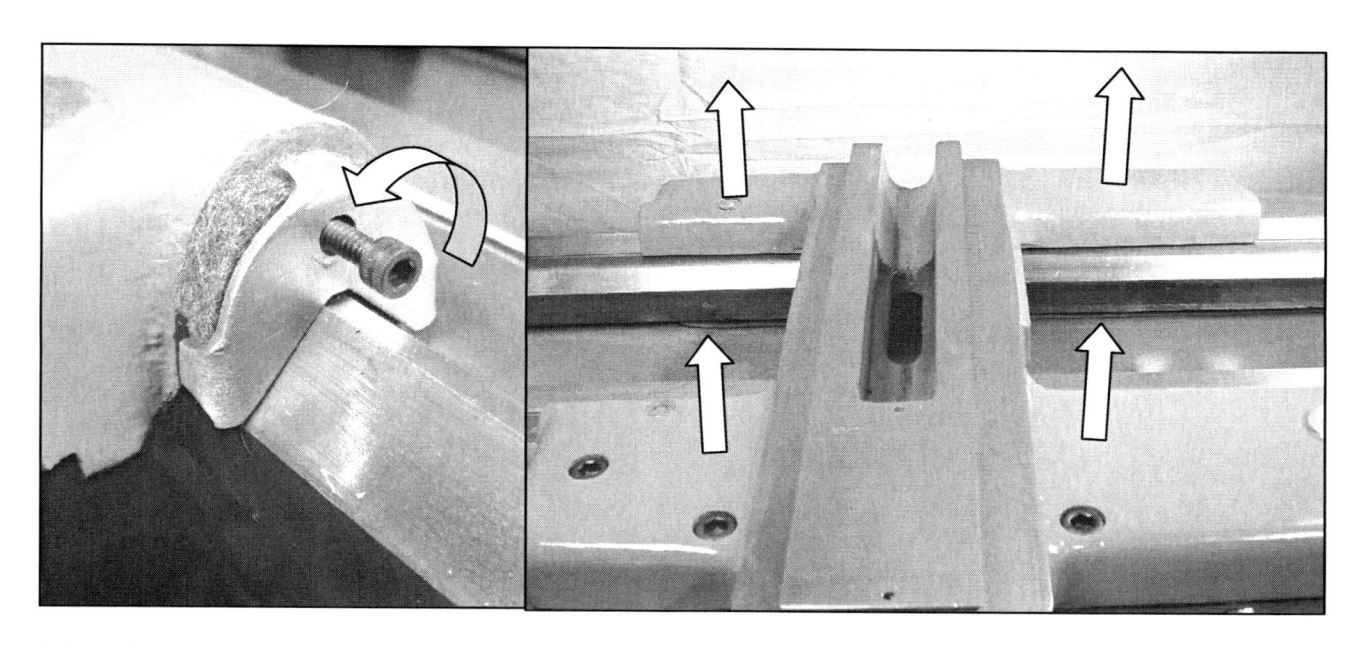

157. Remove the 4 brass retainers and felt bed wipers from the saddle. Lift the saddle straight up and off the bed and set it to the side for now.

Assembly – Saddle and Compound

All parts should be washed in a suitable cleaning solvent to remove grease or oil and if you are stripping and painting the lathe, make sure to paint only the as-cast surfaces and not any surface that has been machined. Use Type C oil to lubricate all components during reassembly.

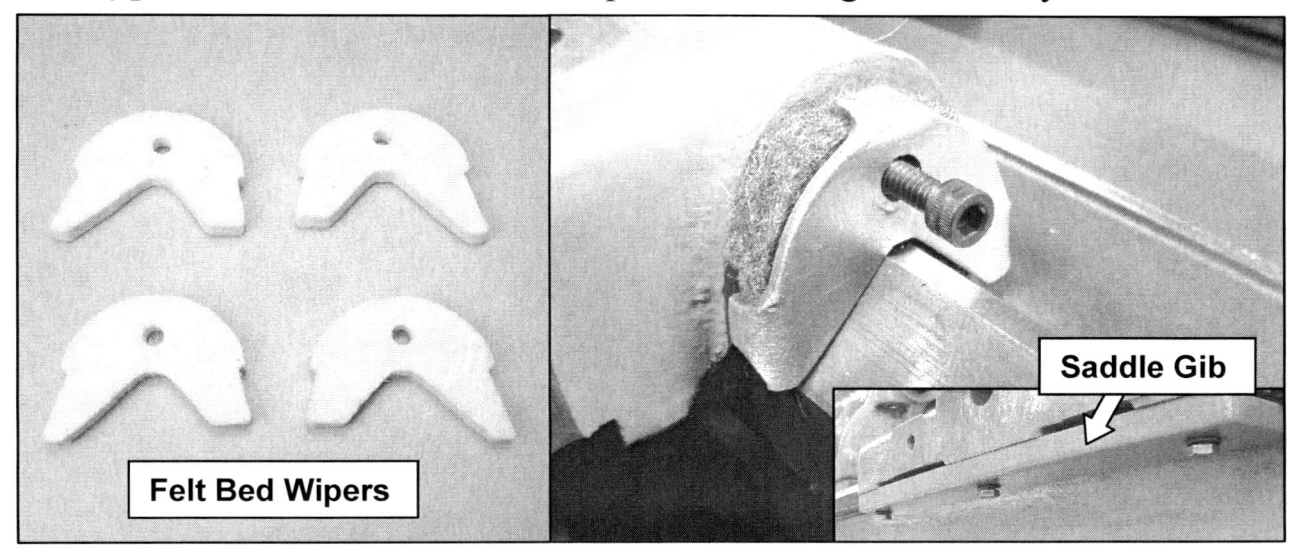

Felt Bed Wipers

Saddle Gib

158. Install 4 new die-cut felt wipers and brass retainers on the saddle. Apply Type C oil to the wipers and seat the saddle on the lathe bed. Install the gib plate and tighten the bolts only enough to contact the bed. If the saddle drags, the gib plate is too tight. Lock-washer tension is sufficient.

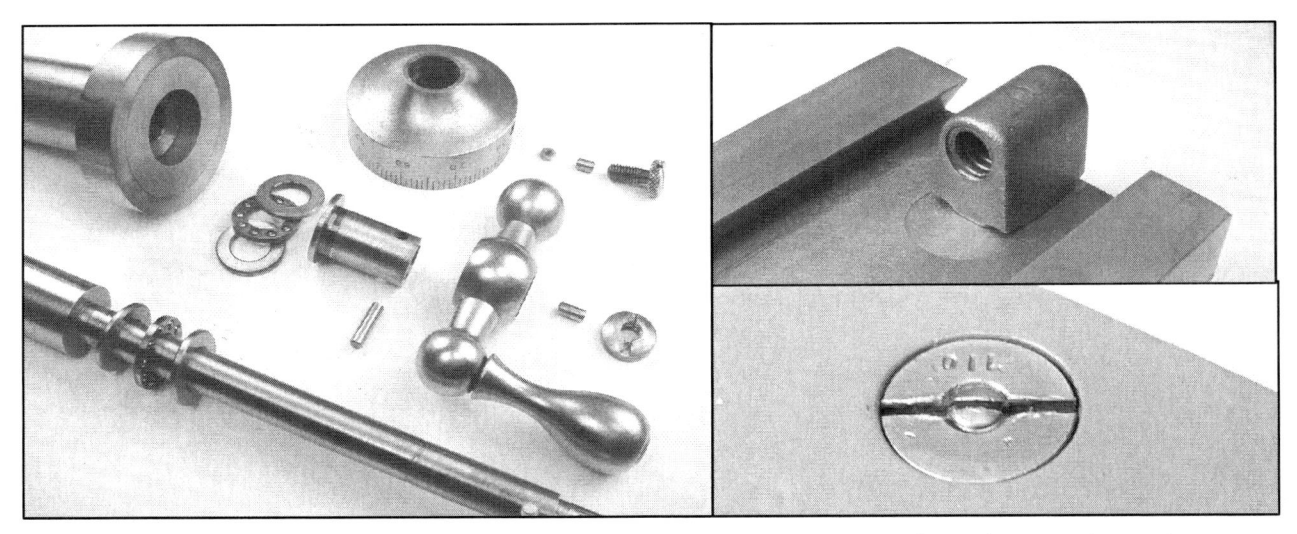

159. Reassemble the feed dials making sure that the thrust bearings and shafts are thoroughly lubricated with Type C oil before assembly. Install the bronze cross feed nut in the cross slide body but only loosely tighten the feed nut locking screw as it will be aligned later. Bolt the chip guard onto the cross slide and make sure the machined lower surface is in line with the cross slide body.

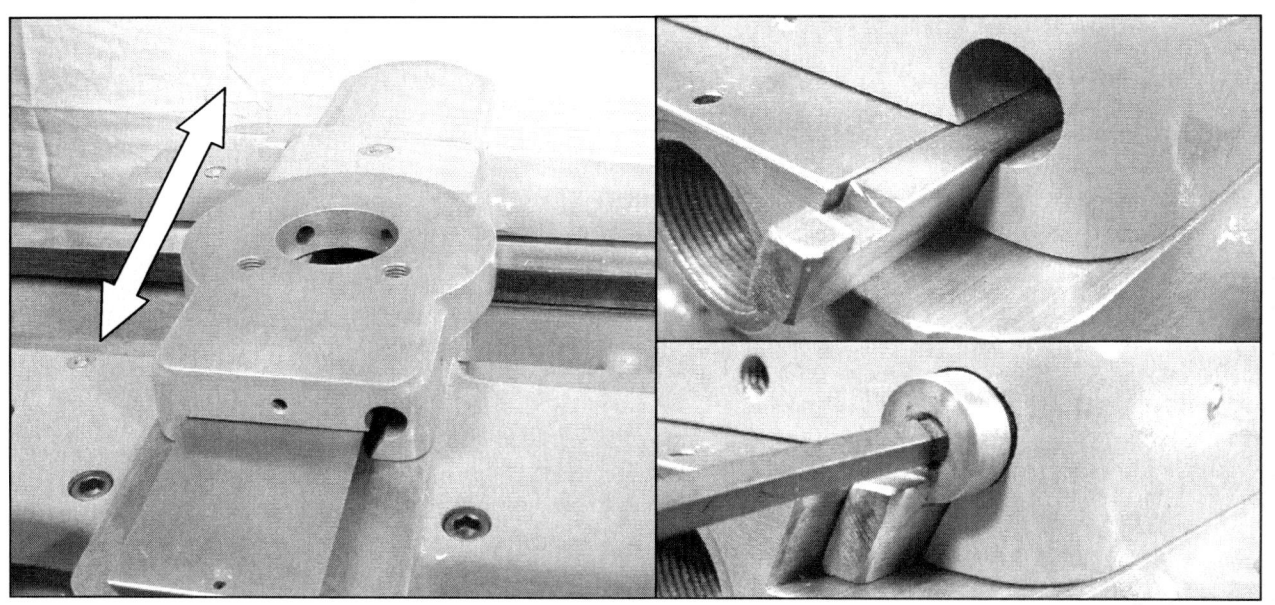

160. Mount the cross slide onto the saddle from the rear of the saddle. Lubricate the gib strip and insert it into the slot. Align and thread the gib screw into the cross slide. Move the cross slide back and forth on the dovetail ways while gradually tightening the gib screw. The movement should be smooth but firm with no lateral play. Install and tighten the brass shoe and set screw to lock the gib screw in position.

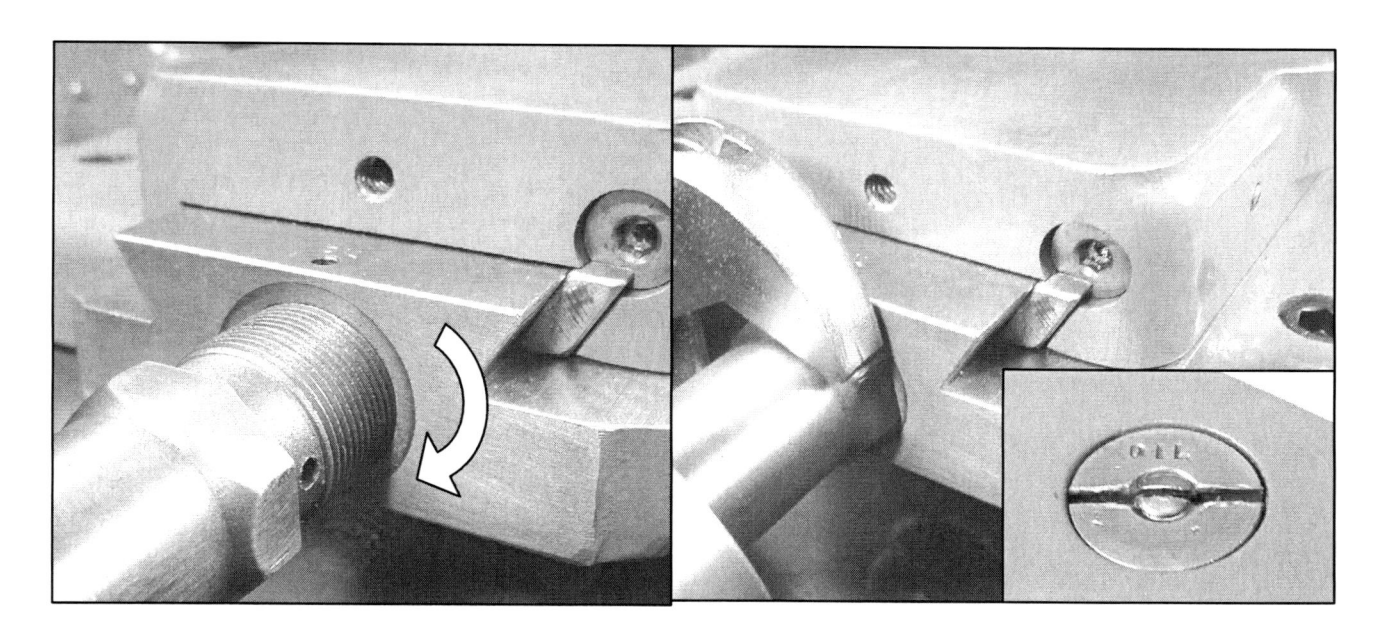

161. Install the cross feed screw into the saddle, turning the ball crank handle counterclockwise to engage the bronze feed nut. It may be necessary to rotate the feed nut slightly to get it started if it is not perfectly aligned. Once the bronze feed nut is engaged, keep turning the ball crank handle counter clockwise while you thread the bushing into the saddle by turning it clockwise. Tighten the bushing. Now tighten the large feed nut locking screw and then install the oil port screw in the center.

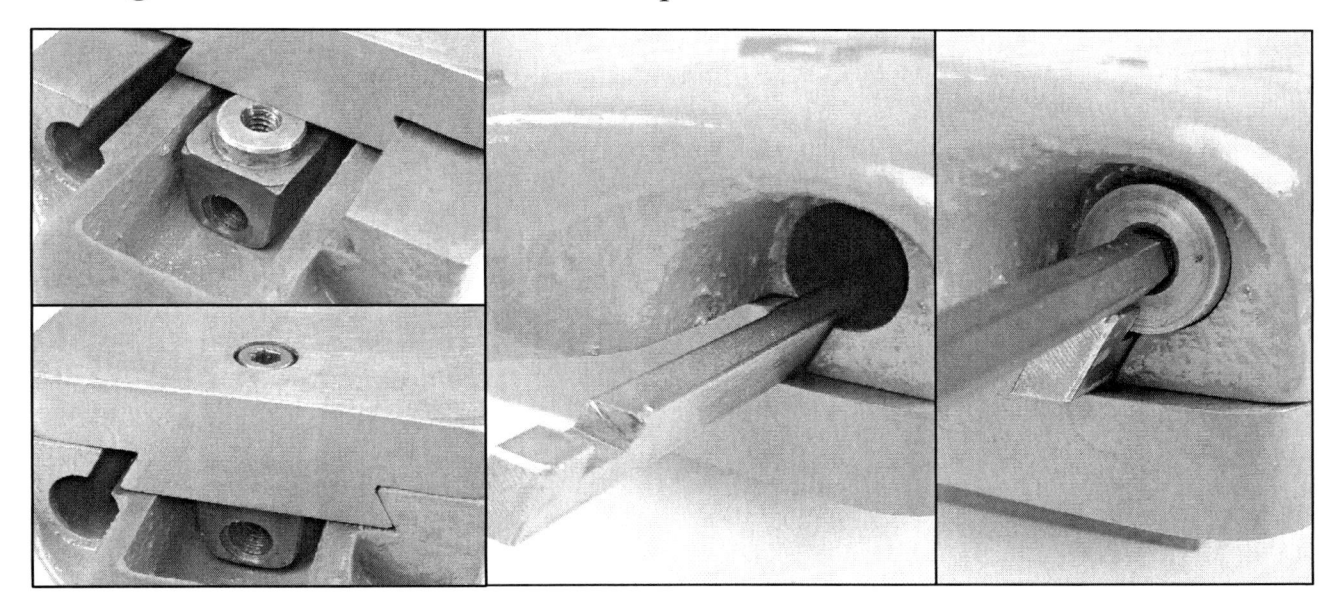

162. Reassemble the compound by installing the nut and installing the socket cap screw loosely. Install the gib strip and gib screw. Test slide the compound body while tightening the gib and then lock in place.

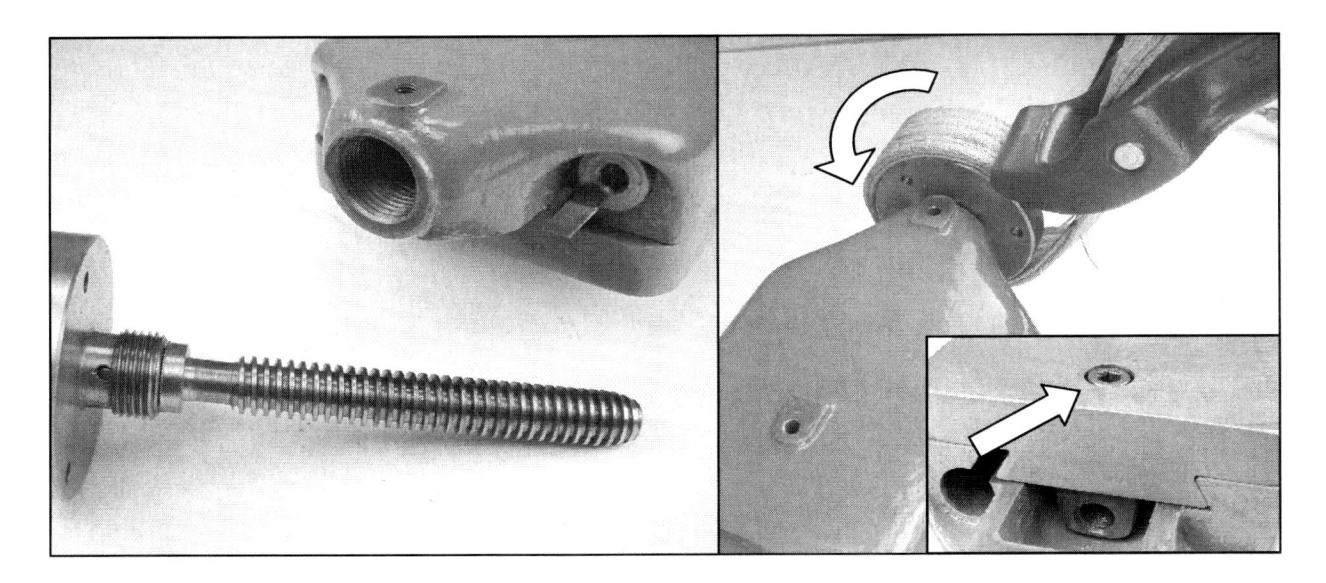

163. Insert the compound feed screw into compound body until it engages with the bronze feed nut. Turn the ball crank handle clockwise until the threaded dial bushing contacts the compound and then screw the bushing into the compound. Tighten the bushing with a strap wrench. Tighten the socket cap screw on the compound based to lock the feed nut in position.

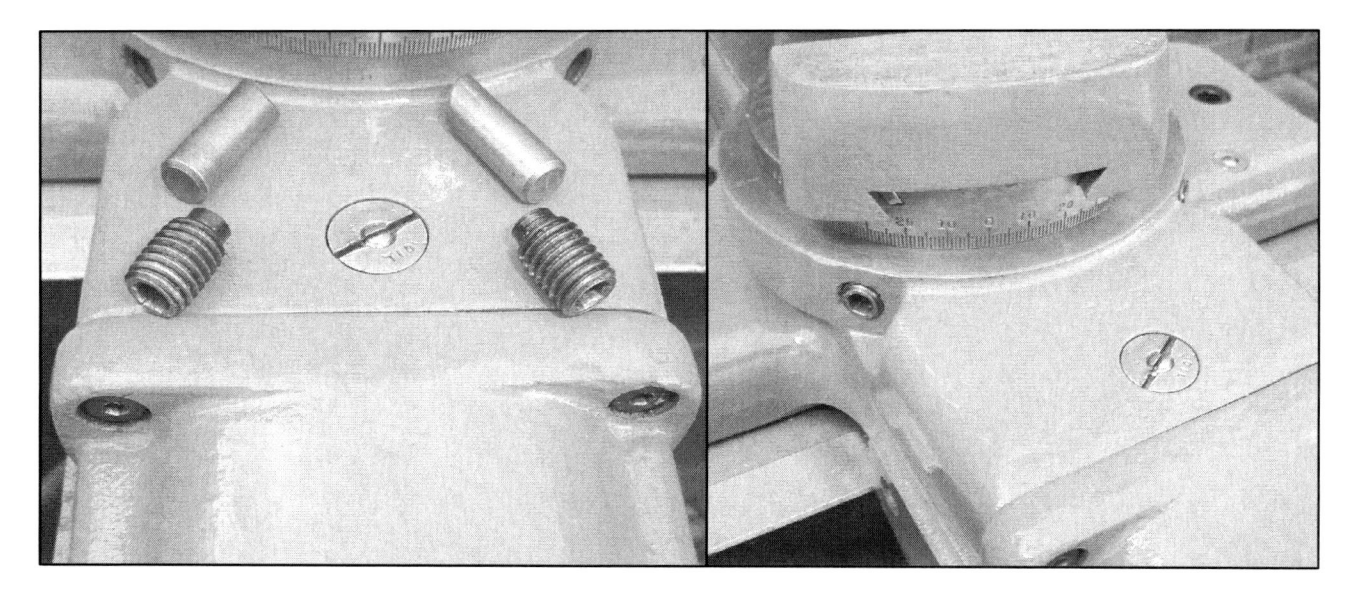

164. Place the compound on the cross slide and drop it into position. Insert the steel angled shoes (bevel pointing down) into the holes followed by the dog-point set screws. Make sure that the beveled shoes mate up with the dovetailed spigot on the compound base. If one set screw goes in further than the other or they protrude from the cross slide housing, then the shoe is not aligned. Pull the compound out and realign.

Section 3 – Headstock & Back Gear

The headstock is the most critical part of the lathe and requires the most attention. Since the headstock and underneath drive unit will be completely disassembled, cutting and splicing the flat drive belt will be necessary. If you are replacing the belt, measure the old belt and then order a new one to that length plus 4 inches. If you don't have the old belt, measure the outer circumference of your pulleys with the belt tensioning lever in the down position and the tension adjusting rod in the approximate center position. Belt lengths and widths vary by model and number of pulley steps.

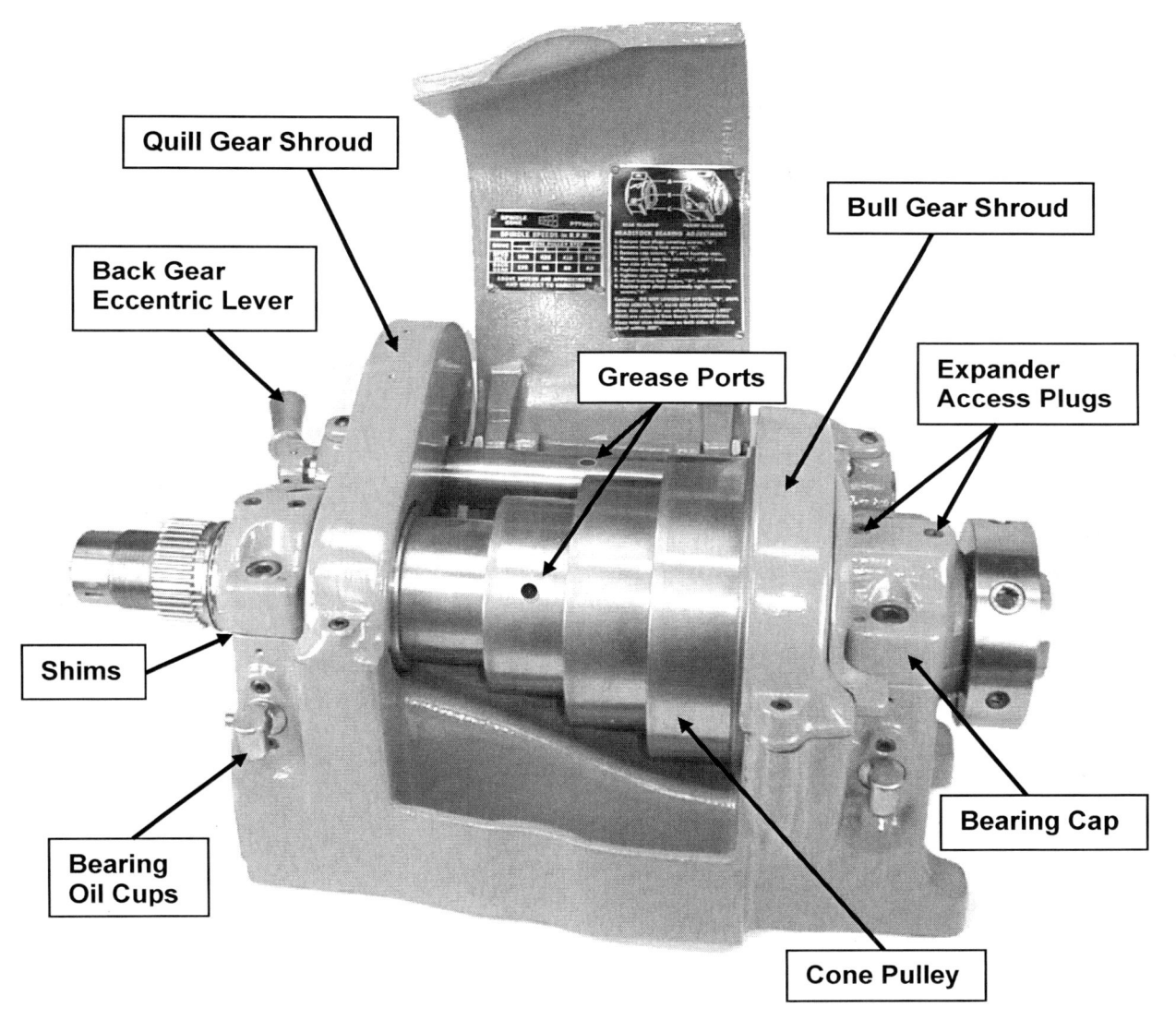

165. Headstock components - 13" South Bend Floor Mounted Lathe. Spindle Nose: D1-4 Cam Lock

Headstock Disassembly

Loosen Belt Tension | **Separate Belt** | **Bull Gear Shroud**

166. Remove tension on the flat drive belt by rotating the hand crank to the "UP" position. Cut the belt at the skived glue joint and pull the belt out through the headstock. Remove the 2 screws securing the bull gear shroud to the headstock and remove the shroud.

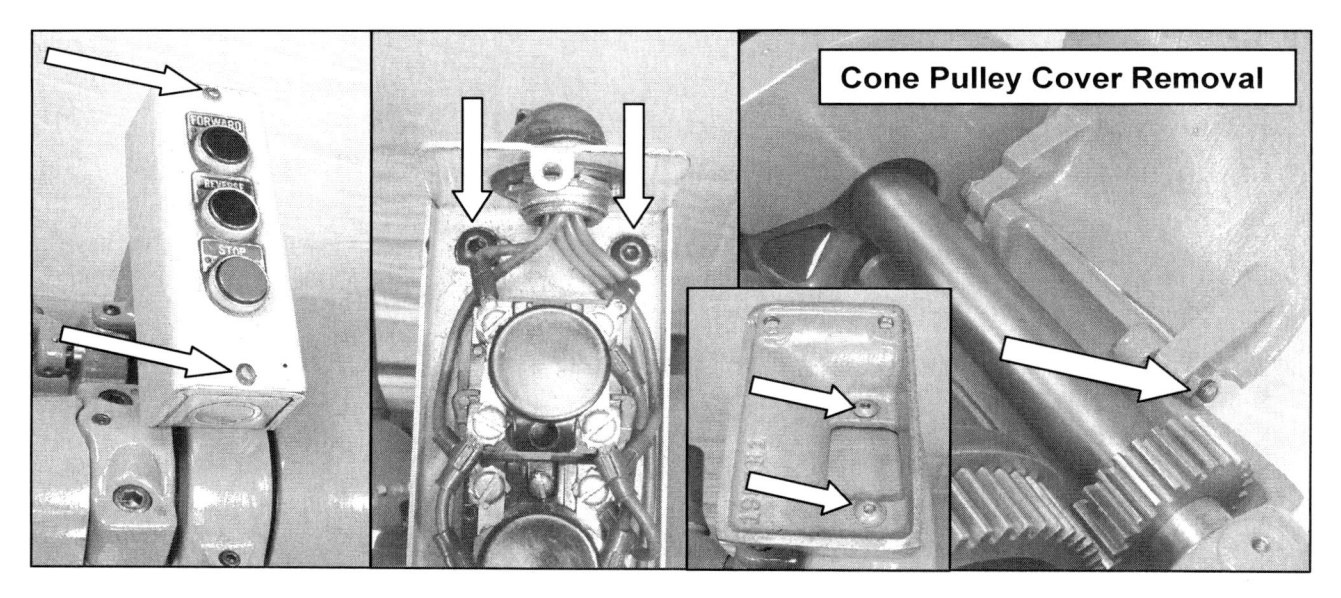

Cone Pulley Cover Removal

167. Make sure the power is disconnected. If the lathe has the motor switch mounted on the left quill guard, remove the cover plate on the switch and then remove two machine screws securing the switch to the mounting bracket. Remove the switch mounting bracket from the left quill shroud (two screws). Take off the cone pulley cover by removing the right side lock nut and cone-pointed set screw from the cover hinge.

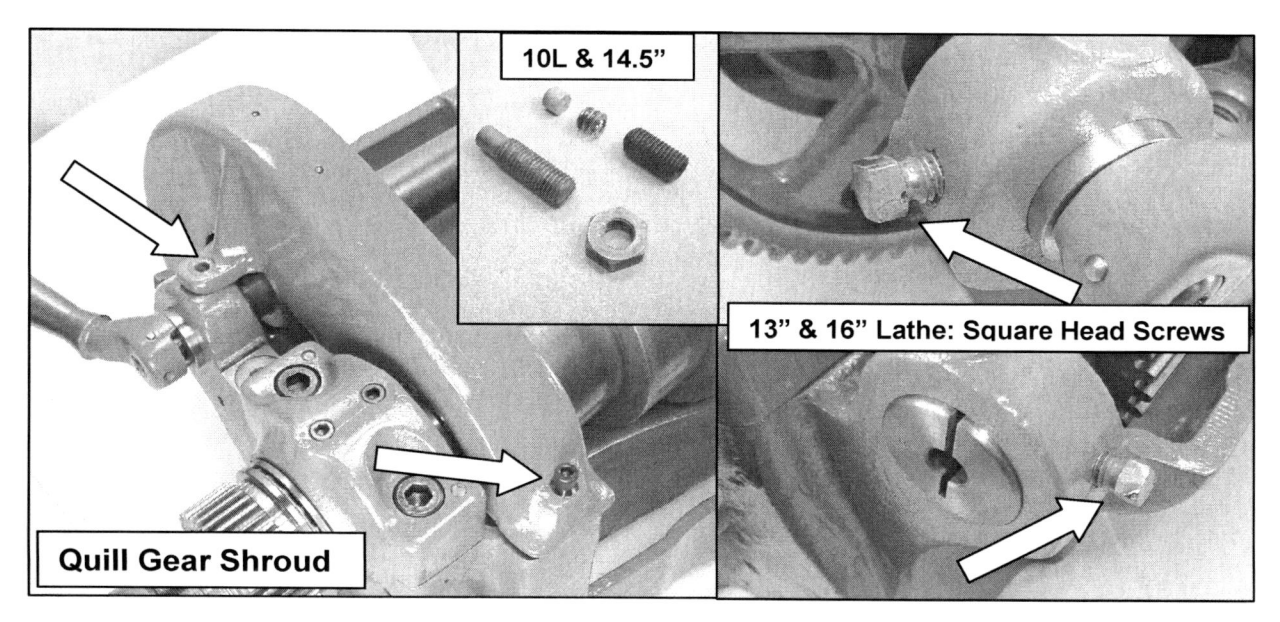

10L & 14.5"

13" & 16" Lathe: Square Head Screws

Quill Gear Shroud

168. Remove the 2 screws on the left side quill gear shroud and remove by rotating it to the rear until it clears the back-gear. Remove the two square-head set screws that secure the split bushing and eccentric lever bushing in the rear of the headstock. [On the 10L and 14.5" model there will be a bolt (or set screw), a spring and a brass shoe on the bull gear side. On the quill gear end there will be a long dog-point set screw with a locking nut.]

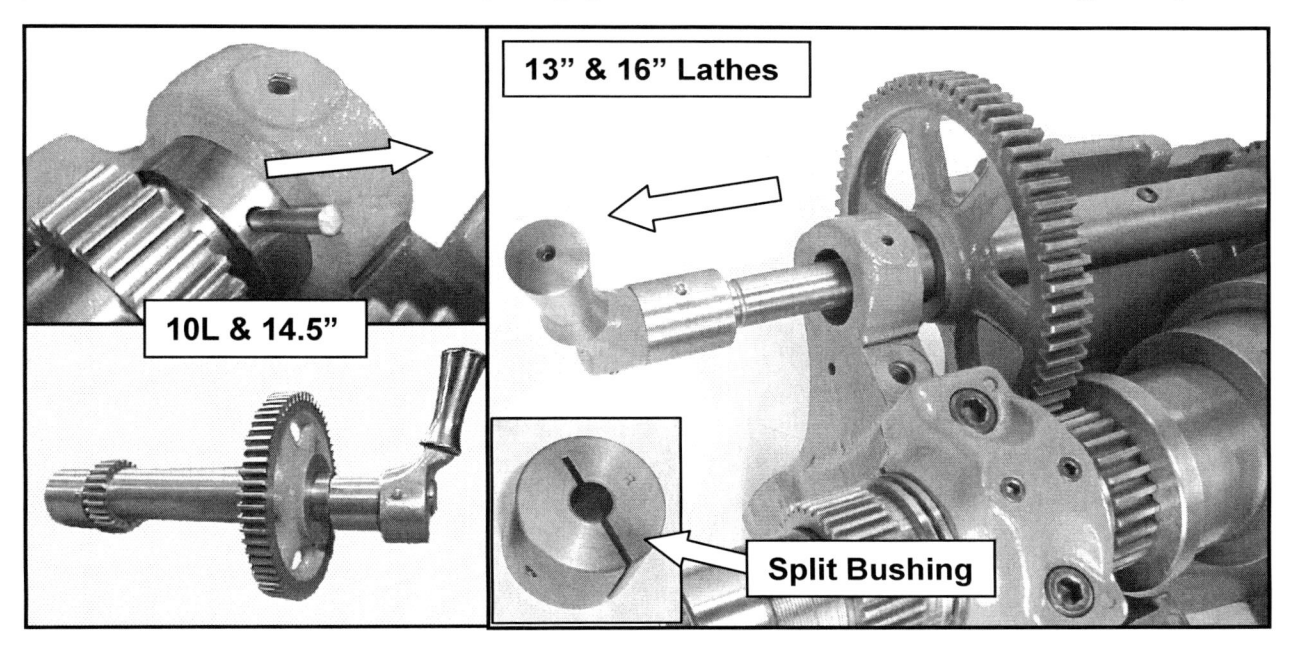

13" & 16" Lathes

10L & 14.5"

Split Bushing

169. [On the 10L and 14.5" lathe, drive the taper pin out of the right side eccentric bushing]. All models: Hold the back gear and pull the eccentric lever & shaft out the left side of the headstock. Lift the back gear out of the head. Tap the split bushing out of the headstock with a brass punch.

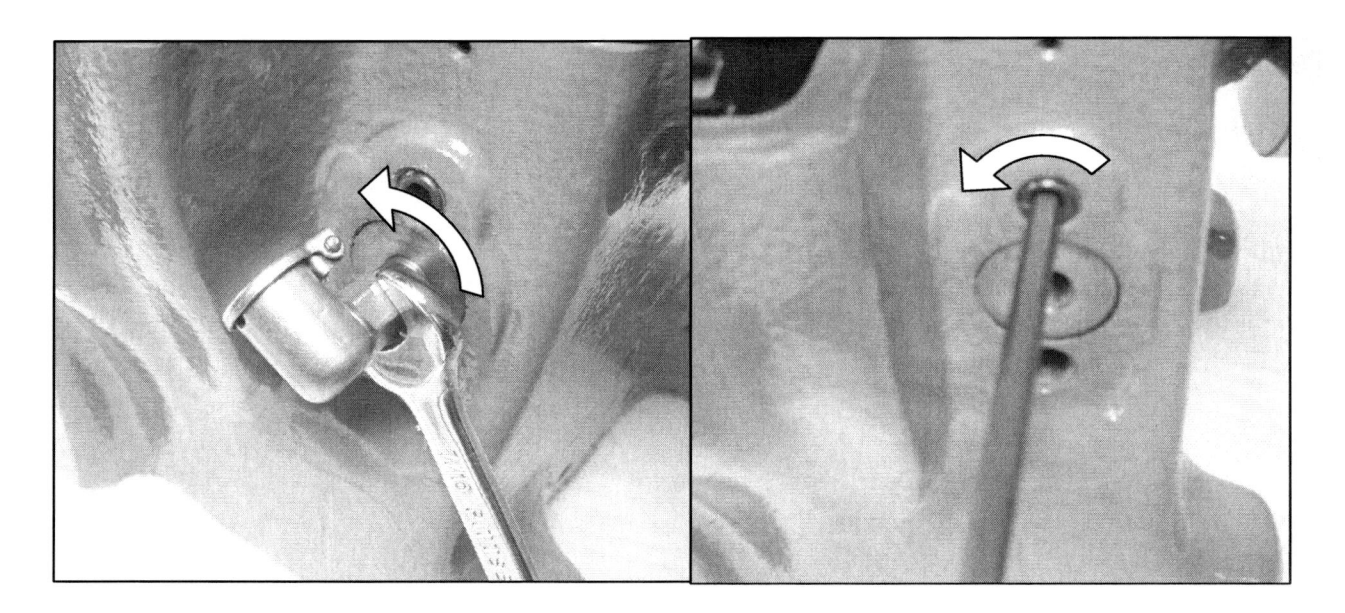

170. Remove the 2 gravity feed oil cups from the front of the headstock to avoid possible damage during cleaning. Remove the two pipe plugs located just above the oil cups.

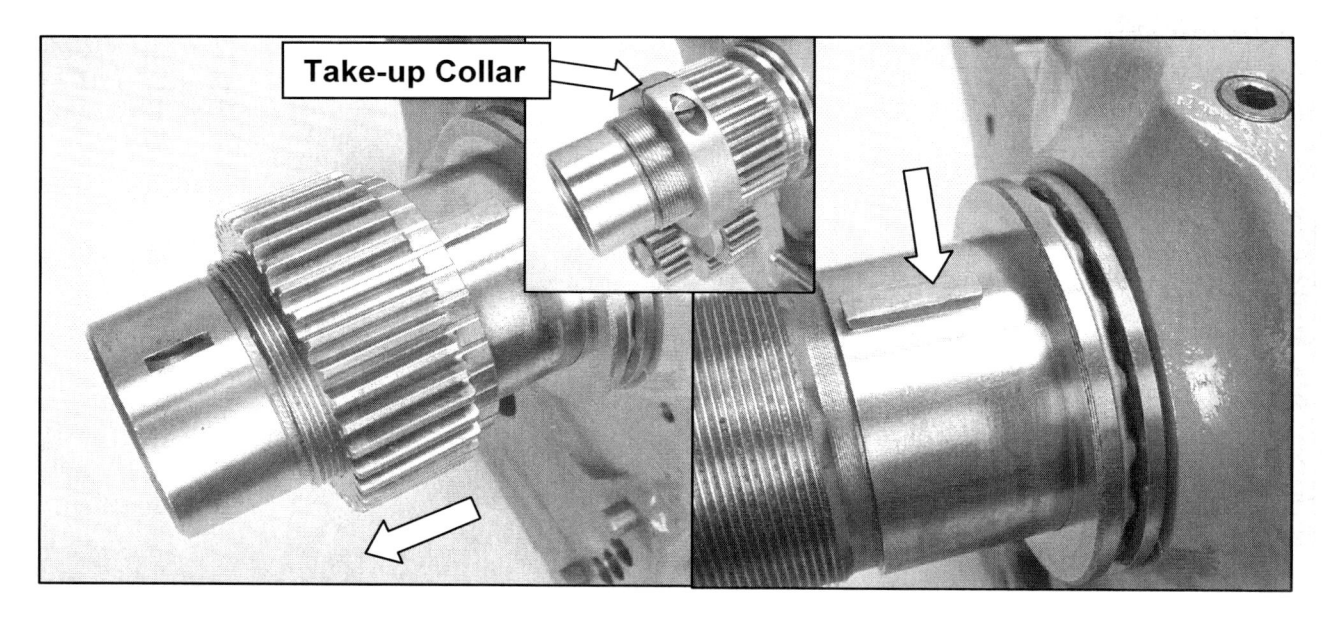

Take-up Collar

171. Remove the spindle gear from the tail of the spindle. Use a gear puller if the gear is tight. Remove the woodruff key from the slot by placing a brass punch on one end of the key and tapping it until it rotates out of its semicircular slot. *[If your spindle looks different than shown and has the take-up collar sandwiched between the spindle gear and headstock (no thrust bearing), simply loosen the lock screw on the take-up collar, loosen the collar a few turns and then proceed to the next step].*

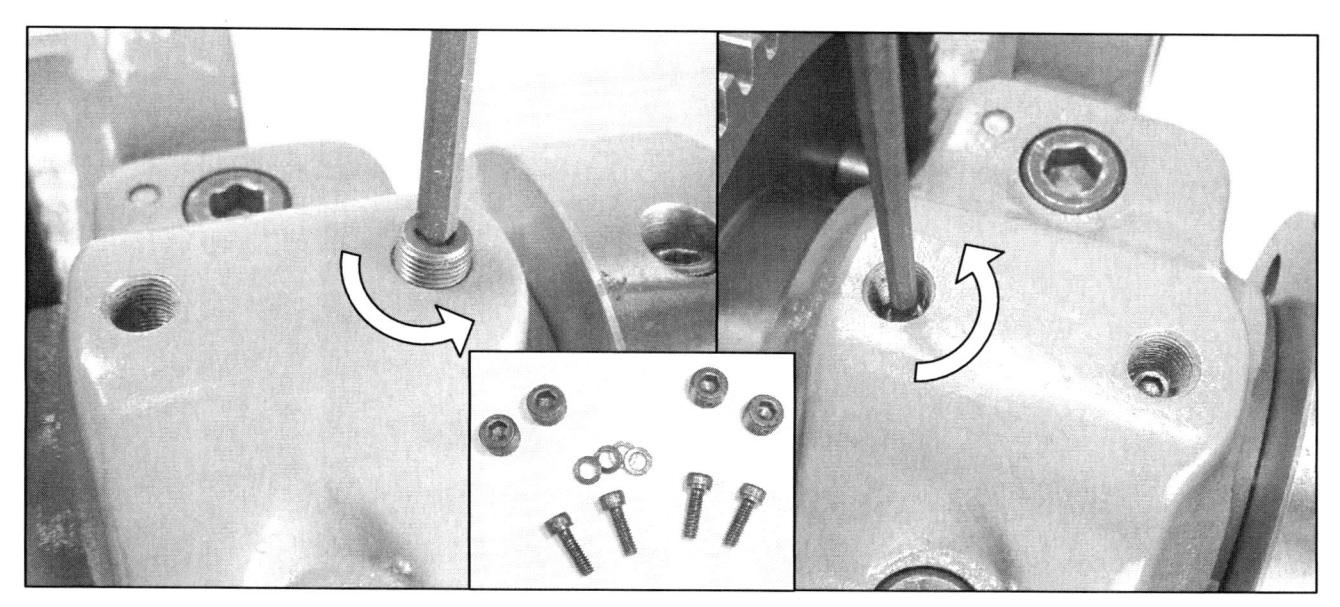

172. On the top of the two bearing caps remove the 4 pipe plugs that protect the expander screws beneath. Remove the expander screws and lock washers from the caps to relax the bearing tension inside the cap.

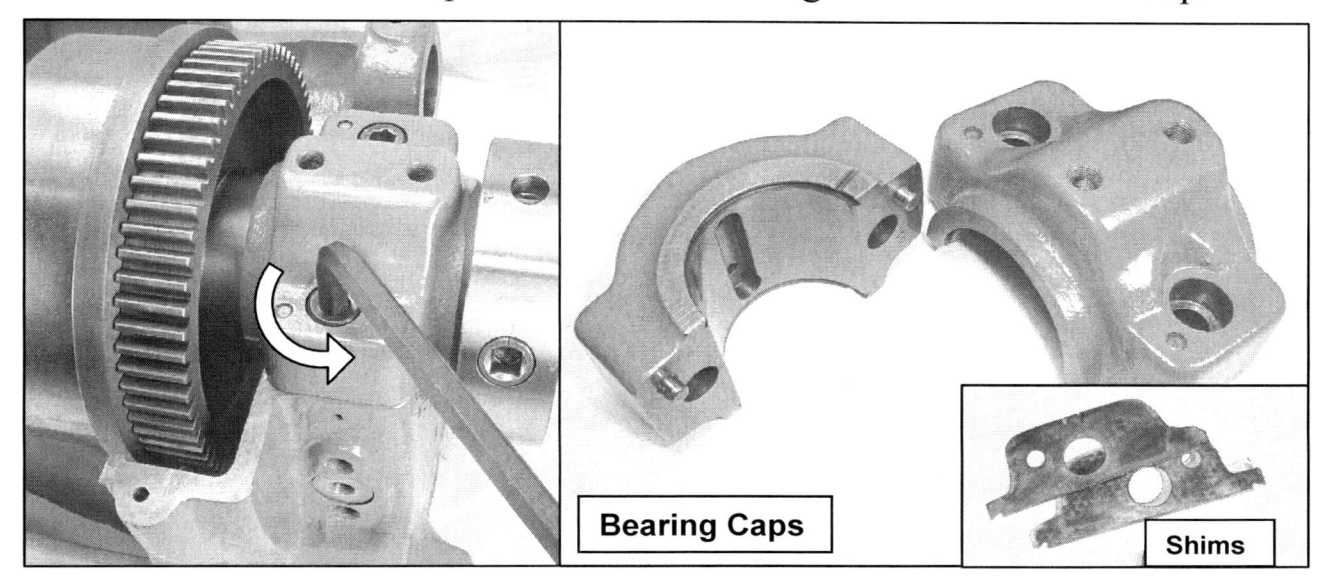

Bearing Caps

Shims

173. Remove the 4 socket cap screws from the bearing caps. [On 16" lathes there is a protective ring over the spindle nose that is secured to the cap and the headstock. Remove the 6 screws, ring and gasket before proceeding]. The bearing caps have two dowel pins that align them to the headstock and they are a snug fit. Put a brass bar into one of the cap screw holes at tap it laterally several time to free it. (No Screwdrivers!) Make sure not to damage the brass shims between the bearing cap and the headstock. Mark the location of the shim with a felt marker for reference at assembly.

174. Slide the 3-part outside thrust bearing off of the tail of the spindle. With the front and rear bearings open, the entire spindle can now be lifted from the headstock. Note: some models only have a take-up nut and washer instead of a thrust bearing. Grasp both ends of the spindle and lift the entire assembly straight up and out of the head. Set the spindle on a soft surface in preparation for removing the bearings, pulley and bull gear.

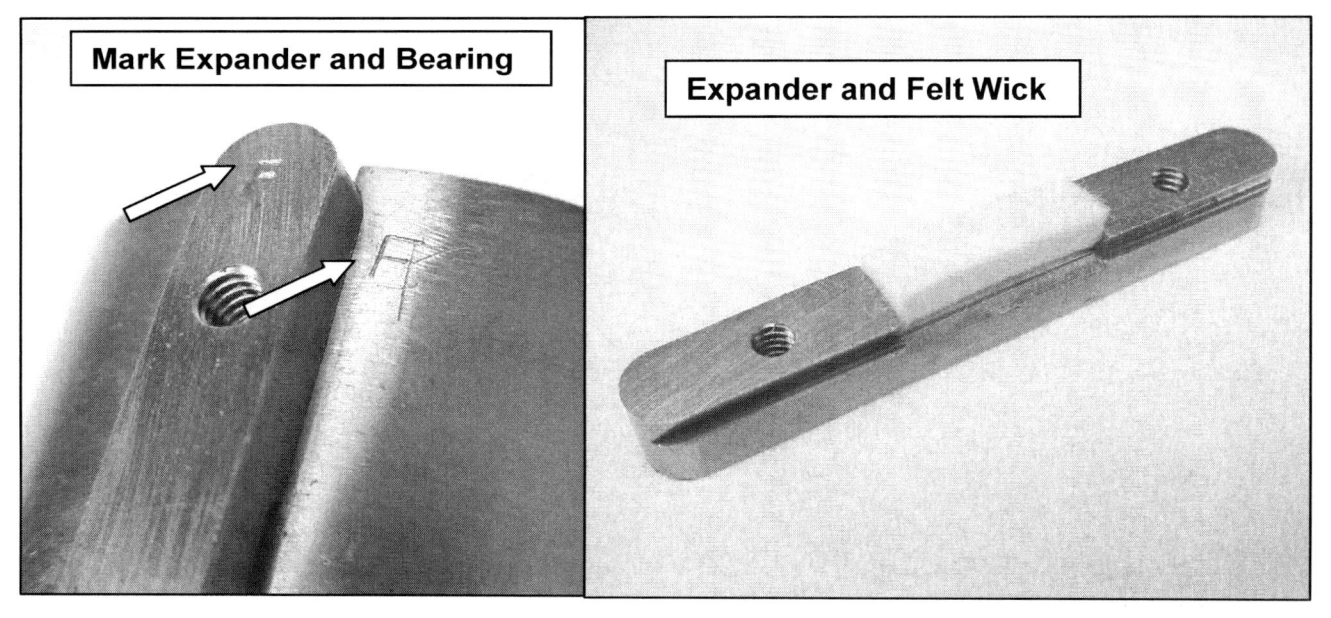

Mark Expander and Bearing

Expander and Felt Wick

175. While the bearings are still on the spindle, make sure to mark the front ("F") on each bearing and expander so that you can return them to the same orientation later. The expanders have a dovetail to spread the bearing as it is pulled up into the bearing cap. There is also a felt oil retaining wick in each expander.

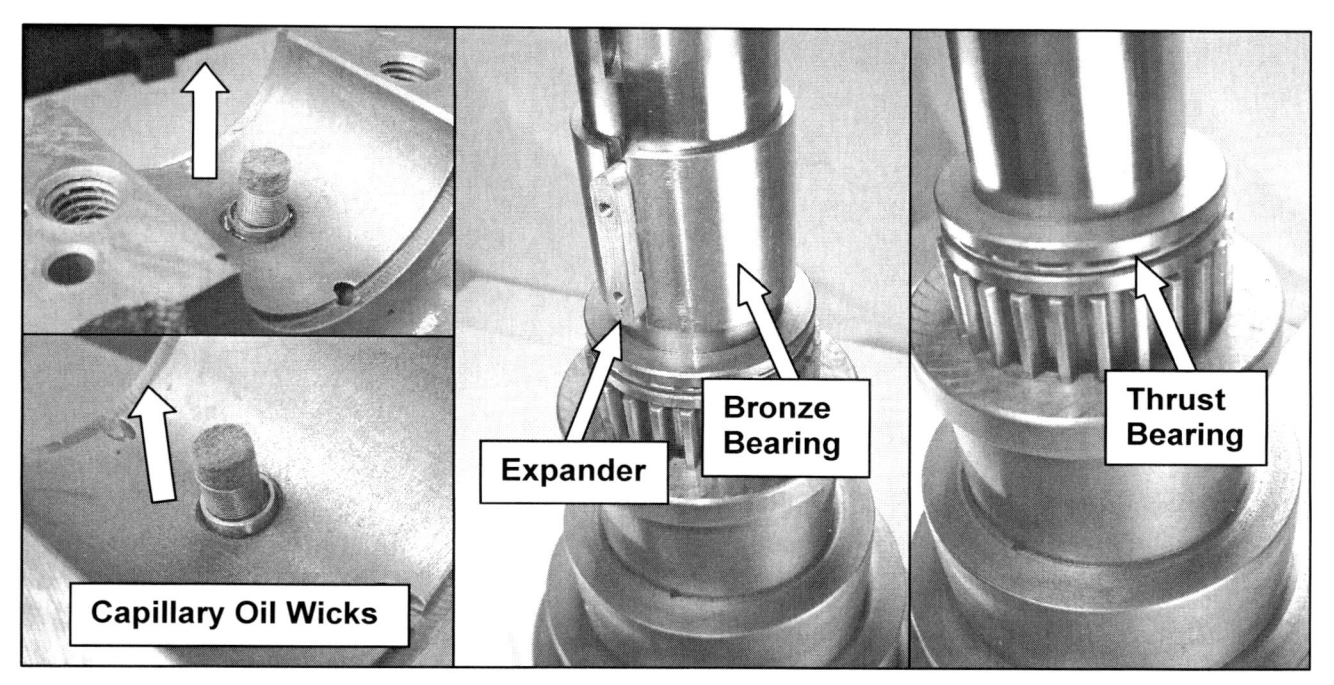

Capillary Oil Wicks

Expander

Bronze Bearing

Thrust Bearing

176. Remove the two spring loaded capillary oil wicks from the brass tube reservoirs just beneath the spindle bearings. Slide the bronze bearing sleeve and expander off of the spindle. Slide the 3-part thrust bearing off of the spindle. Note that this thrust bearing is thicker than the previous one.

Cone Pulley

Key

Bull Gear

177. The large cone pulley should now be free to slide off of the spindle. The bull gear is keyed to the spindle and is a press fit. Place the entire spindle in an arbor press and while supporting the bull gear on its inner collar, press the spindle out of the bull gear. In the absence of a press, a heavy rubber dead-blow mallet will work if the gear is firmly supported.

Remove Socket Cap Screws

178. Slide the last bearing and expander off of the spindle column. If your spindle is a D1-4 cam lock as shown you can remove and clean the locking components. Located and remove the 3 socket hex cap screws.

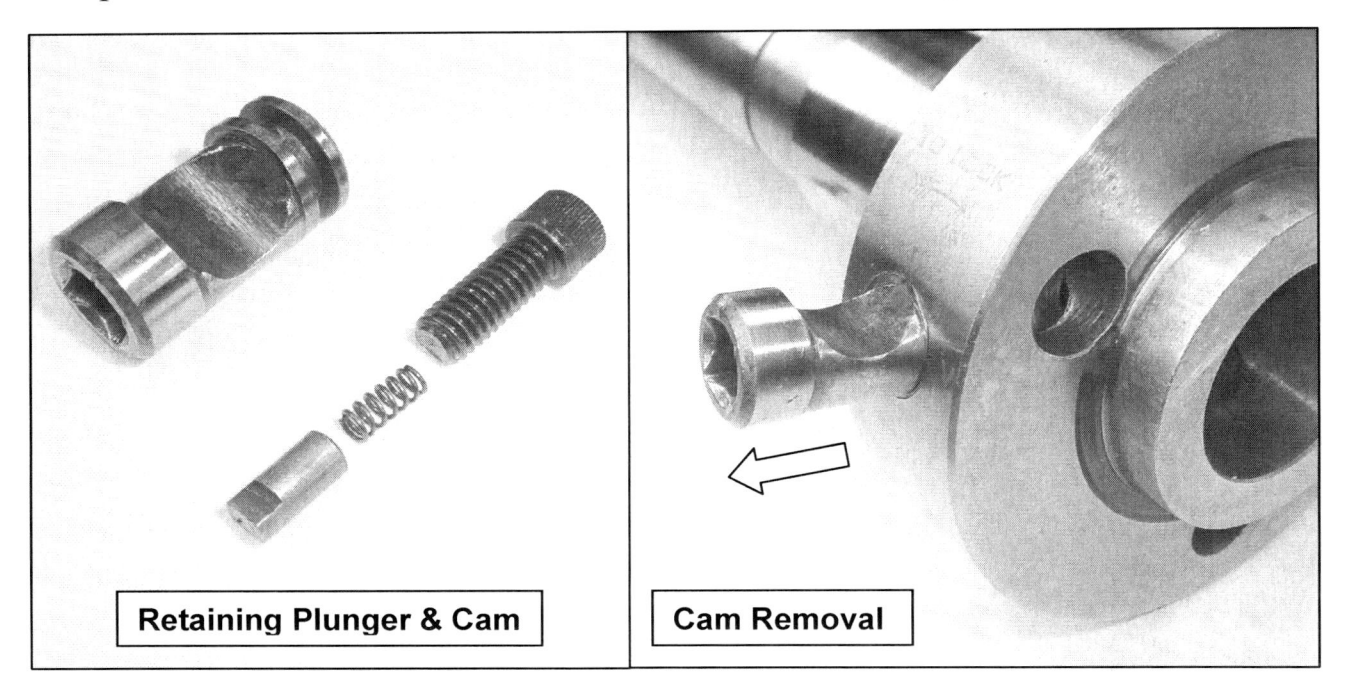

Retaining Plunger & Cam

Cam Removal

179. Below you will find a retaining plunger with a recessed spring. Extract the retaining plunger and spring. Remove the locking cams making sure to number the cams with the corresponding position on the spindle. Be especially careful to protect all spindle bearing surfaces when handling and cleaning. Any dings or nicks can chew up the bronze bearings.

180. Disassemble the bull gear locking clamp by first removing the cotter pin. Remove the plunger, spring and washer from the locking clamp.

Locking Clamp Parts

181. Remove the two cap screws holding the locking clamp gib and remove the gib. The bull gear locking clamp assembly is shown above.

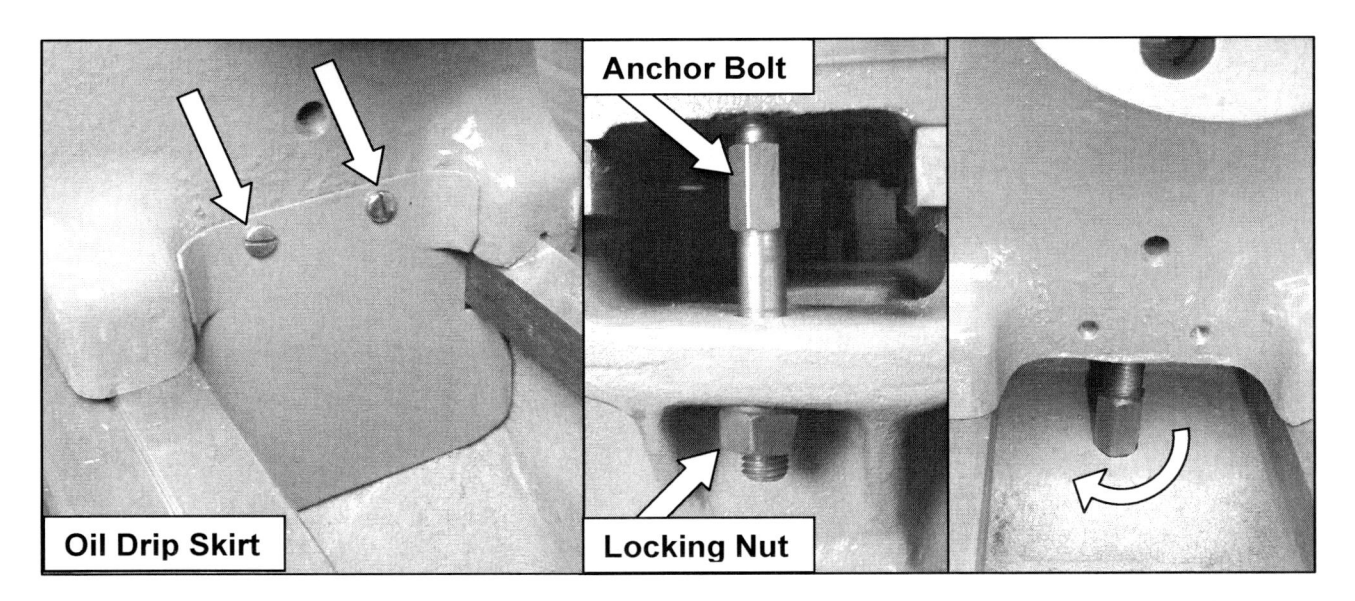

Oil Drip Skirt | Anchor Bolt | Locking Nut

182. To remove the headstock from the lathe bed, first remove the two screws securing the oil drip skirt to the head. Loosen the locking nuts on the 2 headstock anchor bolts from the underside of the lathe bed. Unscrew the mounting bolts from the bottom of the headstock and let the bolts drop down into the hole in the bed. Lift the headstock straight off of the bed.

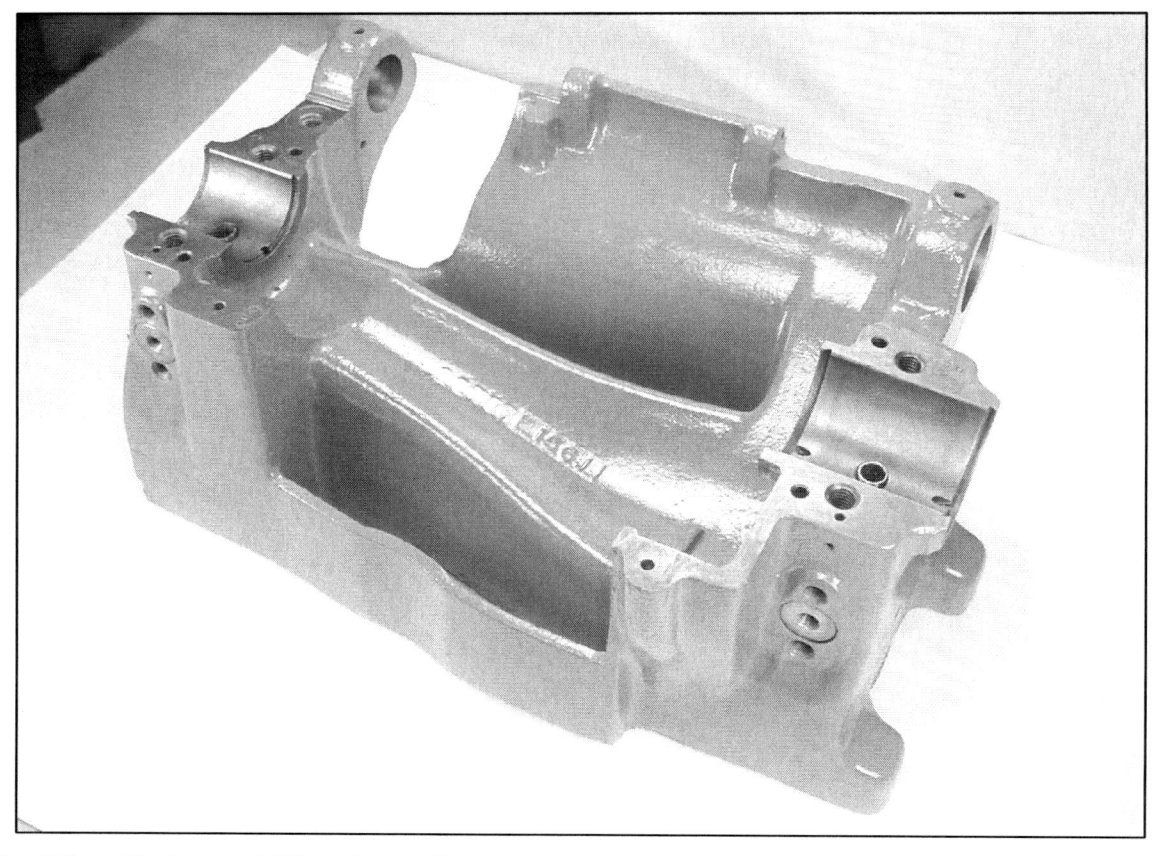

183. The Stripped Headstock

Assembly – Headstock

At this point all headstock components should be cleaned and prepared for reassembly. Make sure not to damage any bearing or mating surface.

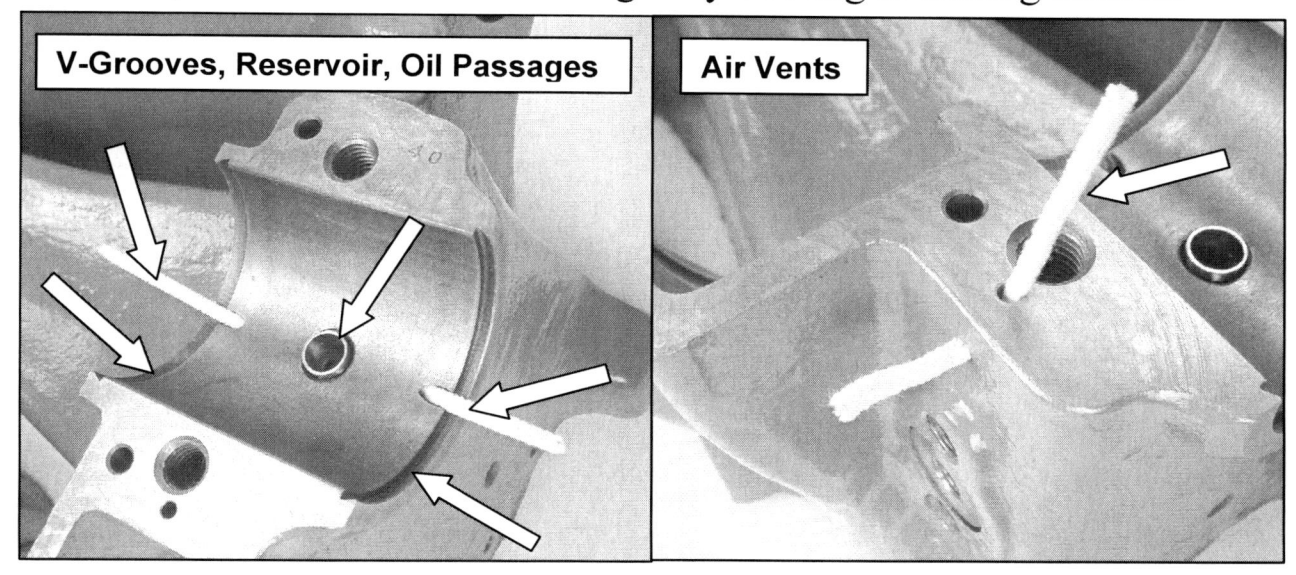

184. Make sure the oil reservoirs which contained the capillary oil wicks are thoroughly flushed with solvent. Clean the oil passages leading to those reservoirs from the 4 "V" grooves around the spindle (shown with pipe cleaners above) and the air vents. If dirt blocks any of these passages then critical components may be damaged over time.

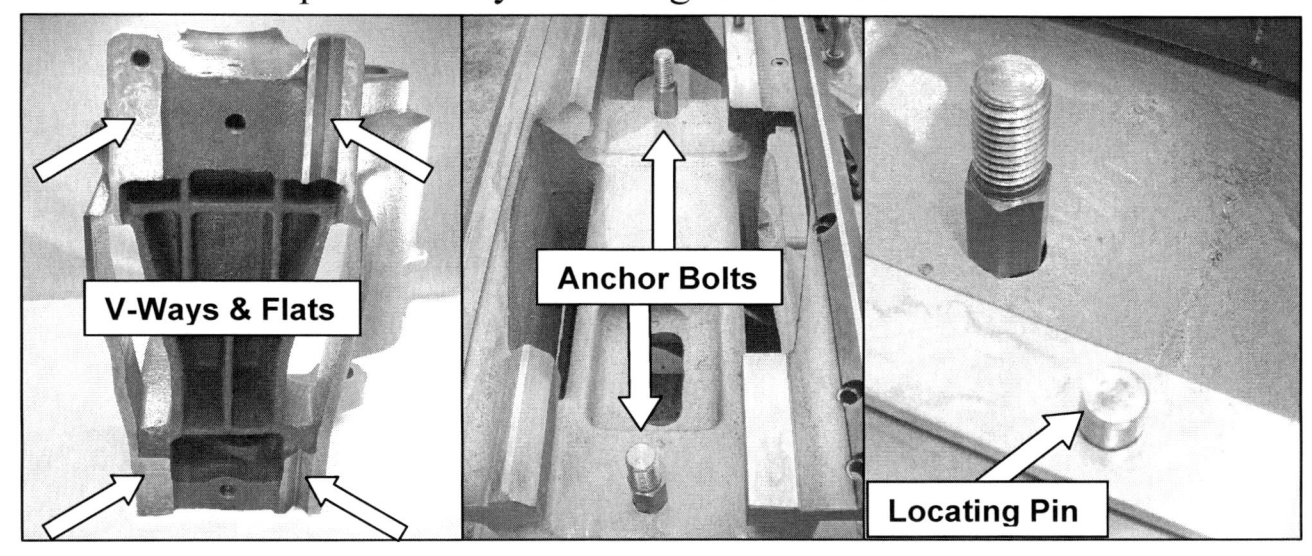

185. Prior to mounting, thoroughly clean the v-ways on the bottom of the headstock and the lathe bed. Drop the anchor bolts into position in the bed. Set the headstock onto the locating pin and bed way and push to the head to the left against the pin. Install the anchor bolts / nuts and then tighten.

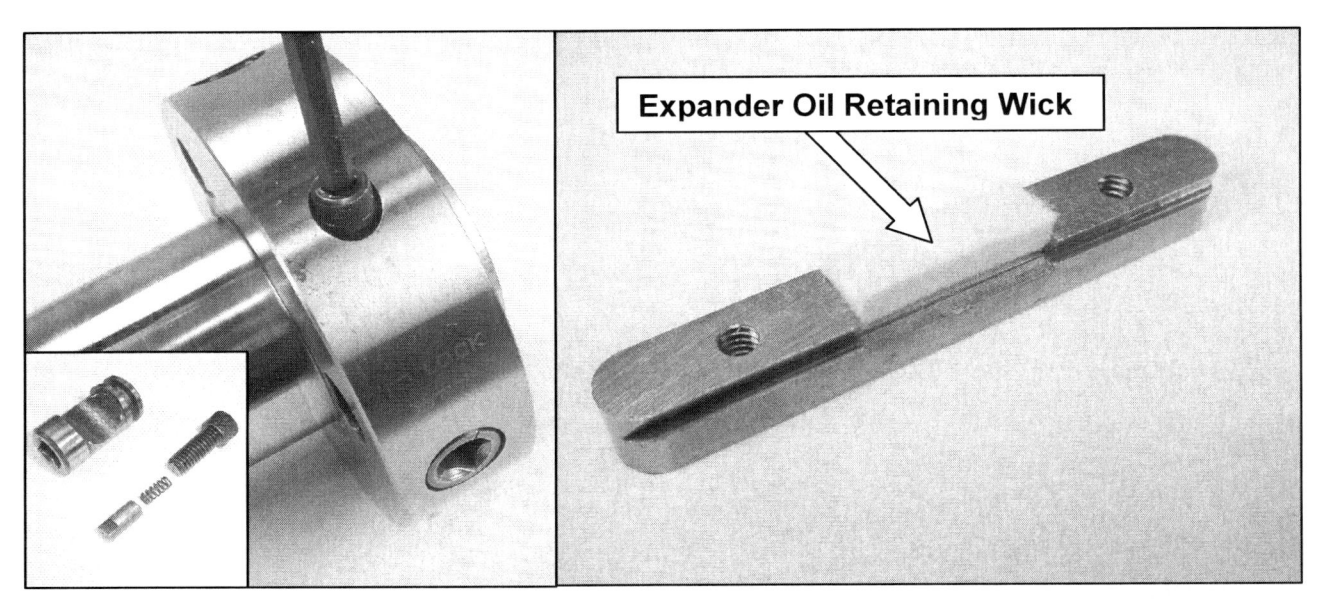

Expander Oil Retaining Wick

186. Reassemble the Cam Lock spindle (if applicable) making sure to put the components back in their original location as marked. Prepare the front bearing expander. Cut and insert a piece of Type 13 felt in the expander and press tightly against the wedge. Soak the felt in Type A oil.

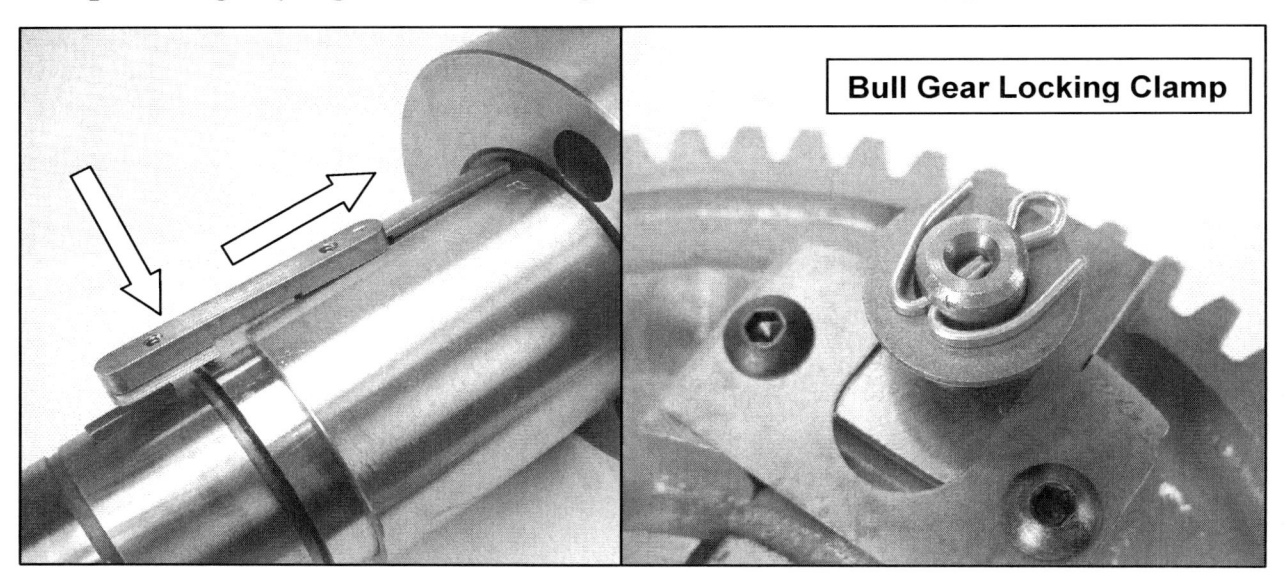

Bull Gear Locking Clamp

187. Clean the spindle bearing surfaces and bronze bearing thoroughly and oil lightly the inner surface with Type A oil. Slide the bronze bearing onto the spindle making sure that the "F" front mark is toward the spindle nose. Slip the bearing expander into the dovetail on the bearing ("F" to the front as well), press down on the felt to compress it against the spindle and then slide it into position on the spindle. Reassemble the clamping pin in the bull gear. Use a new cotter pin and make sure it does not overhang the washer more than 1/16" in any location or it may contact the cone pulley.

188. Clean and oil the bull gear mounting collar. Insert the woodruff key in the keyway (it helps to angle the key down slightly so that the gear does not catch the key during assembly. Start the bull gear onto the spindle and carefully align the key. Mount the spindle in an arbor press and gently press the bull gear into position. The collar on the bull gear should butt the collar on the spindle with no gap. Note that the two 1/8" clearance gaps on either side of the bearing are correct. (You didn't leave anything out)

189. Coat the bronze bushings inside the cone pulley with Teflon Grease and smear a thin film on the corresponding area on the spindle. We will fill the chamber with grease later so no need to pack it now.

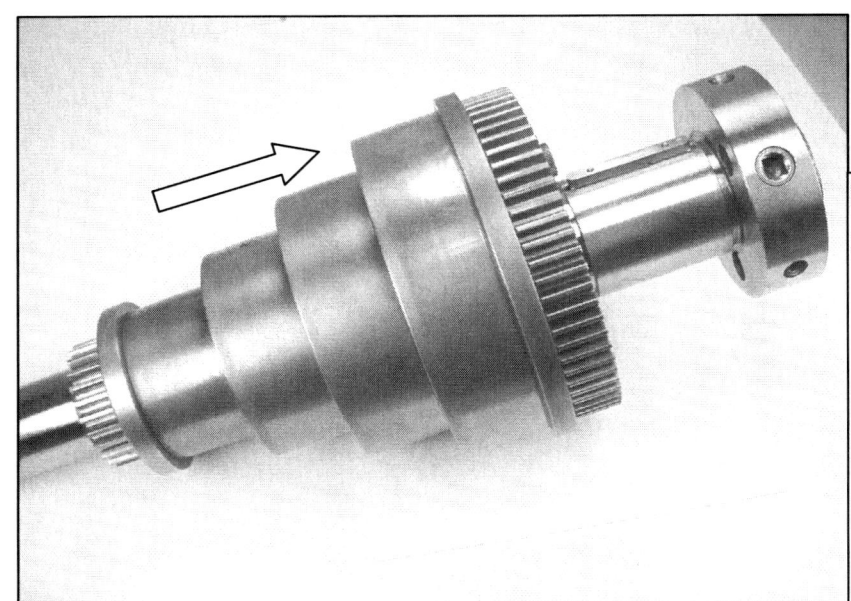

Note the differences in the thickness of the two thrust bearing races !

190. Carefully slide the cone pulley onto the spindle. Double check that the pulley seats against the bull gear and that the bull gear clamp does not interfere with rotation and that it locks/unlocks cleanly. If your spindle was equipped with both an inboard and outboard thrust bearings, make sure to keep them separate. The heavier (thicker) bearing goes on the inboard side and the thinner one on the outboard side. If you do not have an outboard thrust bearing it is not a problem as some models did not come with them.

191. Install the thicker thrust bearing onto the spindle next to the cone pulley. As with the front bearing, install the felt wick in the rear bearing expander and slide both onto the spindle ("F" facing the spindle nose).

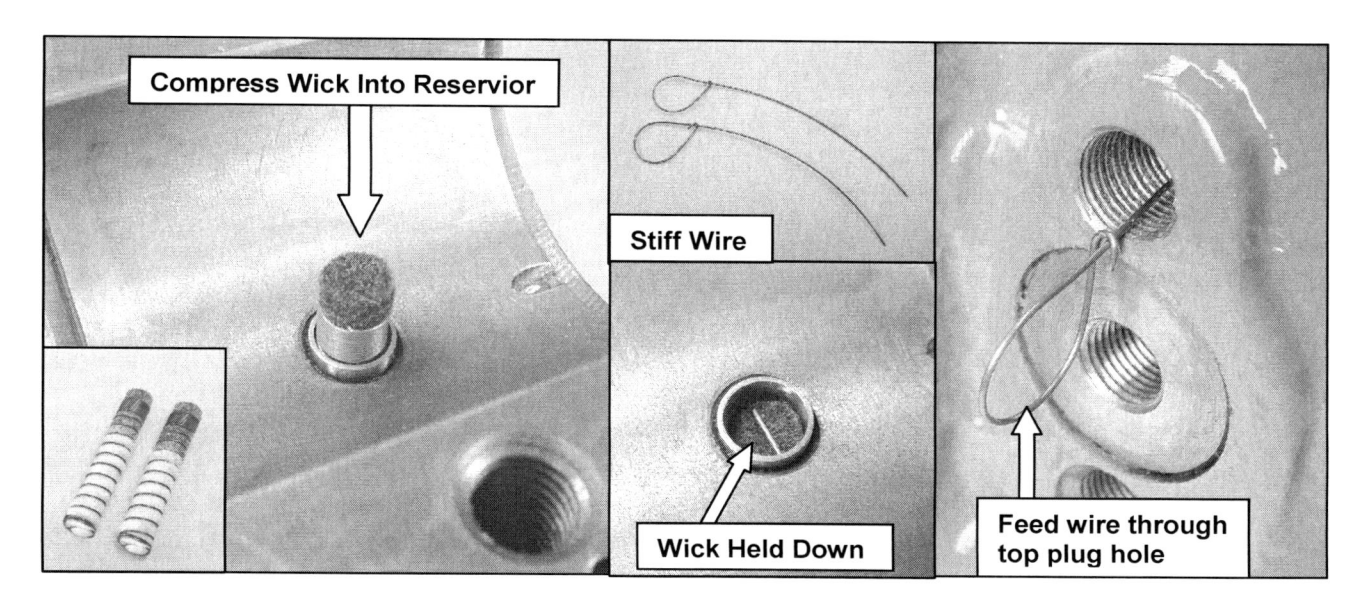

Compress Wick Into Reservior

Stiff Wire

Wick Held Down

Feed wire through top plug hole

192. Soak the new capillary oil wicks in type A oil and place them into the reservoirs. Compress the wick into the brass reservoir about ½" and insert a length of stiff spring wire through the upper threaded hole in the front of the headstock. The spring should go over the top of the wick to hold it down when the spindle is being installed. Wipe down the bearing saddles.

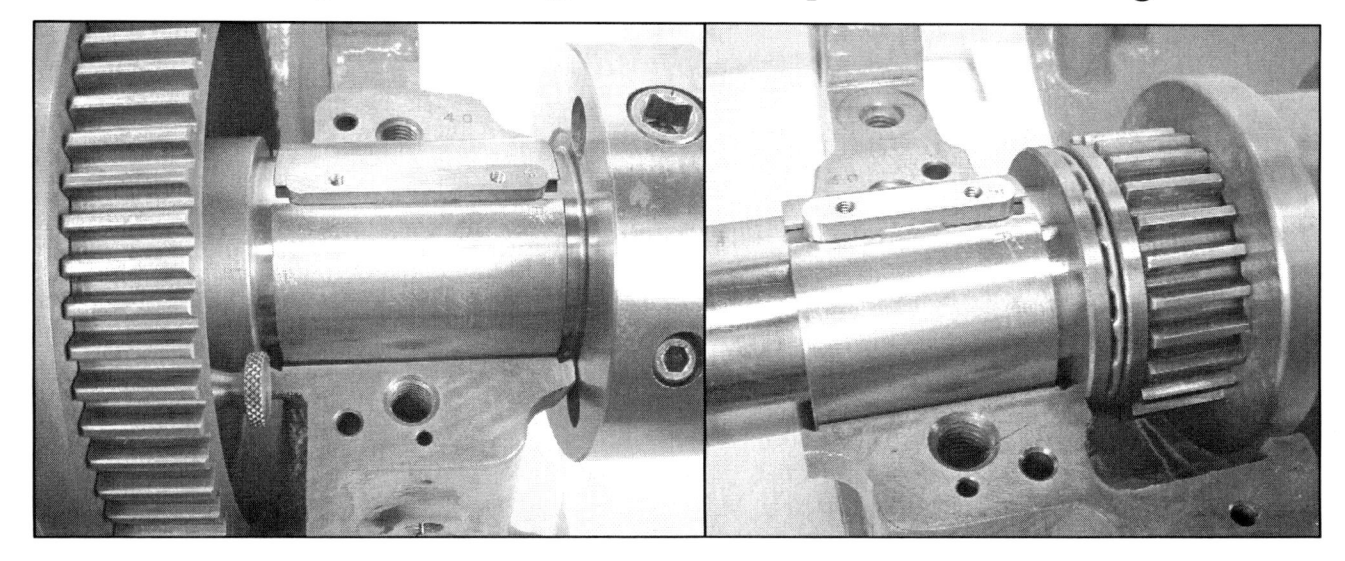

193. On the spindle assembly, center the front bronze bearing in the space so that there is approximately 1/8" on either side of the bearing. Set the rear bronze bearing approximately 1/8" from the thrust bearing. Lower the spindle assembly into the headstock and then gently set the bearings into their saddles. The brass reservoir tubes should fit up inside the holes in the bottom of the bearings so move the bearing around until both bearing shells drop onto the tube. Remove the two wick retaining wires.

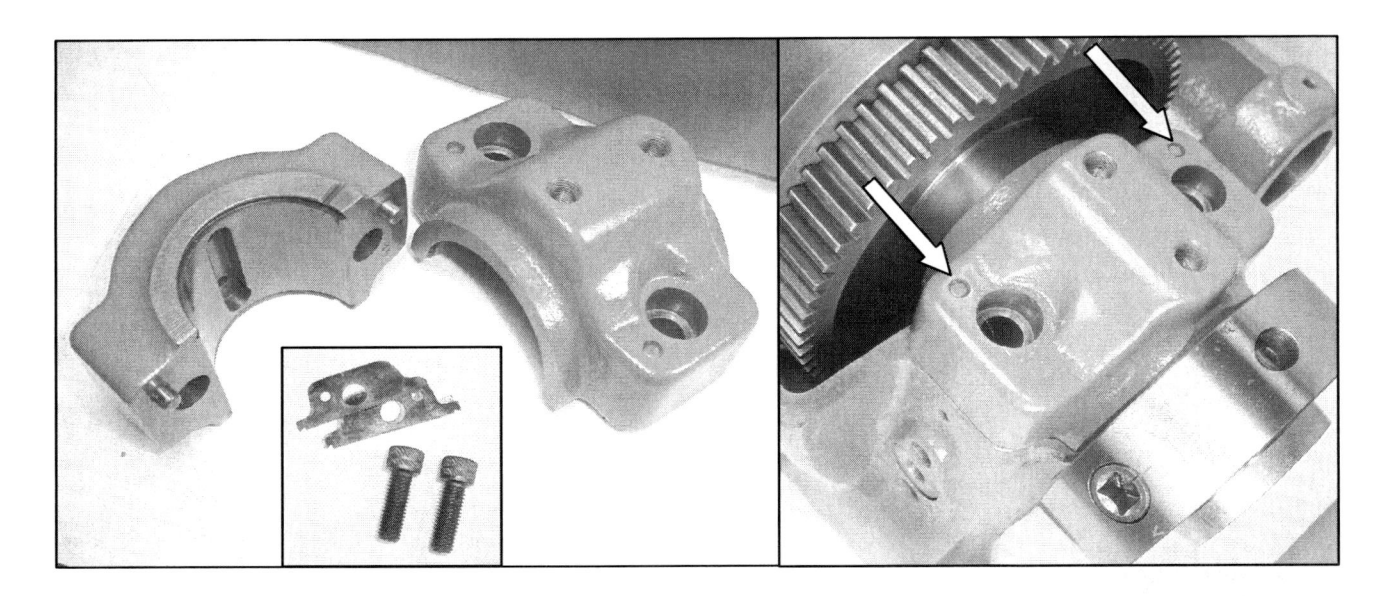

194. Check the alignment of the expanders and that they are centered on the bearing. Make sure the shims are cleaned and properly oriented on the dowel pin inside the bearing caps. Drop the caps into place on top of the bearing expanders. Push down until the caps bottom out on the shims.

Align Holes

195. Install the bearing cap bolts but DO NOT tighten. Look through the expander access ports on top of the cap to see if the threaded holes in the expanders beneath are properly aligned. If not, use a long probe to align the two threaded holes in the expander so that they are concentric with the two bored holes in the cap. Do this by sliding the expander in either direction. Be careful not to damage the threads in the bronze expander.

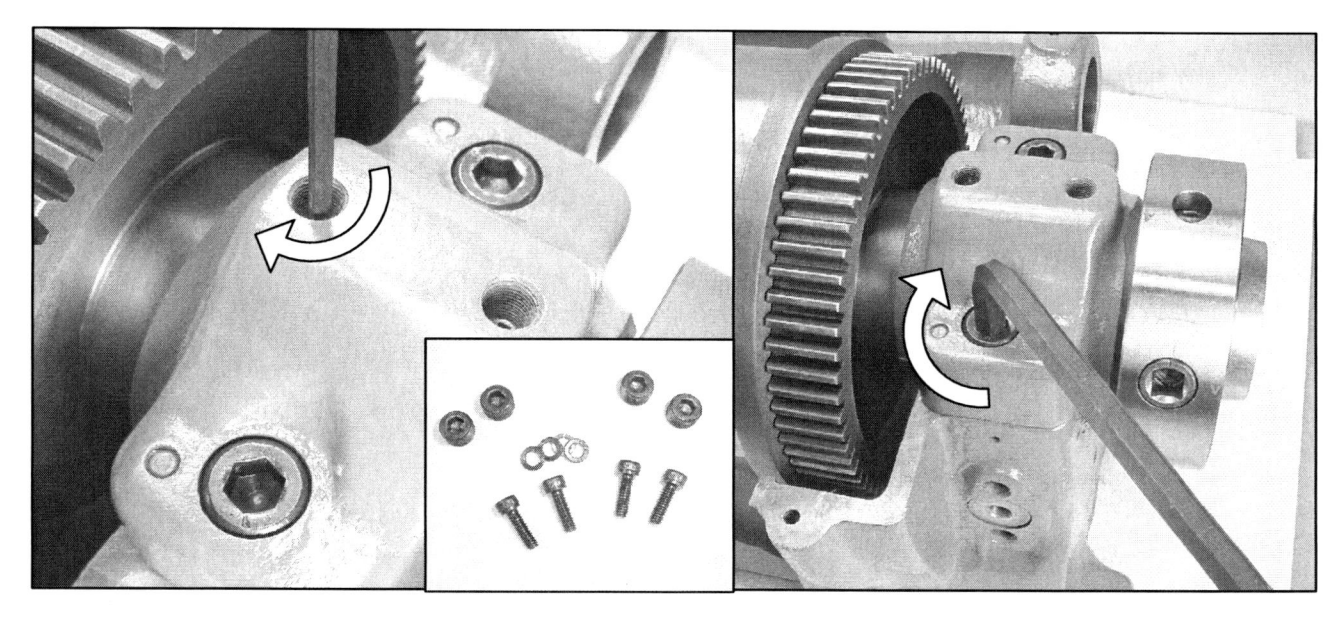

196. Install the 4 small socket cap screws with lock washers in each of the 4 access ports. Thread the screws fully into the expander beneath but DO NOT tighten them yet. Now that everything is aligned, tighten the bearing cap bolts alternating between the two bolts.

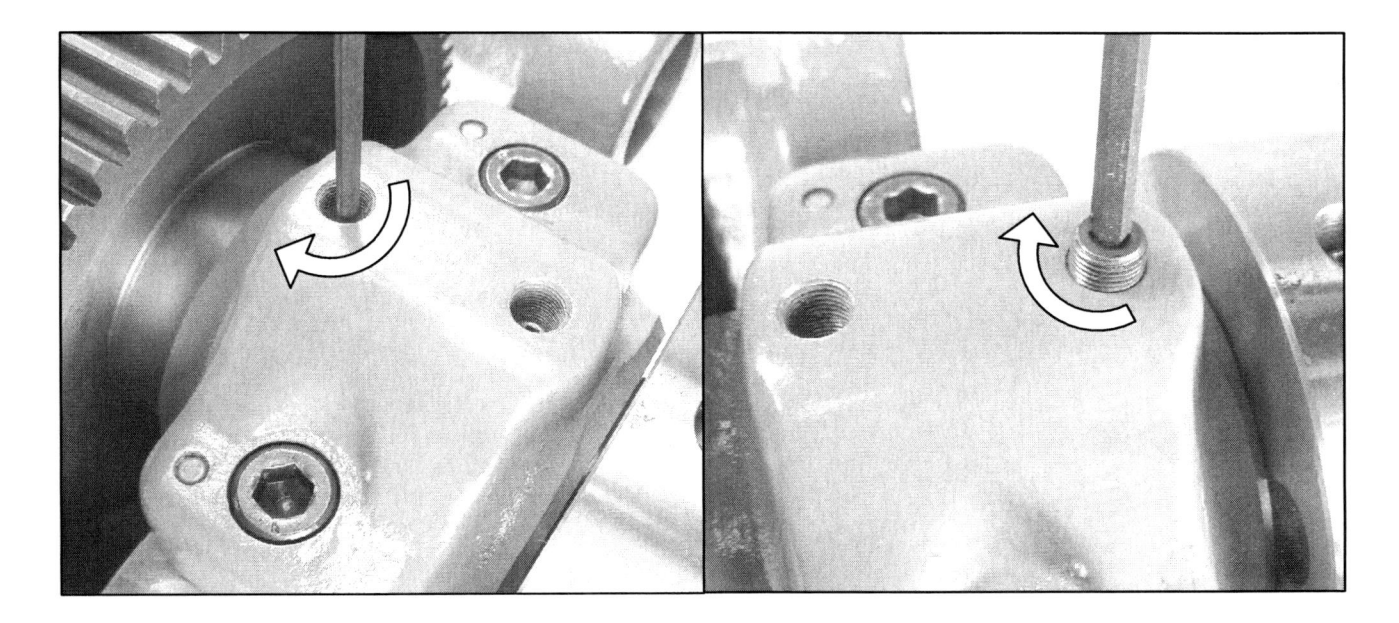

197. After tightening the bearing cap bolts, fully tighten the bearing expander screws. Turn the spindle to make sure it turns freely and does not bind. For now, install the 4 plugs into the bearing expander access ports.

Thrust Bearing, Key, Gear

Locking the Take-up Collar

198. Based on the spindle configuration, install the take-up collar & gear.
A. (No outboard thrust bearing): Install the take up washer and collar against the headstock, tighten it by hand tight and then back off approximately 1/12 of a turn & lock. Install the key & press on the gear.
B. (Outboard thrust bearing): Install the thrust bearing against the headstock, install the key, spindle gear and the locking collar. Hand tighten the collar and then lock in place. Verify that the spindle turns freely.

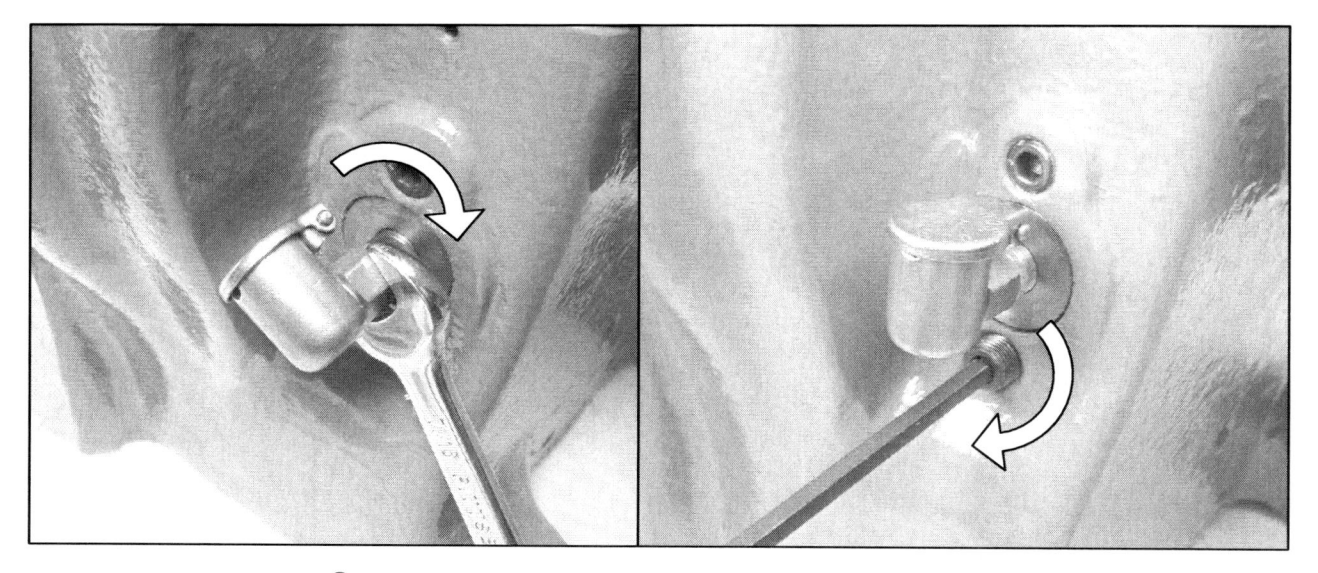

199. Using Teflon® thread sealing tape on all threads; install the upper pipe plugs and oil fill cups for the spindle bearing. Install the lower pipe plugs. Partially fill the oil cups with Type A spindle oil to allow the oil time to saturate the wicks.

Stop Pin

200. Collect all of the back gear components and make sure that the recessed interior of the gear shaft is free of old grease and gunk. If the eccentric handle & bushing was removed from the shaft for cleaning and painting, grease the bushing, remount them the shaft and reinstall the taper pin. Make sure that the dowel (stop pin) moves freely in the lever recess.

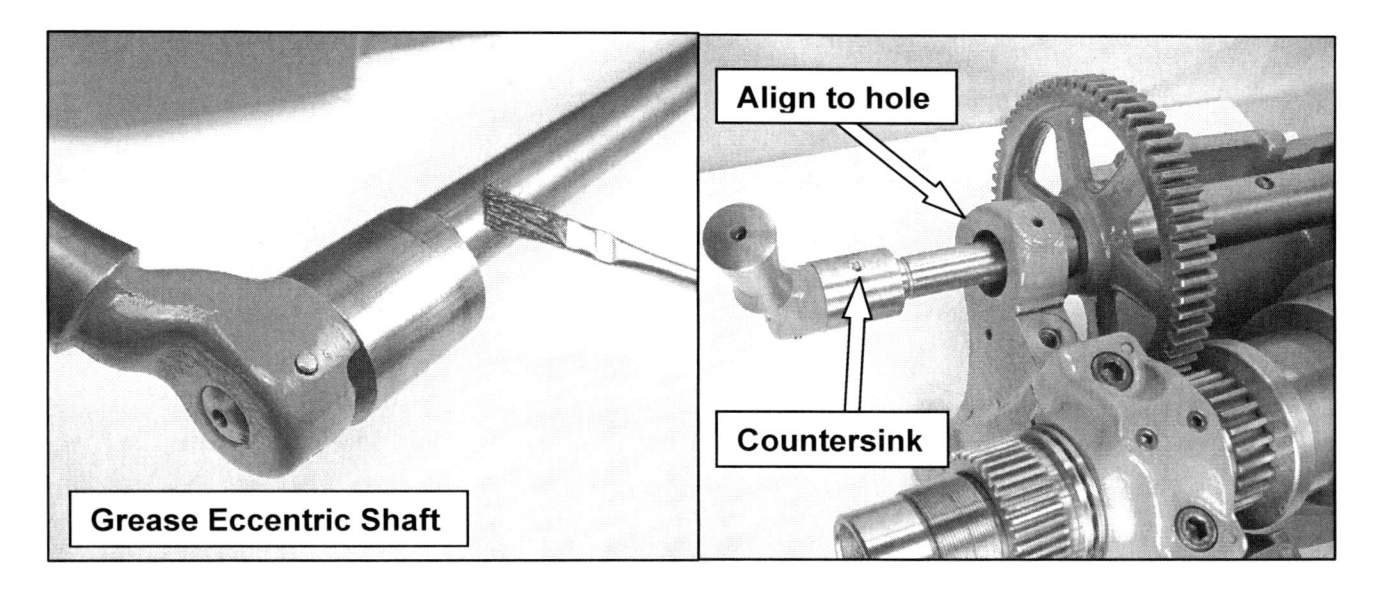

Grease Eccentric Shaft

Align to hole

Countersink

201. Grease the back eccentric shaft with Super Lube® grease. The reservoir inside the back gear shaft will be filled with grease later via the threaded hole in the tube. Position the back gear in the headstock and slide the shaft through the gear. Rotate the bushing on the lever end to align the countersink with the set screw hole on the rear of the headstock.

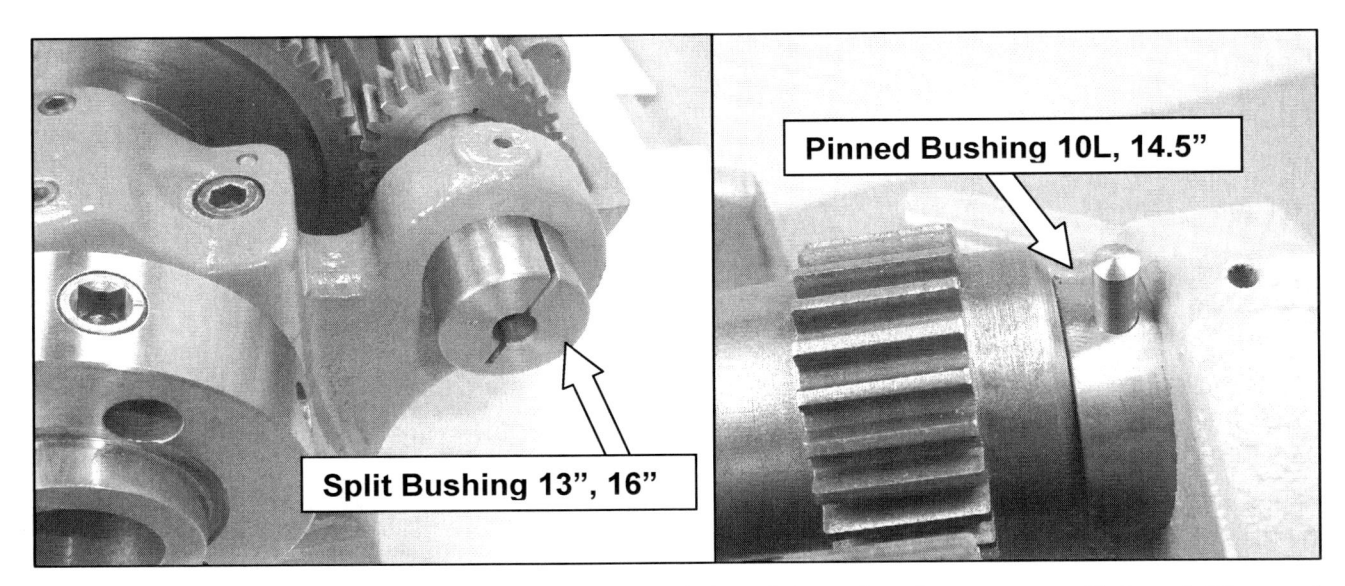

202. Tap the split bushing (or pinned bushing in the case of the 10L and 14.5") into the right side opening and start the eccentric shaft into the bushing. Align the countersink in the split bushing with the set screw hole on the rear of the head. On the pinned type bushing, drive in the taper pin.

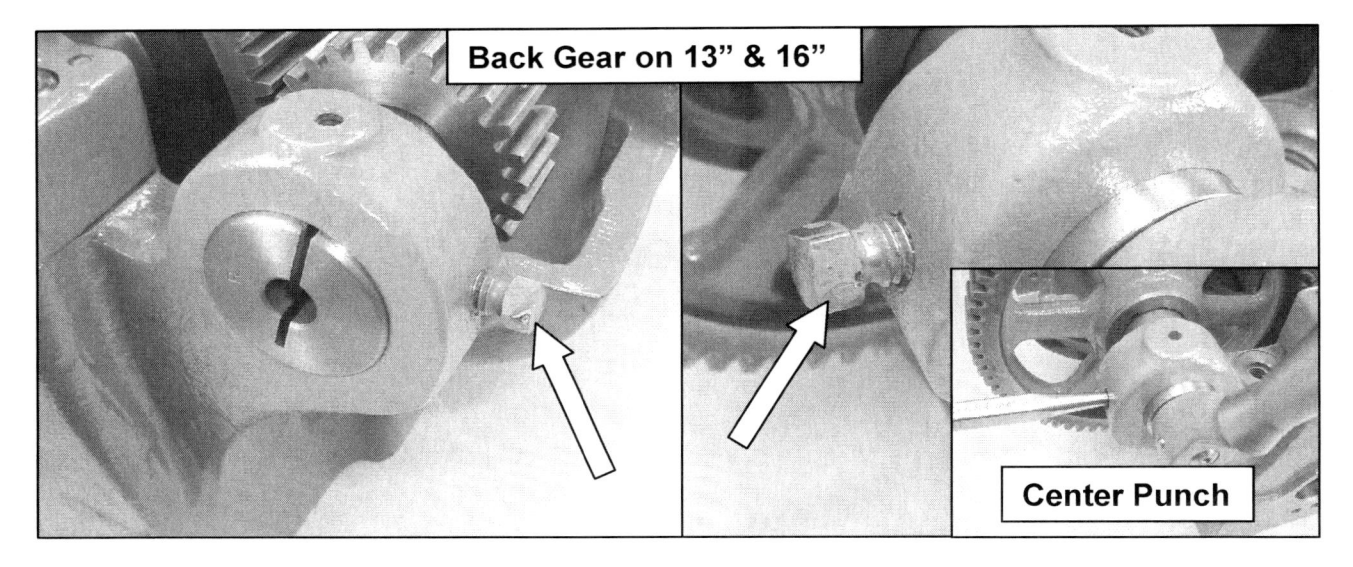

203. For 13" and 16" lathes, look through the set screw hole to make sure the countersink on the split bushing is concentric with the threaded hole. A small center punch works well to assist the alignment. Install the square head, cone point set screws but do not tighten. Tighten the set screw on the eccentric lever side to lock the bushing in place. Test the engagement of the back gear with the spindle several times. Adjust the set screw on the split bushing until the action is firm but smooth. Fine adjustment will be discussed later.

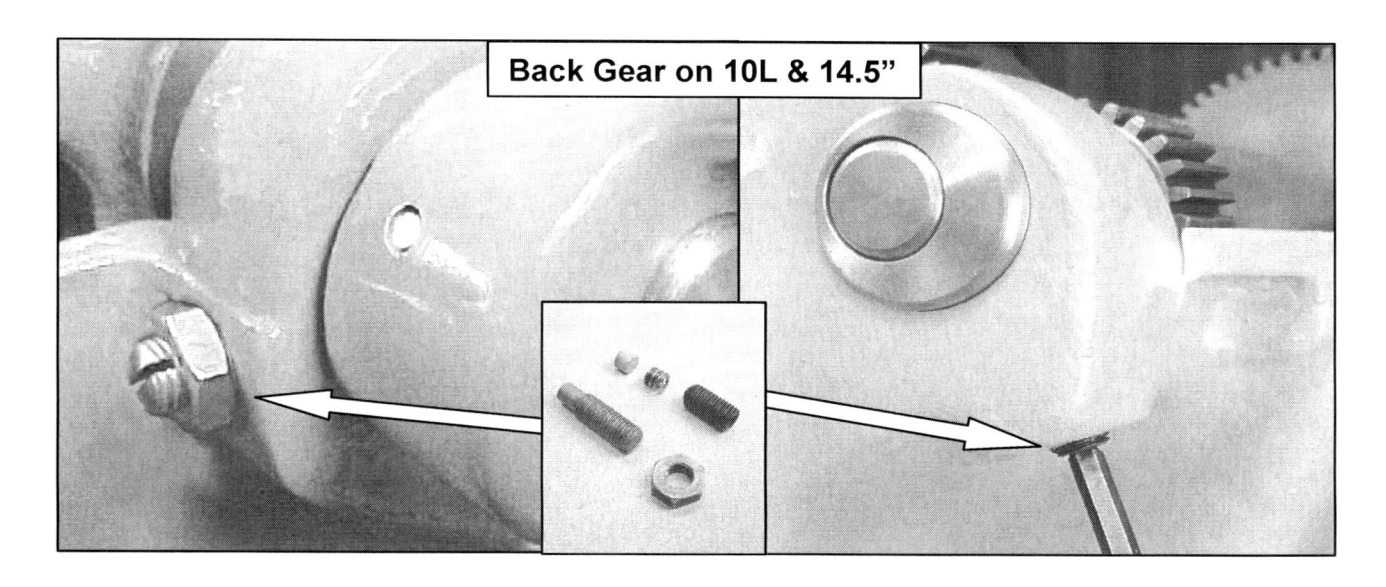

Back Gear on 10L & 14.5"

204. For the 10L and 14.5" lathes insert the dog pointed set screw into the threaded hole next to the eccentric lever. Load the brass shoe, spring and tension bolt into the threaded hole beneath the eccentric bushing. See later section for fine adjustment.

205. Slide the quill gear shroud into position and fasten with the two cap screws. Lubricate the two countersinks in the headstock for mounting the cone pulley cover. Install the left side set screw first and then tighten the right side. Test that the cover does not rub against the quill gear shroud when opening and closing. Adjust until satisfactory and then secure the lock nuts.

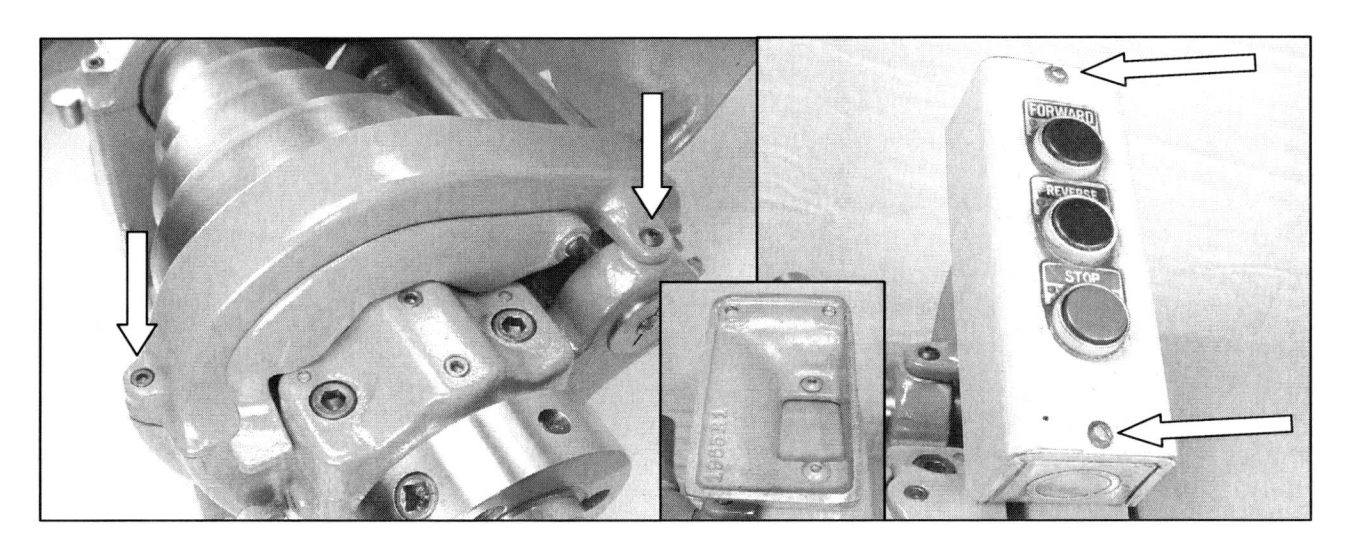

206. Install the bull gear shroud using the two cap screws. Test the cone pulley cover to make sure that it does not contact the bull gear shroud and that the spacing on either side of the cover is approximately equal. If applicable, install the switch bracket on the quill gear shroud and remount the motor control switch.

Grease Fitting Adapter

207. Grease the spindle cone pulley and the back gear by removing the screws from the lube ports as shown and injecting Teflon® based grease into the cavity. You can use an adapter like the one shown above that has a standard grease fitting on a threaded base. Inject only enough to fill the cavity as you do not want grease coming out the ends and fouling the gears or bearings. The headstock is now complete. The drive belt will be installed after the motor drive has been refurbished. Spindle bearing and back gear adjustment is covered in the next two sections.

Spindle Bearing Adjustment Procedure

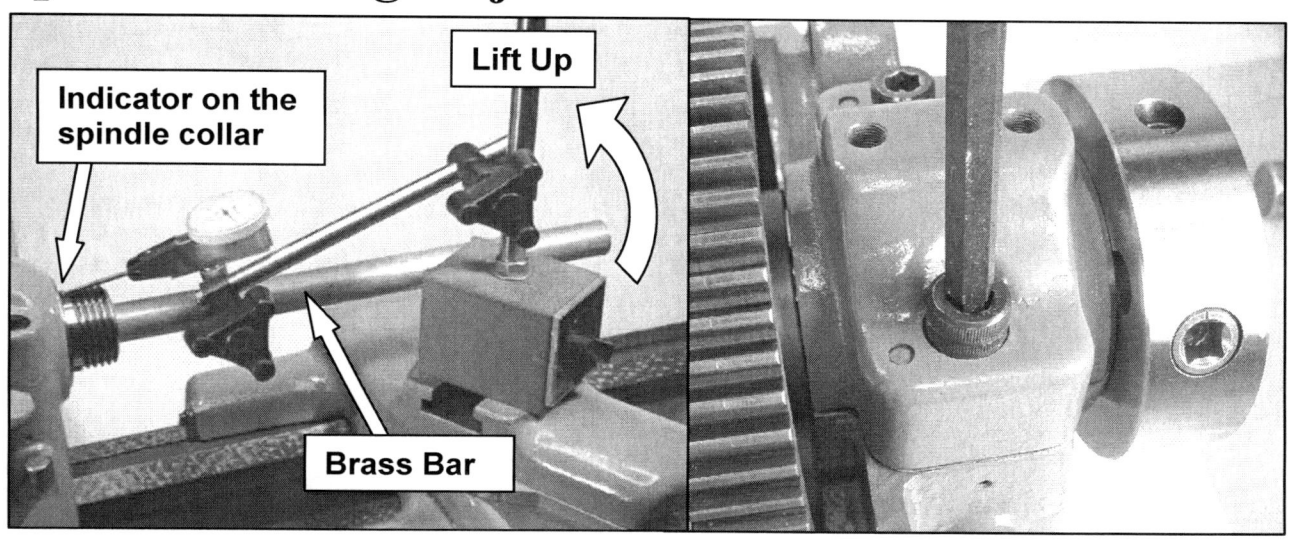

Indicator on the spindle collar

Lift Up

Brass Bar

208. Mount a dial test indicator on the top of the lathe compound with the tip of the indicator contacting the spindle nearest the collar or chuck mounting flange. Place a 2 foot long by 1" diameter brass bar (or similar soft metal) through the spindle. Push down on the bar lightly and zero the indicator. Lift up on the bar with approximately 75 lbs of force and note the reading. **[Acceptable Readings: .0007" min to .0010" max]**

If the clearance is outside of this ranges, then a .0015" brass shim must be added (under .0007") or removed (over .0010") from ***one side*** of the bearing cap only. The shims are usually .0015" thick brass. Remove the expander and bearing cap bolts as before and remove the shim stack. Measure the original thickness of the shims with a micrometer and then add/remove a .0015"shim. Using your wife's best scissors, cut the new brass shim to match the original outline and insert it into the stack. Check the thickness of the shim stack then reinsert them into the headstock. Install the cap bolts, then the expander and tighten. Measure the clearance again. Do not allow the indicated clearance to go below the minimum values listed or there could be issues with proper spindle lubrication. The minimum clearance specified is necessary to maintain the oil film that protects the spindle bearing surfaces, so a little too much clearance is better than too little clearance since low clearance can starve the spindle of oil and damage the bearings. Repeat the test procedure on the other end of the spindle by clamping the dial indicator on the headstock casting and placing the indicator contact on the smooth outer collar of the spindle.

Back Gear Adjustment Procedure

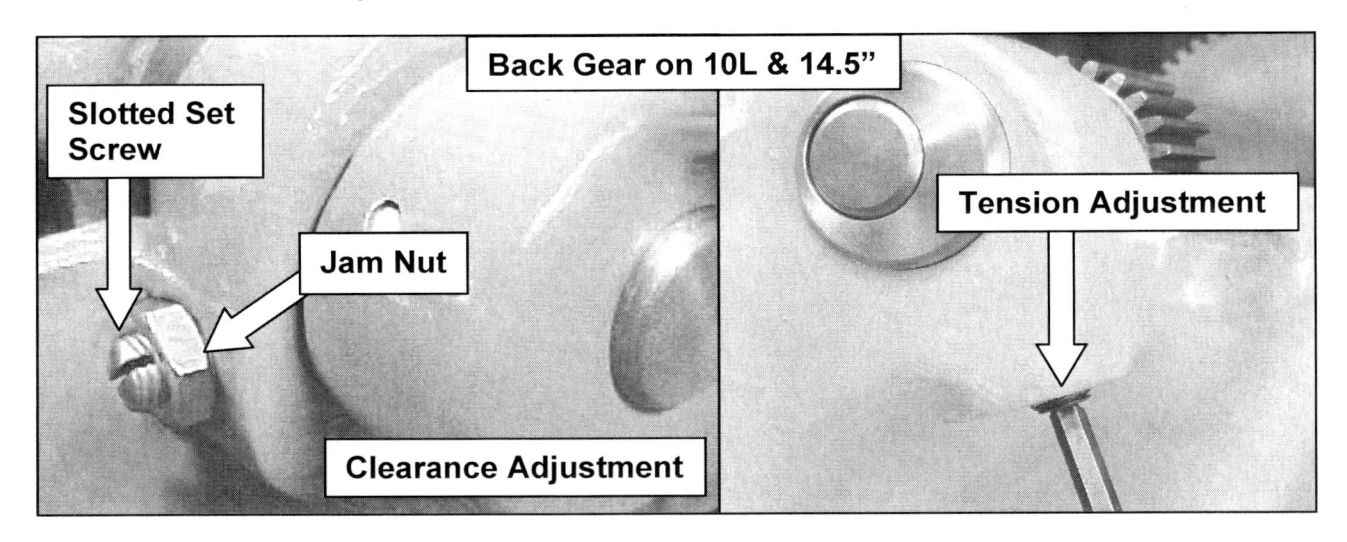

Back Gear on 10L & 14.5"

Slotted Set Screw

Jam Nut

Tension Adjustment

Clearance Adjustment

209. Model 10L, 14 ½": Engage the back-gears using the eccentric shaft lever and allow the mating gears to bottom out. Back off the eccentric lever until you feel a slight rock between the gears when the back gear is rotated. Tighten the slotted set screw and jam nut beside the eccentric lever. Tighten the tension adjust screw against the internal spring to put enough pressure on the bushing so that gears will be held in mesh on heavy cuts, but not so tight that the eccentric shaft lever is hard to operate. If there is significant gear rattling noise during operation, the gear clearance is too great. Adjust by slightly unscrewing the slotted set screw (to bring the gears closer together) and test it again. If the gears produce a growling noise, the gear clearance is too low. Adjust by turning the slotted set screw clockwise (to push the gears apart) and then tighten the jam nut. If the gears pop out of engagement during operation or heavy cuts, increase the tension.

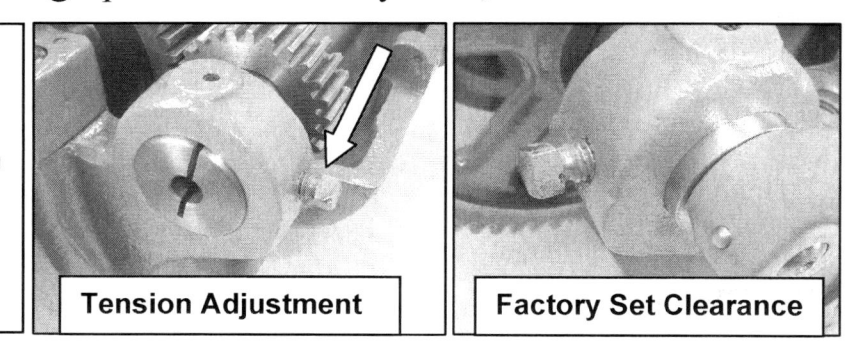

Back Gear on 13" & 16": Note that the gear clearance is preset by the position of the stop pin in the bushing on the eccentric lever. The bushing in turn is positioned by the countersink beneath the pointed set screw.

Tension Adjustment

Factory Set Clearance

210. On the 13" and 16" lathes, gear depth is set at the factory by the position of the bushing on the eccentric lever. Tension is adjustable by tightening the split bushing. Adjust tension as described above.

Section 4 – Motor Drive System
Motor Drive Unit Disassembly

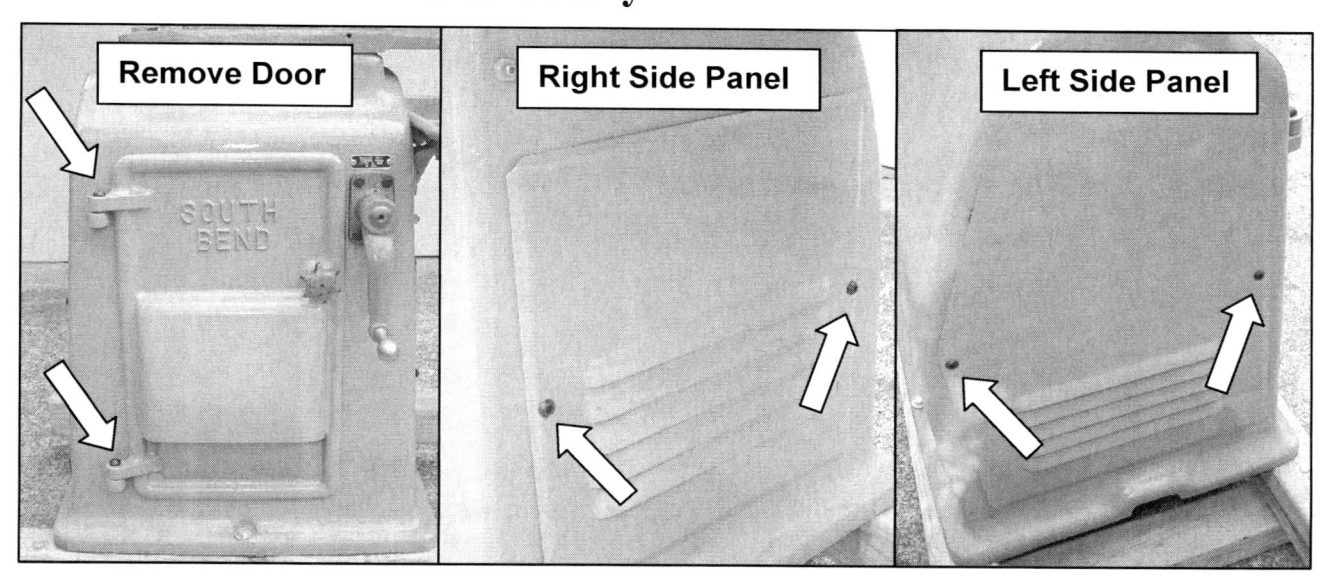

211. To access the motor drive unit, first remove the front door by driving out the two hinge pins, then remove the two access panels located on either side of the pedestal base. These may be cast or sheet metal.

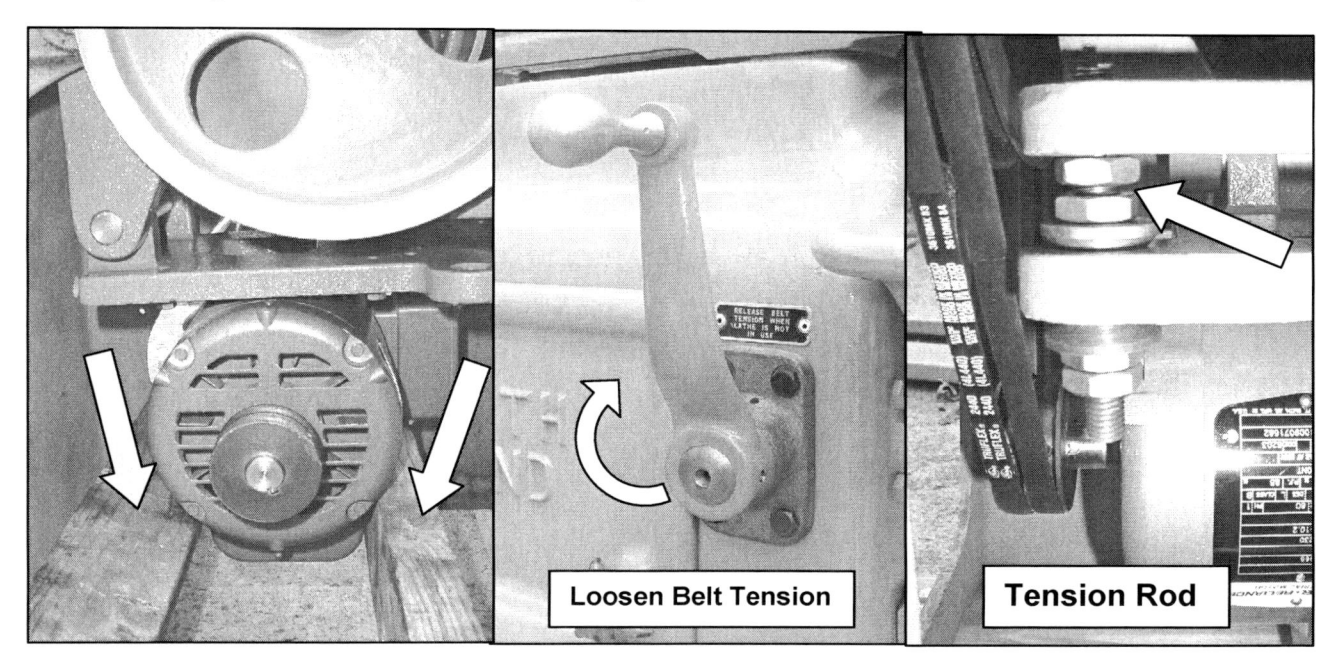

212. Place wooden blocking underneath the motor & drive unit to help support the weight during removal. It is best to disassemble one section at a time because of the weight and access limitations. Place the belt tensioning lever in the "up" position to relieve the spring tension. Loosen the V belt tension by first loosening the locknuts on the tension rod.

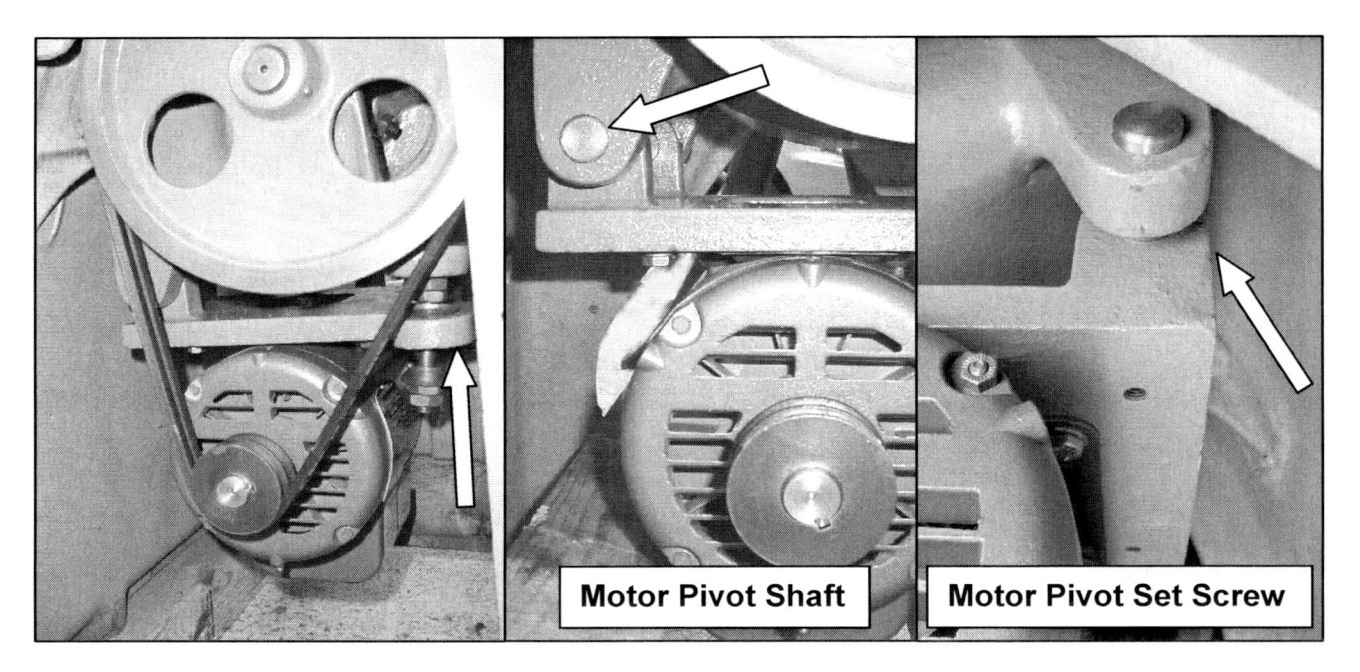

Motor Pivot Shaft **Motor Pivot Set Screw**

213. Remove the V belts by lifting the motor plate and slipping the belts off of the larger pulley while rotating it. The motor mounting plate pivots on a shaft that is connected to the pulley cradle. Locate the set screw on the right rear side of the cradle casting that locks the motor plate pivot shaft and remove it. Disconnect the power cable from the motor.

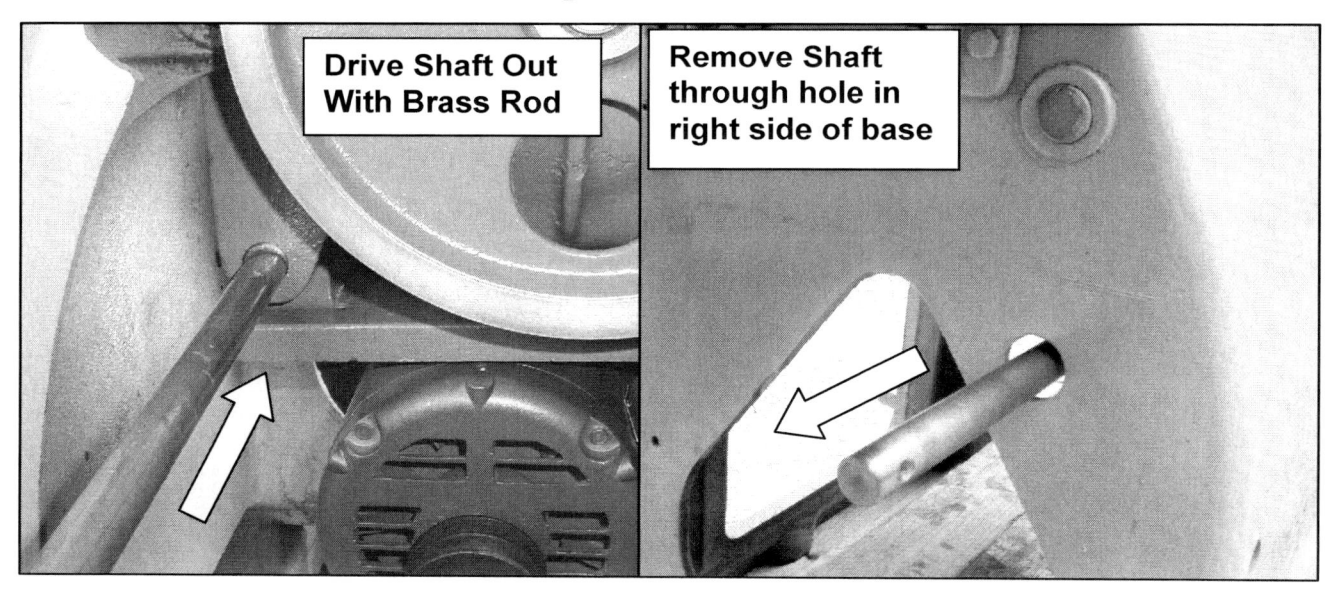

Drive Shaft Out With Brass Rod

Remove Shaft through hole in right side of base

214. Make sure that the motor is well supported from below. Use a 2 ft. long x ¾" diameter brass rod to drive the pivot shaft out the hole in the right side of the base. The brass rod will replace the shaft as you drive it through and keep the motor suspended until you are ready. Remove the rod carefully and slide the motor out of the base on the wooden blocks.

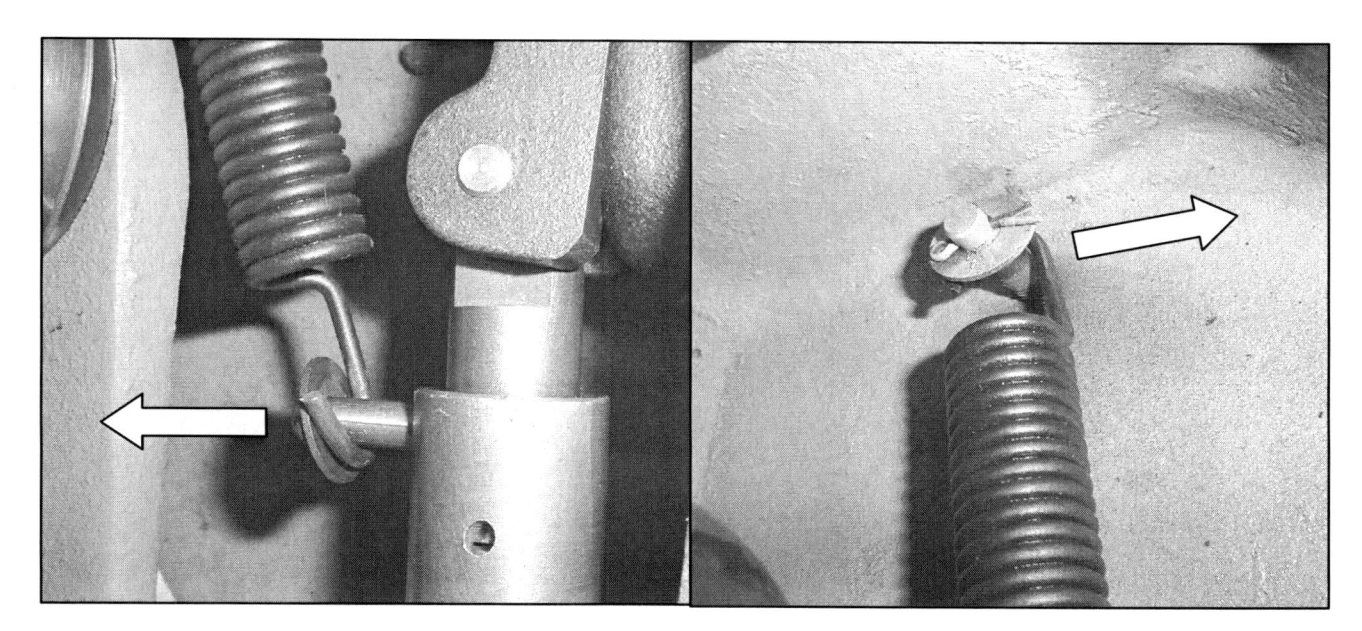

215. Remove the counter balance spring by first making sure that you have eye protection. We usually install a long tie wrap around the spring for safety in case the spring was to come off unexpectedly. Remove the cotter pin in the spring mounting stud and slide the washer off of the stud. Using a loop of wire, hook the spring and pull downward to slide it off of the end of the stud. Unhook the spring from the upper mount.

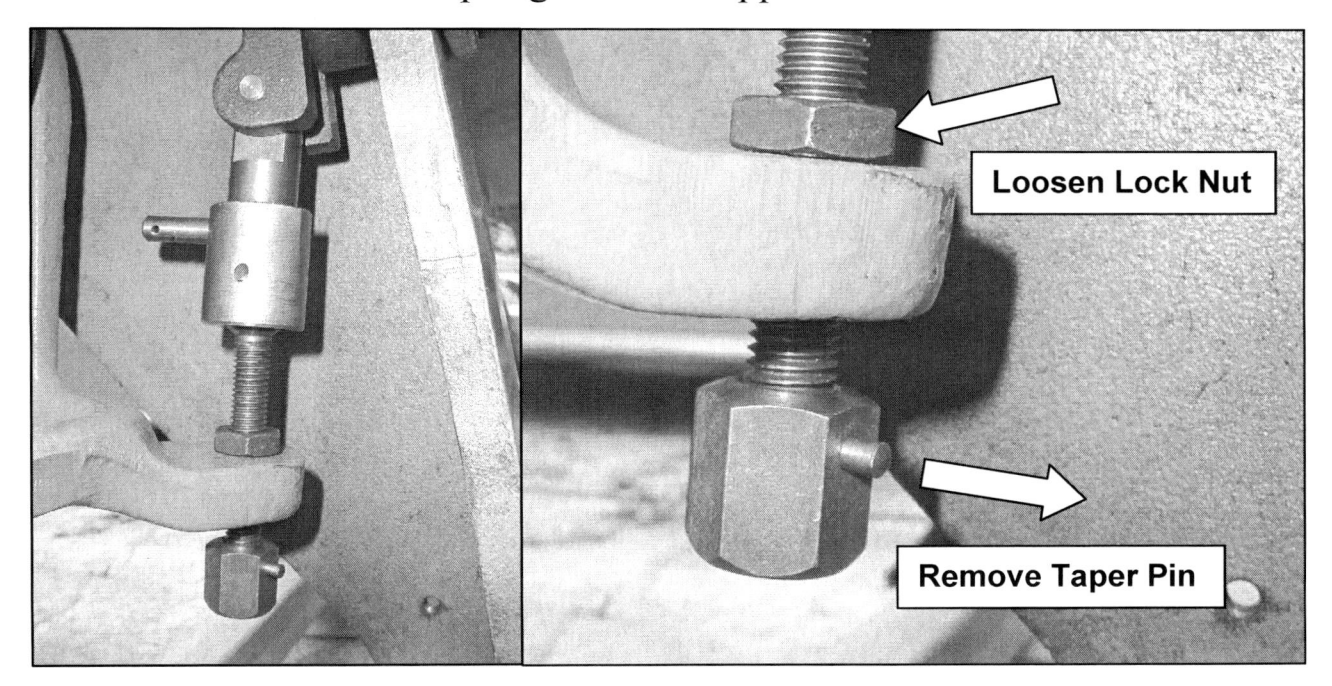

216. Support the cradle. Loosen the tension rod lock nut located next to the cradle. Locate the taper pin in the adjusting nut on the bottom of the rod and drive the taper pin out. Unscrew the adjusting nut from the rod.

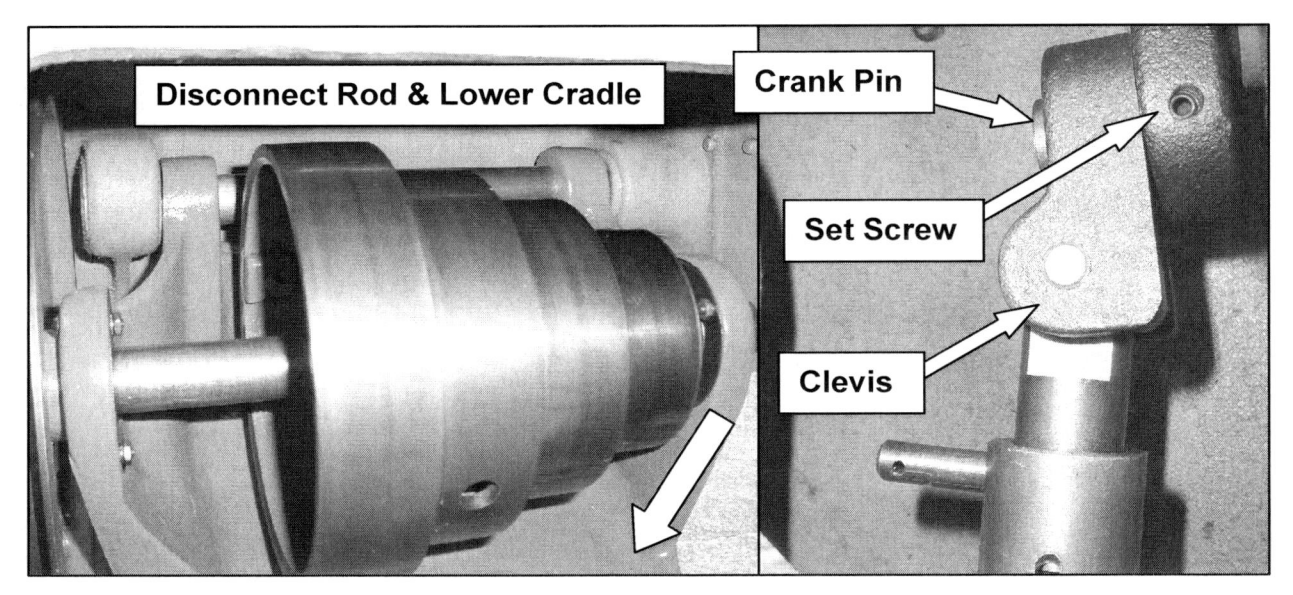

217. Gradually lower the cradle while simultaneously unscrewing the rod. After the rod disengages from the cradle, gently lower the cradle until it stops against the base side. Remove the set screw from the side of the crank shaft. Once removed, slide the crank pin and clevis assembly out of the crank shaft.

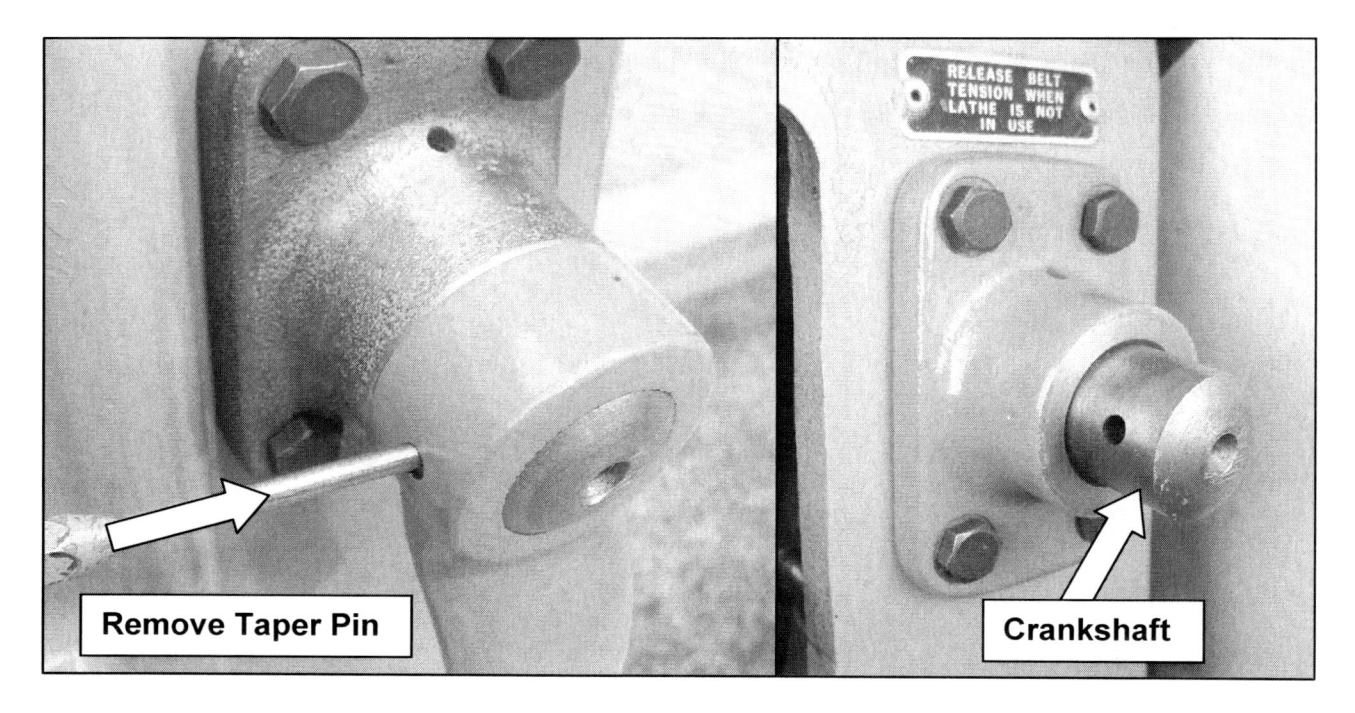

218. Drive the taper pin out of the belt tensioning crank handle and slide the handle off of the crankshaft. Push the crankshaft out from the front and then remove the mounting collar from the base.

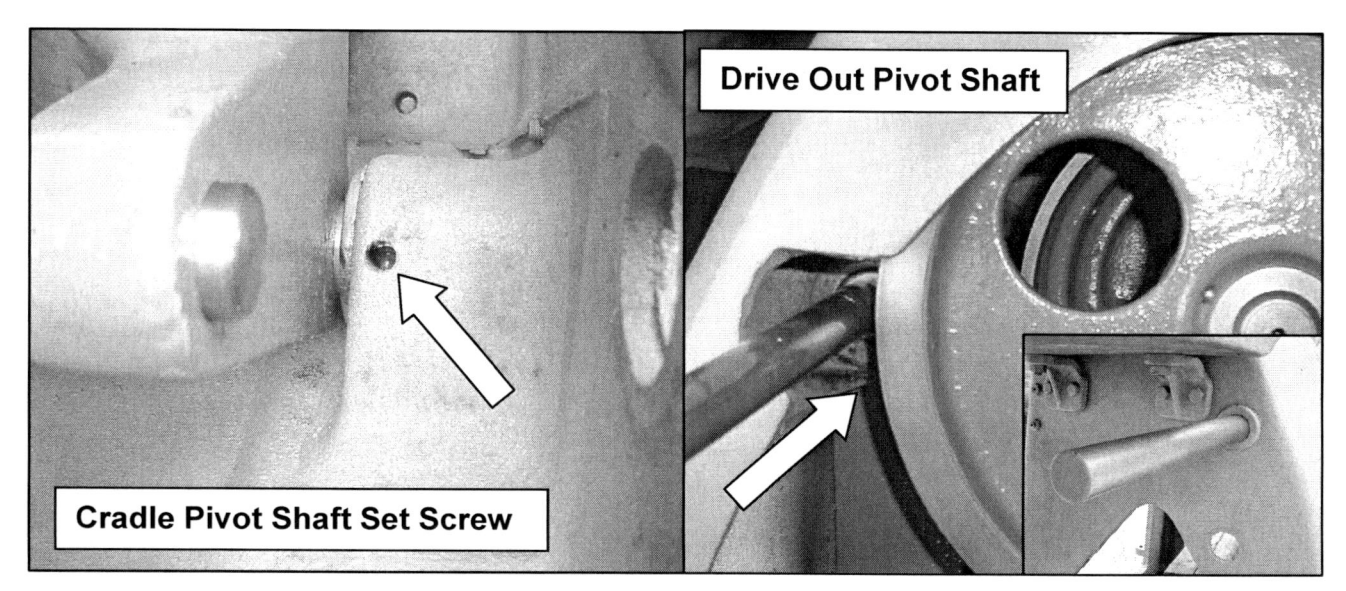

Drive Out Pivot Shaft

Cradle Pivot Shaft Set Screw

219. Locate the set screw on the upper right side of the base casting that secures the cradle pivot shaft and remove the set screw. Using the brass rod again, drive the pivot shaft out of the cradle from left to right and extract the shaft from the right side of the casting. The pivot bearings are poured-in-place soft Babbitt metal, so be careful not to damage them.

Babbitt Bearings

Remove Taper Pin

220. Carefully remove the brass rod and lower the cradle onto the wood blocking. Slide it out of the base. Set the cradle assembly on the workbench and locate the taper pin on the large pulley. Drive the taper pin out and use a gear puller to extract the pulley from the shaft. See appendix if you have difficulty removing this taper pin.

Jam Nut & Preload Nut

Cone Pulley Set Screw

221. Inside the cone pulley, locate the two set screws that lock the pulley to the shaft and loosen the jam nuts. Remove the set screws with a long Allen wrench. On the right end of the shaft, use two box wrenches to remove the jam nut, bearing preload nut and washer from the shaft.

222. Remove the 3 round head machine screws, lock-washers and nuts from both ends of the cradle housing. These screws hold the two bearing retaining rings in place. Use a rubber dead blow mallet to rap the right side of the shaft. This should push the bearings out of their pockets. If they are tight, mount the cradle in an arbor press and press the shaft out.

223. Use a gear puller to remove the bearing from the left (flywheel end) of the shaft. Slide the cone pulley on the shaft toward to the left end, tilt the pulley away from the cradle and pull the shaft out of the pulley. If the pulley is seized on the shaft you will need to mount the whole cradle in an arbor press and then press the shaft back out through the right side.

224. Remove the four hex cap screws and washers holding the motor to the mounting plate. Remove the set screw(s) in the pulley collar. Use a gear puller to remove the pulley. Clean all components in a suitable solvent, strip and repaint as desired. Acquire new replacement sealed ball bearings if the old bearings have rough spots, or are hard to turn.

Motor Drive Unit Assembly

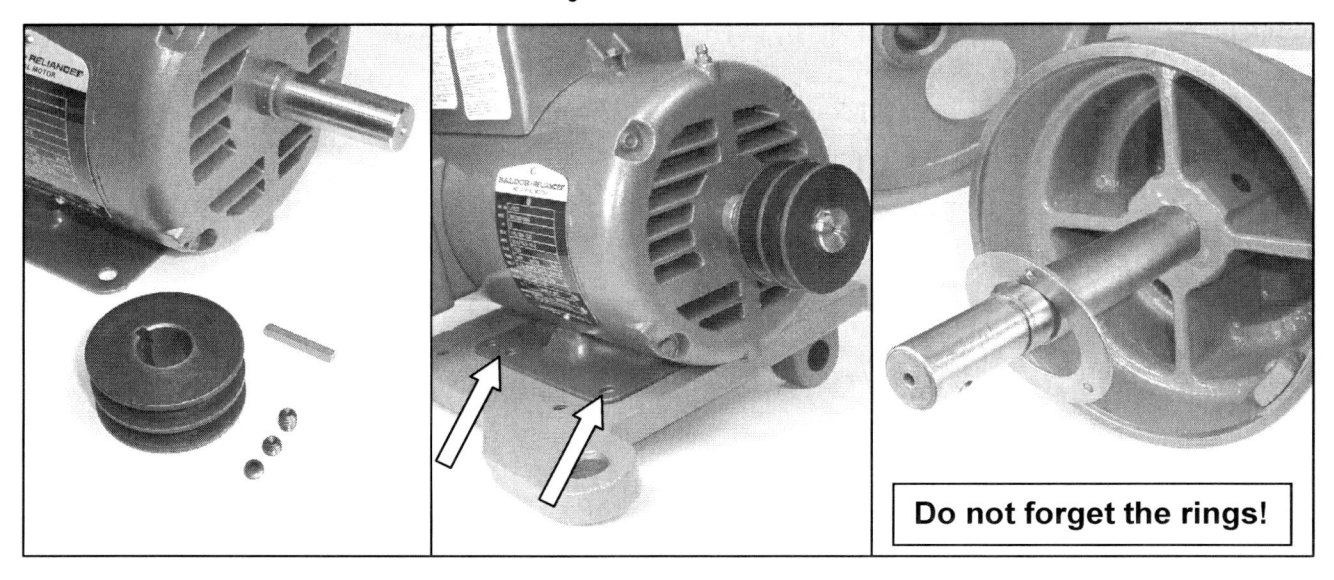

Do not forget the rings!

225. Install the motor pulley and key on the motor shaft. Install the set screws and loosely tighten. (The pulley must be aligned to the flywheel later so do not lock in place yet). Assemble the motor onto the base plate using 4 hex cap screws and lock washers. Slide the cone shaft into the cone pulley as shown. Slip a bearing retaining ring on each end of the shaft.

226. Position the cone pulley & shaft inside the cradle as shown. Position one sealed bearing on the left end of the pulley and press onto the collar. When pressing on the bearing use a length of steel pipe so that the pressure is only placed on the inner race of the bearing. Pushing on the outer race or shields may damage the bearing.

227. On the treaded end of the shaft press the 2nd ball bearing onto the shaft collar. After assembly, this bearing will not necessarily contact the shaft collar as on the other end. The threaded nuts on this end of the shaft preload the bearing to remove any play in the assembly so there may be a slight gap here. From the flywheel end, gently press the shaft and bearings into the cradle. If necessary, use a small brass punch to tap the outer race to seat it in the cradle housing. Slide the pulley out of the way if needed.

228. Check that the bearings are flush with the inner machined faces of the cradle. Slide the bearing retaining rings into position and install the 3 round head machine screws on each end. Mount the flywheel pulley on the shaft, align the taper pin holes and install the taper pin.

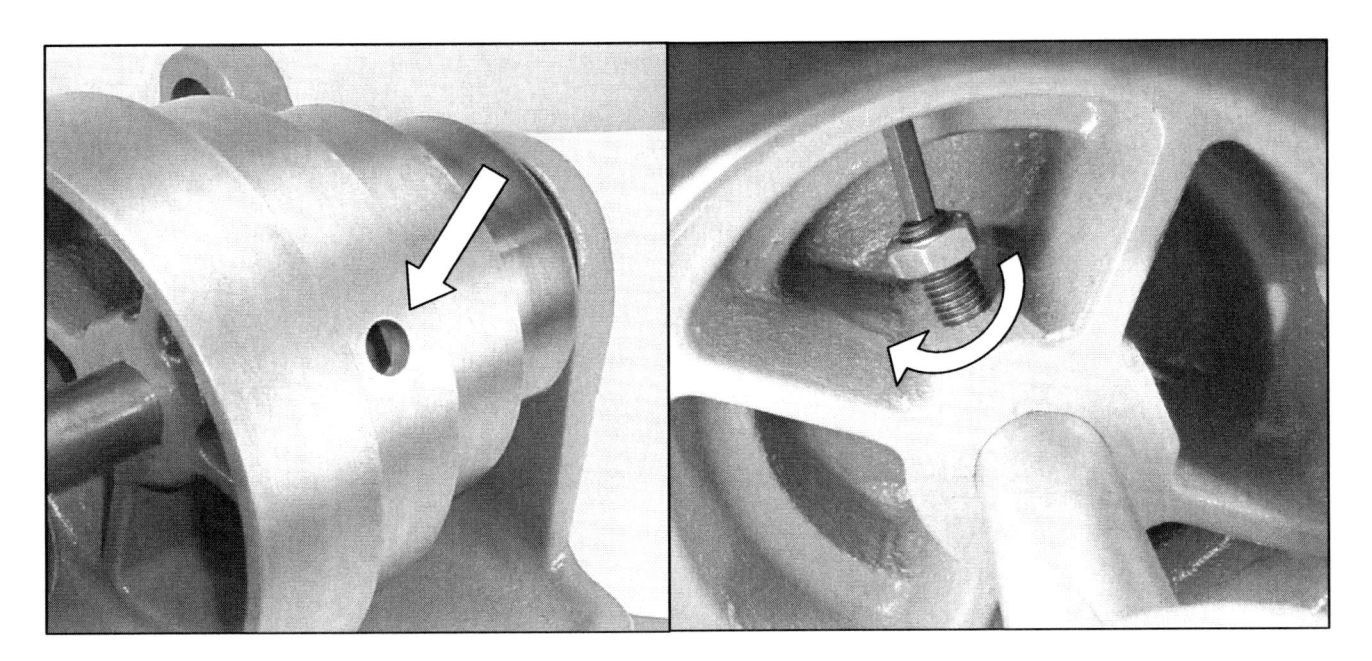

229. Using a flashlight, look through the pulley set screw holes and rotate or slide the pulley along the shaft until both countersinks on the shaft align with the 2 set screw holes. Loosely install the set screws and jam nuts. Once the set screw makes contact, rock the pulley back and forth slightly while tightening to make sure that the set screw is entering the countersink properly. Once both set screws are seated tightly, lock with the jam nuts.

230. Thread the preload washer and nut onto the pulley shaft. Tighten lightly and test the rotation of the pulley. Continue tightening until a slight drag is felt and then back off 1/12 turn. Install and tighten the jam nut. Test again to make sure the pulley spins freely.

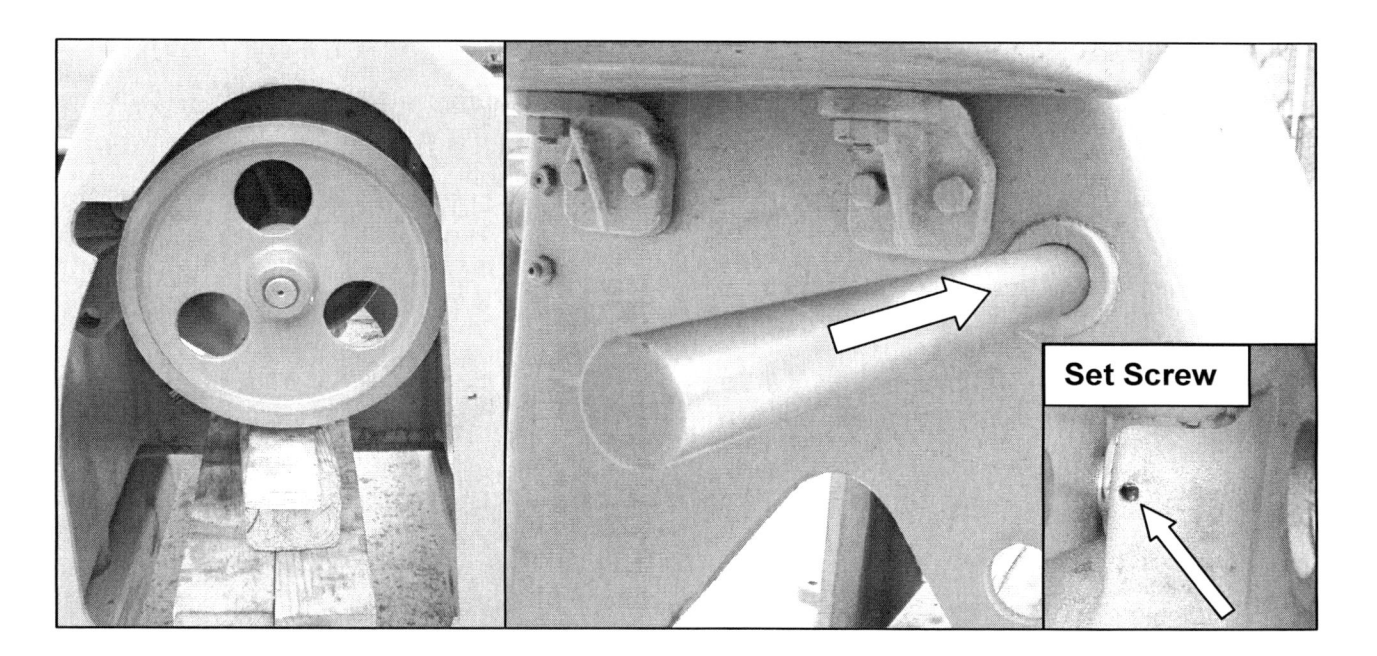

Set Screw

231. Position the cradle inside the base casting and align the mounting holes using the brass rod. With the set screw countersink point downward, start the cradle shaft through the right side of the casting and gradually push it through the cradle and into position. Look through the set screw hole to align the countersink and then install & tighten the set screw.

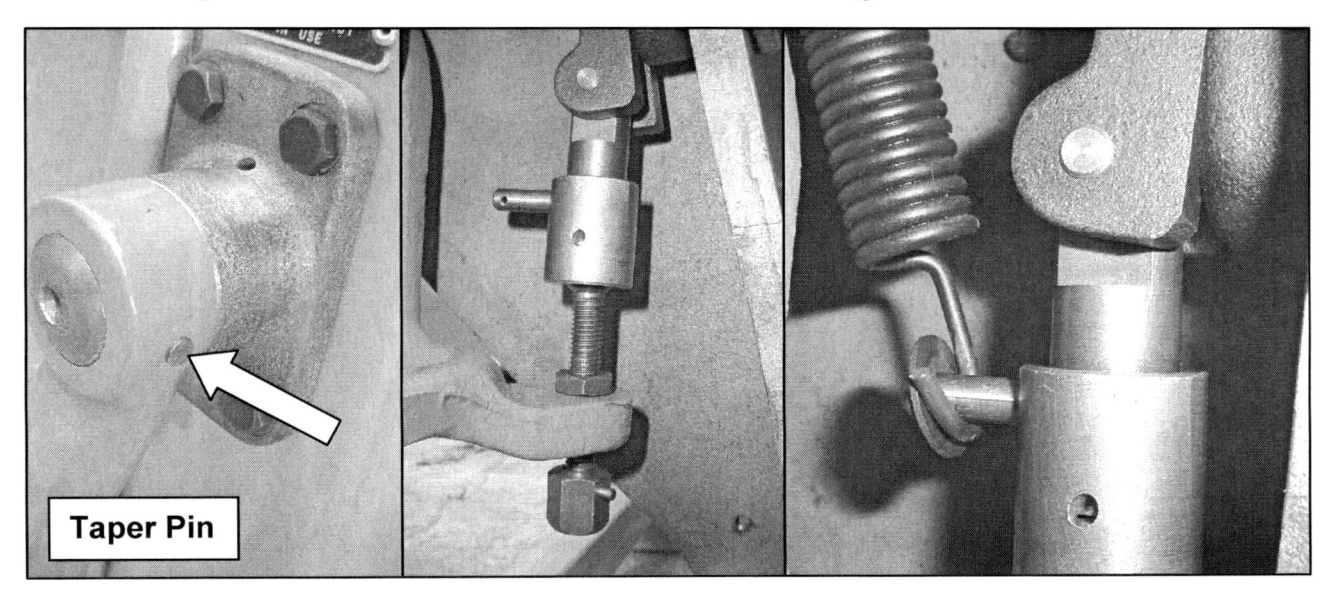

Taper Pin

232. Install the crankshaft mounting collar in the base. Lubricate the crankshaft, insert it into the collar and then pin the crank handle in place. Install the clevis and tension rod assembly by supporting the cradle and threading the tension rod through the threaded hole. Install the adjusting nut and pin it in place with the taper pin. Stretch the tension spring as shown previously and secure it to the studs using a washer and cotter pin.

Set Screw

233. Start the motor plate pivot shaft into cradle from the right side of the base. Block the motor at the approximate correct height and work the shaft through the motor plate. The countersink on the shaft should face to the rear so that it will line up with the set screw hole. Tighten the set screw once the shaft is in position.

Align Pulleys

234. Use a long straight edge to vertically align the motor pulley with the flywheel pulley above. Once they are aligned, tighten the set screws in the motor pulley. Slip the v-belts onto the motor pulley and then catch the edge of the large pulley with the belt and rotate it to pull the belt into the groove. Install the tension rod and lock nuts as shown. Install the left and right side base covers and then set the access door back on the hinge pins.

Tailstock – 13", 14 ½", 16"

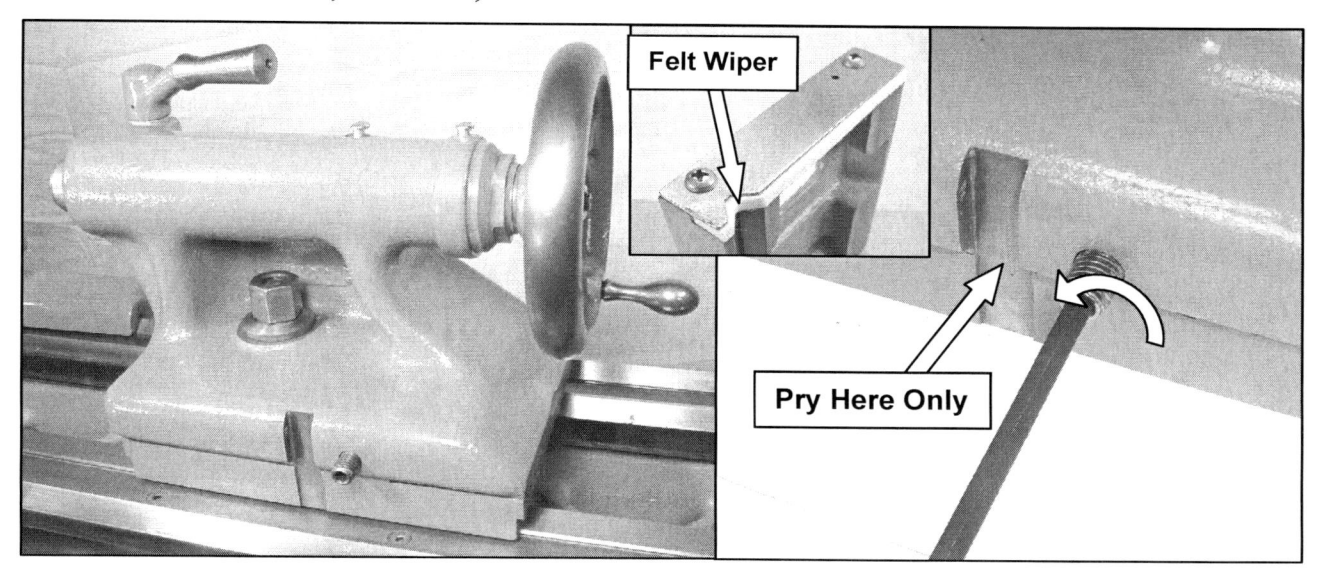

235. With the tailstock removed from the bed, free the base plate by first removing the two lateral adjusting set screws from the front and rear of the tailstock. Pry the two pieces apart by inserting a narrow wood chisel into the slot as show so as not to damage any of the scraped mating surfaces. Replace the felt wipers in the base of the tailstock by removing the two machine screws and cover plate.

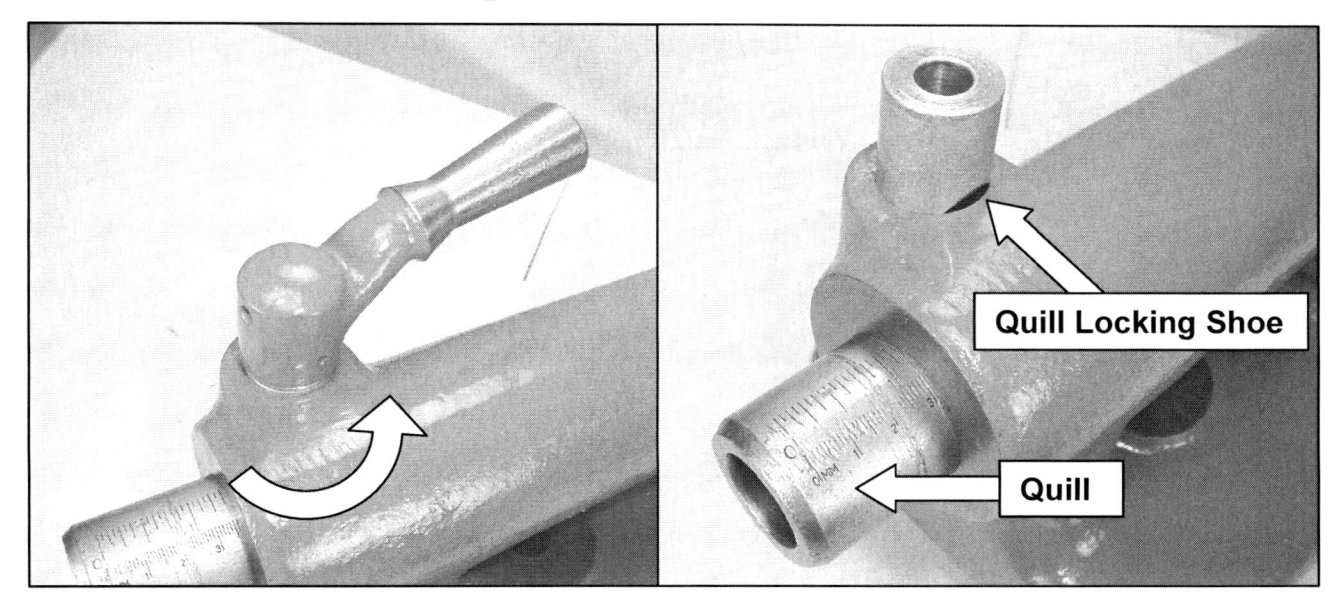

236. Unscrew the quill locking lever from the tailstock and remove. Pull out the top half of the quill locking shoe through the opening in the top. If tight, wait until the quill is removed and then push it out from the bottom.

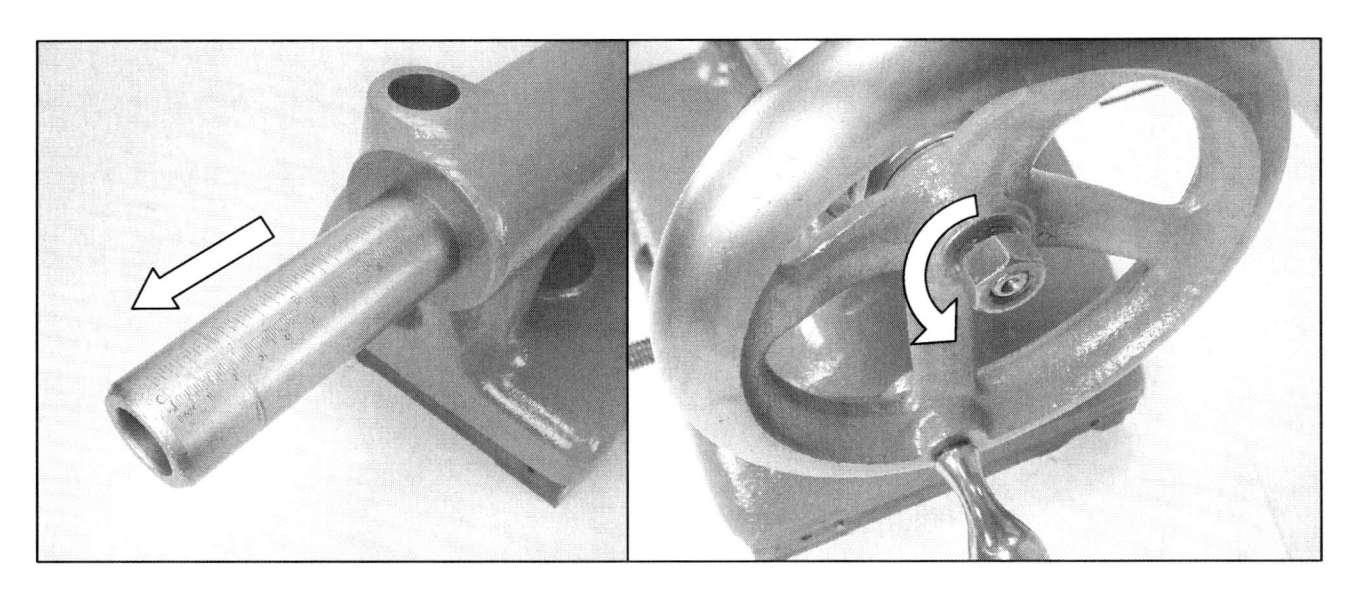

237. Rotate the handwheel clockwise until the quill disengages from the screw and stops moving. Slide the quill out of the tailstock. Remove the locking nut from the center of the tailstock handwheel.

Round Key(s)

238. Beneath the handwheel you will find either a square keyed shaft or round key(s) that locks the handwheel to the tailstock screw. Gently tap the handwheel from the rear. If it does not come off easily use a gear puller. Make sure not to shoot the key across the room and lose it. Unscrew the tailstock nut from the body using a large wrench on the flats. Extract the screw shaft from the tailstock nut. Clean all components in solvent making sure that all oil passages from the oil hole covers on top of the tailstock are clear. The tailstock nut typically has a felt plug inside to retain oil.

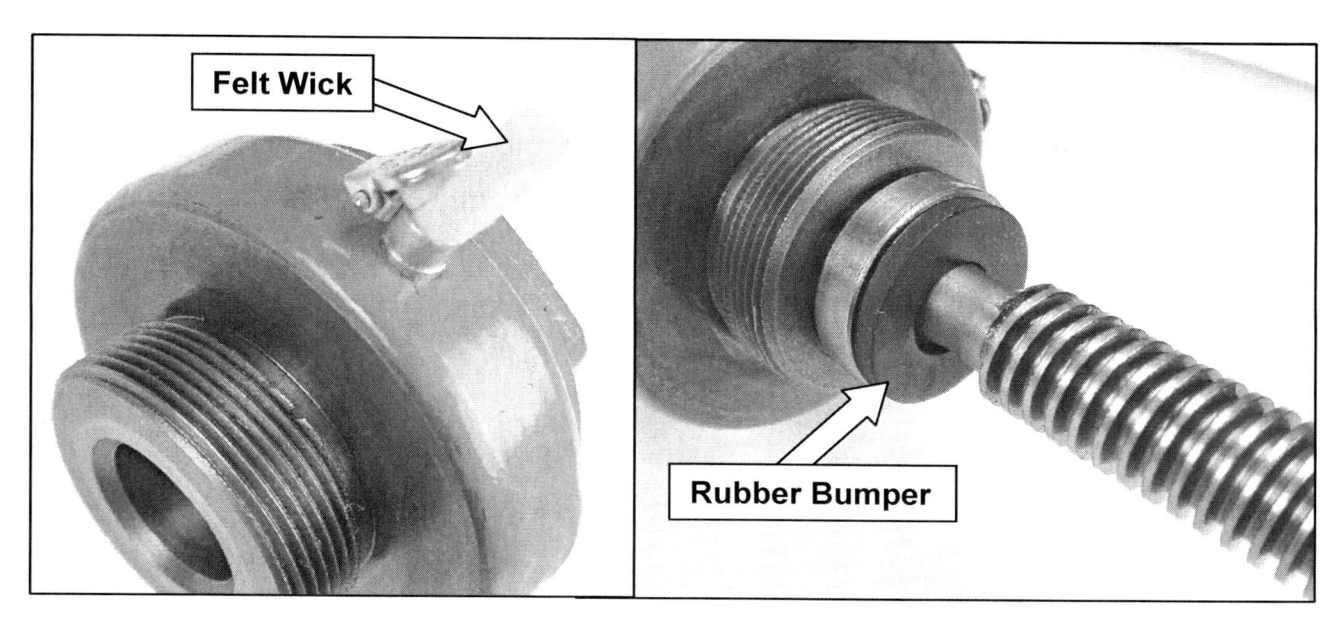

239. Replace the felt plug inside the tailstock nut with a ¾" length of Type 7 felt cord. If necessary, use a thin wire the pull the plug through the hole and stop flush with the inner surface. Lubricate and install the quill screw. Install a new rubber bumper over the threads and against the rear stop. This bumper prevents the quill from jamming tight against the stop.

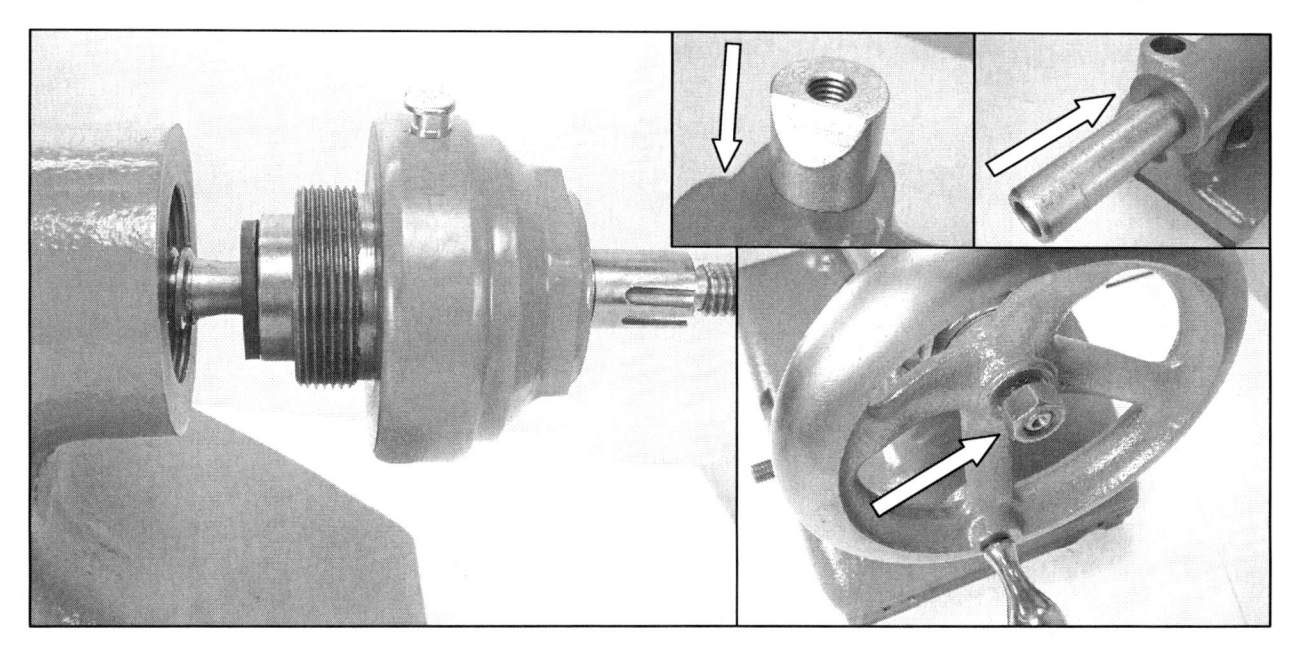

240. Reinstall the tailstock nut and shaft into the tailstock housing and tighten with a large wrench. Insert the lower quill locking shoe (threaded), and then slide the quill into the housing and engage with the tailstock screw. Install the upper locking shoe and the locking handle. Install the handwheel with keys and locking nut. Install the base and two set screws.

Tailstock – 10L

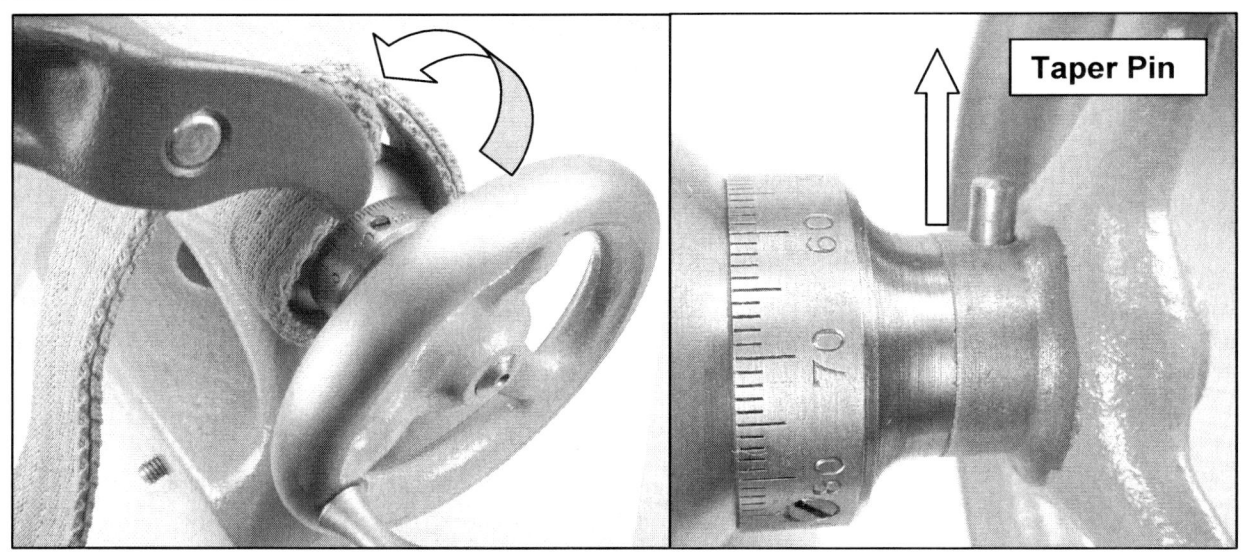

241. The 10L tailstock is a bit different from the other models. The base, quill and quill lock removal is the same as before. To dismantle, use a strap wrench to unscrew the collar behind the hand wheel. Remove either the **taper pin** or **lock nut** on the handle and pull the handle off of the shaft.

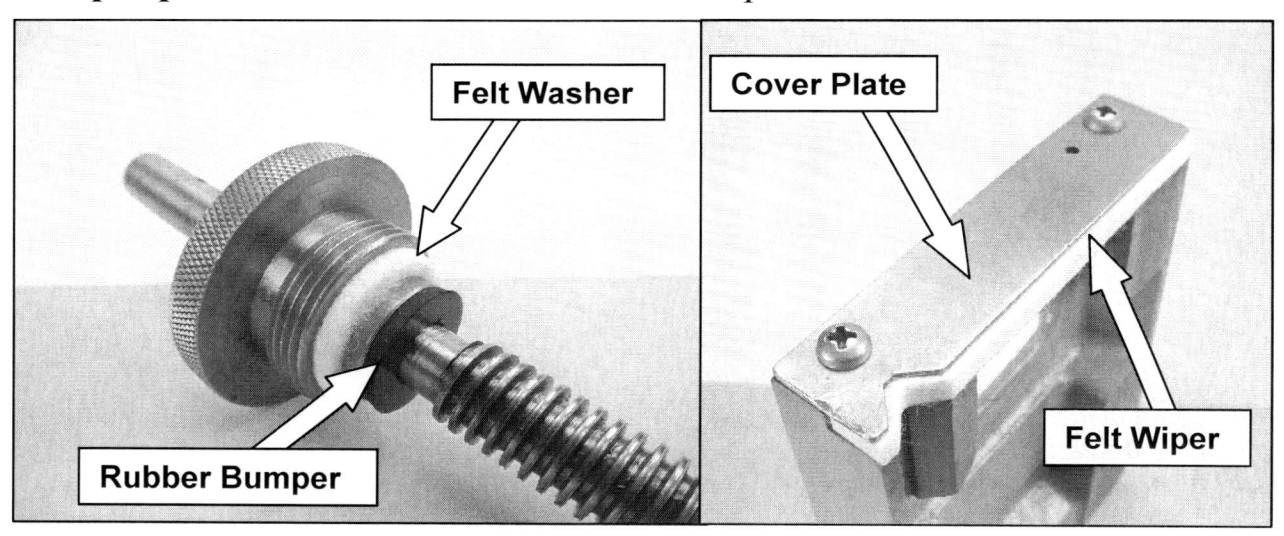

242. Loosen the locking screw on the graduated dial. Remove the dial and collars and clean thoroughly. Replace the felt washer on the feed screw and replace the rubber bumper. This bumper keeps the quill from jamming against the feed screw stop. Oil all of the components and reassemble. Replace the two bed wipers on the base of the tailstock by removing the machine screws and cover plates. Align the die cut felt wipers (center them on the v-way) and mount the plate. Oil the wipers and bolt the tailstock on the lathe bed.

Final Assembly & Belt Installation

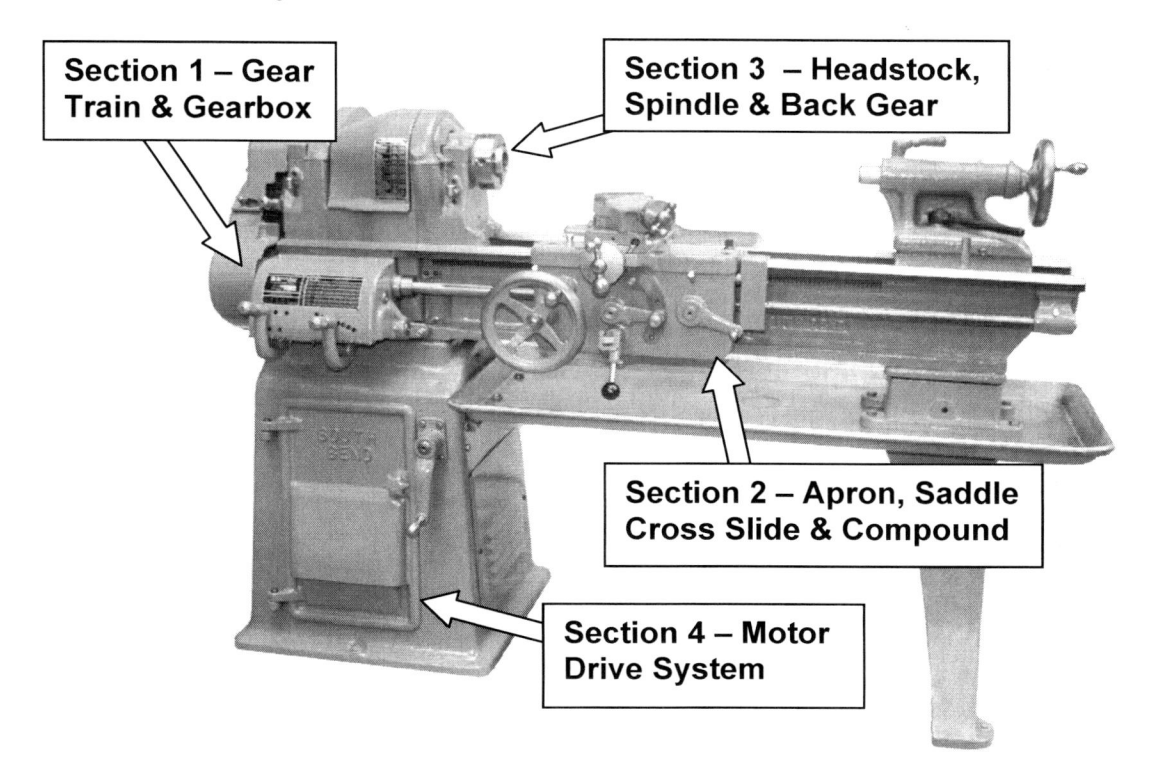

243. Reinstall the sub-assemblies in reverse order of removal.

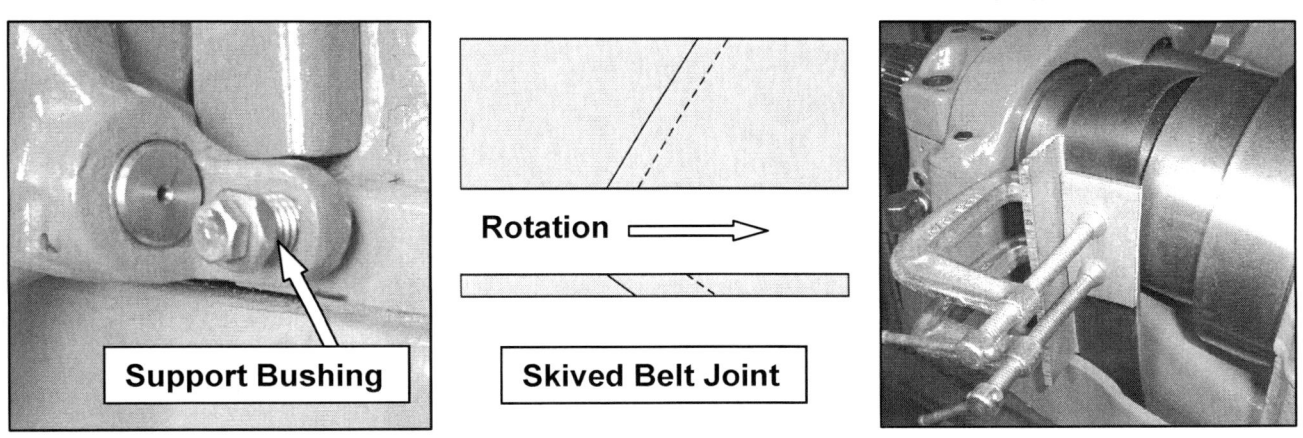

244. Special Notes: When mounting the gearbox, tighten the 3 bed bolts first and then install the gearbox support bushing. After the bushing contacts the bed, tighten 1/4 turn more and then install the bolt. To install the flat belt, skive the ends at an angle as shown to increase glue surface area. Feed the belt through the cradle, head and cone pulley. Apply cement to the joint and then clamp in an angle iron fixture until cured. The angle iron helps keep the belt edges parallel so that it will run true in operation.

Appendix 1

A Brief Guide to Refinishing Industrial Machinery

For those of you who have been around metalworking machinery for awhile, you already know the difference between a really well finished machine and one that has had the paint slathered on with a 4 inch brush. If you are not sure about the difference, look around ebay® for awhile and you will begin to understand what is meant by this term. When you look at a lathe and see the normally polished outer rim of the cast iron hand wheels painted gray, or see knurled plunger knobs painted, it is an indication of a rush job or it is because someone didn't know any better. If there is one fundamental rule on what to paint and what not to paint it is simply this:

If the surface in question is in the rough "as-cast" state, paint it.
If the surface has a machined or ground finish, do NOT paint it.

This rule will always serve you well going forward and your machine will tend to look as it originally did when it left the factory. There are many different ways to achieve a nice looking finish on your machine, so we will describe one of the approaches for achieving a durable finish that will apply not only to these lathes, but to other machine tools as well.

Preparation for a Good Finish

The cleaning and preparation steps are important. On older equipment, you should assume that the paints may contain lead so care should be taken in the stripping and removal of the old finish. Respiratory protection should always be used during the process. Two approaches for stripping the old finish:

1. Chemical – Use of commercial paint stripping solutions.
2. Mechanical – Use of a needle scaler, abrasive brushes or flap wheels.

The chemical method tends to be easier but it is really a personal preference. Always follow the manufacturer's directions for using chemical strippers. It should be noted that a filler compound was often used on the machine castings at the factory to fill in imperfections prior to painting. Because of this, industrial finishes are usually thicker and may take more than one pass with the chemical stripper so it helps to hit the filled thicker surfaces with a needle scaler first. Air powered needle scalers can be purchased from many suppliers but Harbor Freight currently sells one for about $30 (#96997) that does the job just fine. Make sure to wear eye and hearing protection when using a needle scaler. It is very important not to contact any of the machined surfaces of your lathe with any of the mechanical abrasion tools. The scaler, brushes, and flap wheels can damage the machined surfaces so mask them off with thick tape if necessary. The scaler should not be needed and should not be used on small delicate parts. After using a chemical stripper, go back over the surface with a wire brush and a cleaning solvent to remove the residue. The final step would be to go over the as-cast surfaces with a small abrasive flap wheel to reveal some virgin metal and give the surface some "tooth" that the paint can grab. If there are significant imperfections found in the castings after using the flap wheel, you can use standard Bondo® auto body filler and apply it directly to the abraded surface. Sand the filler level after it has cured and then re-apply as necessary. With the filler, you can spend an hour or a day here, and it just depends on the quality of final finish you want. Keep in mind that this is industrial equipment.

On priming, there may be a preference to prime the surface before painting but with modern industrial enamels it is not always necessary if the surface is well prepared. We do not use primers typically and have not had a problem with paint peeling off of a properly prepared surface but we will leave this step up to the discretion of the owner.

Painting Machinery

On the subject of paints, keep it simple: High-Quality Industrial Alkyd Enamel. With respect to color, we have seen *quality* paint jobs on lathes in a wide variety of colors ranging from Jet Black to Royal Blue and they all looked great. Color is your choice but "light machinery gray" is typical. Paints that we have used with very good results: Industrial 7400 series enamel from Rustoleum® and Benjamin Moore P22 Urethane Alkyd enamel. You normally have to purchase this type of paint from an industrial supplier as this is not the same paint found in hardware stores.

When painting, pay close attention to the interfaces between the cast surface and machined surface. Cutting a nice straight line here is the difference between an OK job and an excellent job. You don't have to mask and spray the paint to be neat. In fact, most good industrial paints go on just fine with a small high-quality fine-bristle brush and the brush strokes will self-level as the paint dries. This approach has the advantage to putting down thicker layers of paint so usually two coats is more than enough to give a smooth industrial grade finish. Always paint with overlapping strokes in an "X" pattern and then knock down the remaining ridges very lightly with back and forth strokes. On small parts use a 1/8" round detail brush. Let the paint encroach on the machined surface slightly. Take a shop towel with a small amount of paint thinner on it, wrap it tightly around your finger and then let your finger trace the machined edge just like the tool that machined it originally. You'll be surprised how clean and sharp it looks if you take your time. Of course masking and spraying the paint is fine if you have the compressor, sprayer and other equipment so this is just one approach to a good finish. Overly simplified:

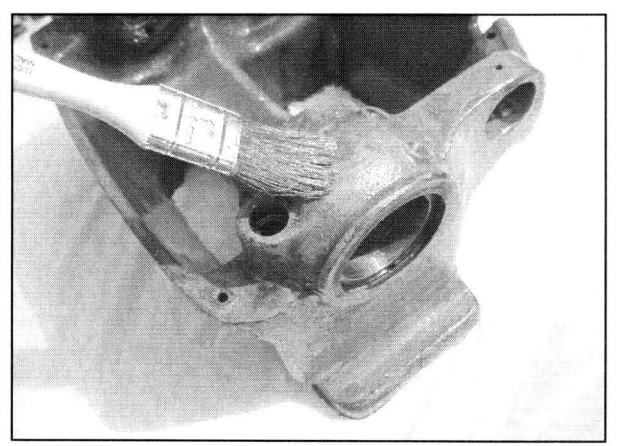 

Photo 1: Strip Old Paint & Filler   Photo 2: Abrade & Apply Filler

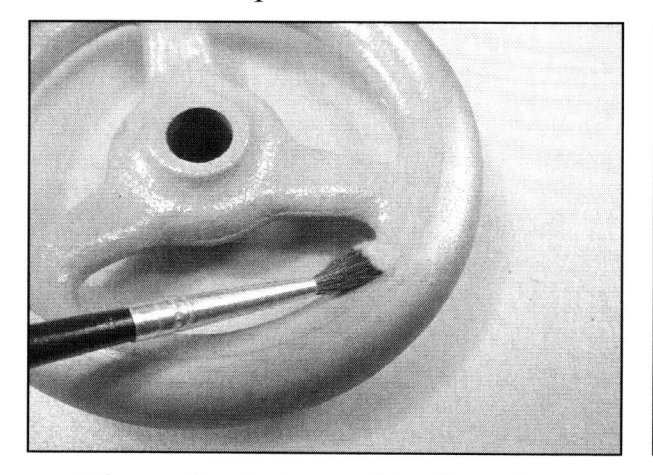 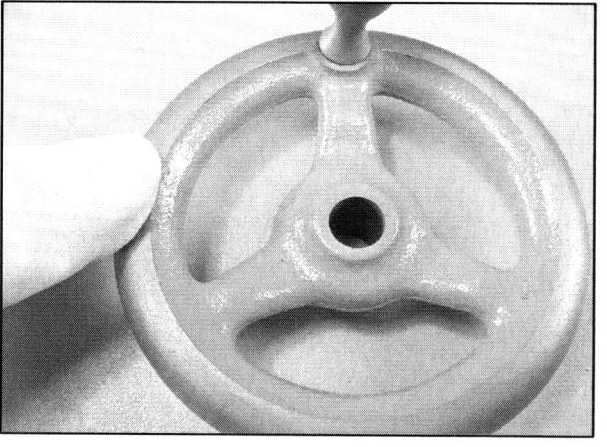

Photo 3: Paint with Overlap   Photo 4: Cut the Line

Appendix 2

<u>**Taper Pins**</u> – After hearing from quite a few people struggling with taper pins, we are including a short treatise on how to handle those nefarious little fasteners that were used on many South Bend Lathe assemblies. These are most commonly found on hand-wheels, back-gear bushings, shift levers, half-nut levers, and in the gearbox. If you have never had to deal with taper pins before, you're in for a treat so patience is absolutely essential. Taper pins only pop out easily on the first Tuesday of any calendar month that contains the letter "N", so make sure to schedule your lathe refurbishing work accordingly (this is a joke).

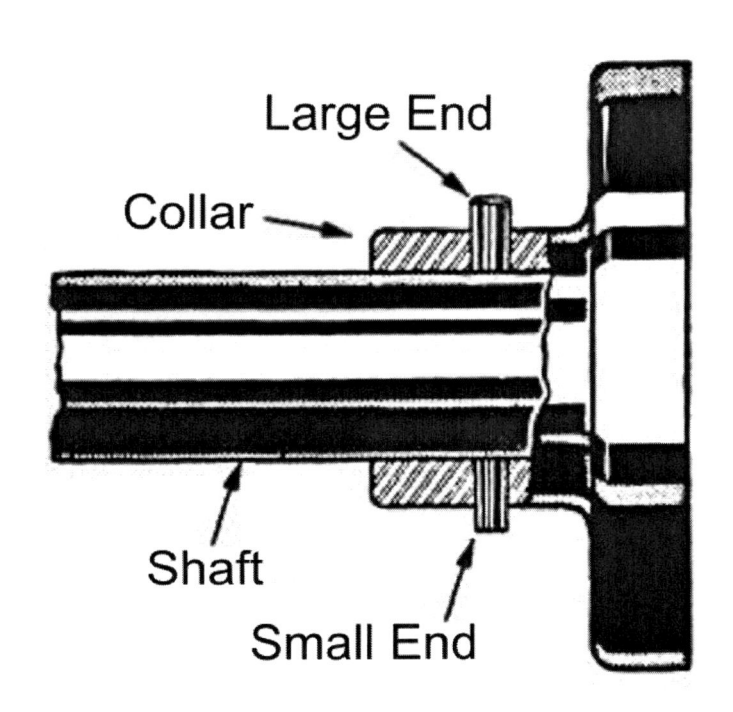

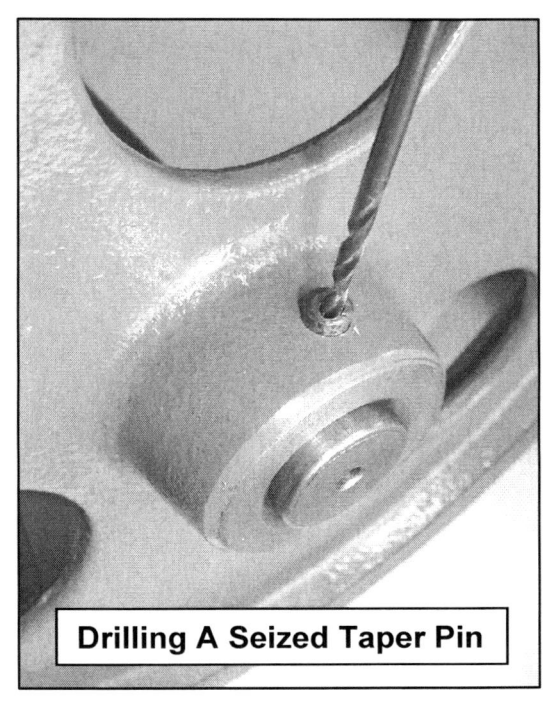

Drilling A Seized Taper Pin

Taper pins are essentially a conical wedge that is driven into a reamed through-hole that has the same taper angle. On flywheels and collars that do not have to be removed to disassemble the lathe, it is best to leave them in place and not touch them. If removal is necessary, the first step to extracting a taper pin is to make sure that you can identify the large end from the small end since these pins can only be removed in one direction. If the pin stands proud of the adjoining surfaces and it has been removed before, the ends may be "mushroomed" and hard to measure. If the head is damaged, it is best to grind down the ends of the pin slightly with an angle grinder until the deformity is removed.   Use a caliper and a magnifier to measure the two ends. Occasionally, the manufacturer ground the ends of the pins flush with the surface (which also tended to smear the metal together) and often the pin has been painted over so you have to look carefully. If the pin has been ground down and is not readily visible, strip away the paint with a wire brush, dab on some layout dye and then wipe it off. The dye will help decorate the interface so that the end of the pin is barely visible. Once the small end has been identified place a flat-faced steel pin punch (slightly smaller in diameter than the pin) squarely against the small end and strike firmly with a heavy hammer.   There is no substitute for mass here so use a 5 pound hammer (dead-blow style if possible). If you are lucky, the pin will shoot out the other side on the first blow. Often you can judge progress by sound. If the sound is "dead" when the pin is struck there is still progress being made. If the pin is seized, it will have more of a ringing sound each time you hit it since it is essentially monolithic.   If after five or six firm hits, the pin does not budge it is time to reassess. It is not advised to continue pounding away with the hammer. The force may be bending your punch or deforming the taper pin, thus making it harder to remove. If the pin mushroomed, touch off the ends of the pin with a grinder to clean up the deformation and move to the next phase.   Heat the shaft and collar slightly with a propane torch and then firmly strike the pin again. If that fails then it is usually best to drill the pin out. Replacing a taper pin is cheaper than replacing a broken shift lever or a damaged shaft. To drill out the pin, first center punch both ends lightly to provide a starting point for the drill bit. Using a long length high-speed steel drill bit approximately half the diameter of the small end of the pin, drill straight into the end of the pin until you are about half-way through the length. Flip it over and drill from the other end as straight as you can. Drilling the pin out substantially weakens it and several good hits should complete the pin removal process. You should not have to resort to the next step but in the event that the pin will simply not come out after drilling, the last resort is to purchase a taper pin drill bit & reamer and increase the taper pin to the next largest size. Simply step drill through the hole already created in the previous step making sure the old taper pin is completely drilled out. Ream the new hole and fit the new taper pin size and you're good as new. Now there are just 12 more pins to go…

Appendix 3

● <u>Machine Oil Specifications</u>

Lubrication Chart is shown on the next page.

(Units = Saybolt Universal Seconds Viscosity at 100°F)

Type A (Spindle):   100 seconds (Mobil Velocite 10, ISO 22)
Type B (Gearbox / Drive):   150-240 seconds (Mobil DTE, ISO 32)
Type C (General Purpose): 250-500 seconds (Mobil DTE, ISO 68)
Way Oil: 300-500 seconds (Mobil Vactra Medium Way)

● <u>Wicks, Wipers, Capillary Oilers:</u>

Type 1......................... 1/16" x 1/8" rectangular cross section
Type 2......................... 1/16" x 3/16" rectangular cross section
Type 3......................... 3/32" x 3/16" rectangular cross section
Type 7......................... 3/16" Round cross section
Type 13......................1/8" x 1/4" rectangular cross section
Type 14......................1/8" Round cross section
Capillary Oil Wicks......... 0.40"D x 2.125"L spring uncompressed
Tailstock Wipers.............3/16" Die Cut Felt (2 pcs.)
Way Wipers..................1/4" Die Cut Felt (4 pcs.)

● <u>Additional Resources Available on the Internet:</u>

Practical Machinist: www.practicalmachinist.com – SBL Forum

Yahoo Groups: http://groups.yahoo.com/group/southbendlathe/

SBL Site: **www.wswells.com** - A site dedicated to South Bend®
          Machinery. List of surviving SBL lathes & serial numbers.

● <u>Parts: (New and Used OEM Parts):</u>

South Bend Lathe Co.®: www.southbendlathe.com (Successor Company
to LeBlond Ltd. and the original South Bend Lathe Corporation)

eBay®: www.eBay.com – Business and Industrial Section - Metalworking

Lubrication Chart

For 10", 13", & 16" Lathes

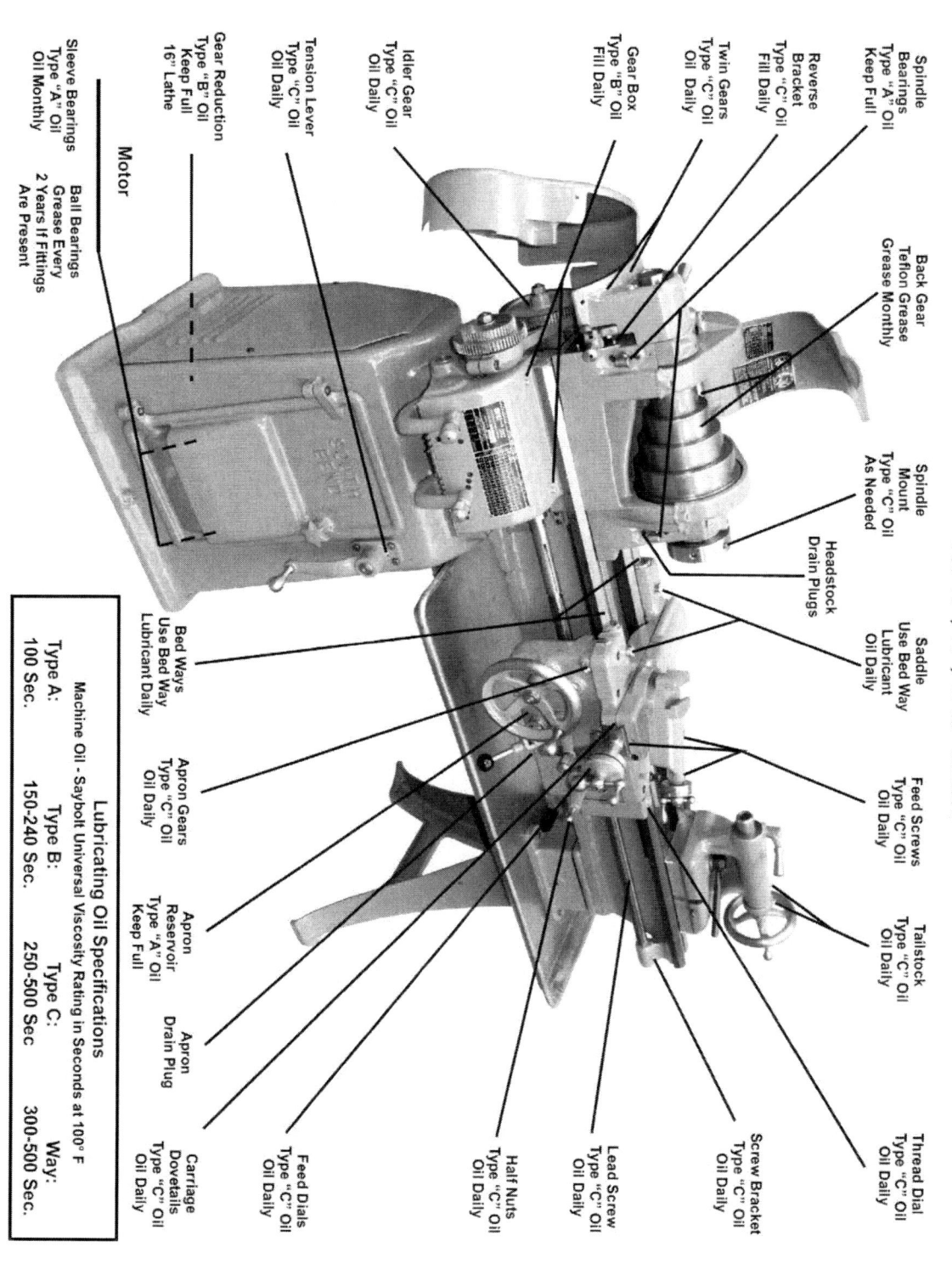

Spindle
Bearings
Type "A" Oil
Keep Full

Reverse
Bracket
Type "C" Oil
Fill Daily

Twin Gears
Type "C" Oil
Oil Daily

Gear Box
Type "B" Oil
Fill Daily

Idler Gear
Type "C" Oil
Oil Daily

Tension Lever
Type "C" Oil
Oil Daily

Gear Reduction
Type "B" Oil
Keep Full
16" Lathe

Motor

Sleeve Bearings
Type "A" Oil
Oil Monthly

Ball Bearings
Grease Every
2 Years If Fittings
Are Present

Back Gear
Teflon Grease
Grease Monthly

Spindle
Mount
Type "C" Oil
As Needed

Headstock
Drain Plugs

Saddle
Use Bed Way
Lubricant
Oil Daily

Feed Screws
Type "C" Oil
Oil Daily

Tailstock
Type "C" Oil
Oil Daily

Thread Dial
Type "C" Oil
Oil Daily

Screw Bracket
Type "C" Oil
Oil Daily

Lead Screw
Type "C" Oil
Oil Daily

Half Nuts
Type "C" Oil
Oil Daily

Feed Dials
Type "C" Oil
Oil Daily

Carriage
Dovetails
Type "C" Oil
Oil Daily

Apron
Drain Plug

Apron
Reservoir
Type "A" Oil
Keep Full

Apron Gears
Type "C" Oil
Oil Daily

Bed Ways
Use Bed Way
Lubricant Daily

Lubricating Oil Specifications

Machine Oil - Saybolt Universal Viscosity Rating in Seconds at 100° F

Type A:	Type B:	Type C:	Way:
100 Sec.	150-240 Sec.	250-500 Sec	300-500 Sec.

Recommended Reading:

Most of the books below can be found as reprints by Lindsay Publications (www.lindsaybks.com). The Lindsay catalog number is shown in [ ]. Lots of other great resource material may be found in their catalog as well.

[21150] How to Run a Lathe (1942 by South Bend Lathe)

[4708] Running An Engine Lathe (Fred Colvin)

[22482] Machine Shop Projects (1954 edition by South Bend Lathe)

[21583] South Bend Lathe Booklets (1942 by South Bend Lathe)

[23861] South Bend Lathe Maintenance Pamphlets (Various Dates)

[23268] The Screw Cutting Lathe (1907 by James Hobart)

[21052] Care and Operation of a Lathe (1942 by Sheldon Machine Co.)

[22962] Lathe Work for Beginners (1922 by Raymond Yates)

Lathe Notes (Volume 1-6) (From early 1900's Machinery Magazine)

Recommended Viewing:

A great resource for vintage video and other relevant published works is www.archive.org There you can find old industrial videos, books and photos.

● Consumable Parts & Special Tools:

Specialty tools, manuals, and consumable items such as wicks, wipers, felt cord, and gaskets as shown below can be purchased individually or as kits directly from:

ILION Industrial Services, LLC
PO Box 80502
Raleigh, NC 27623-0502
email: ilion@bellsouth.net

Shopping On-Line:

http://stores.ebay.com/stevewb
(All items currently available are listed in our ebay store)

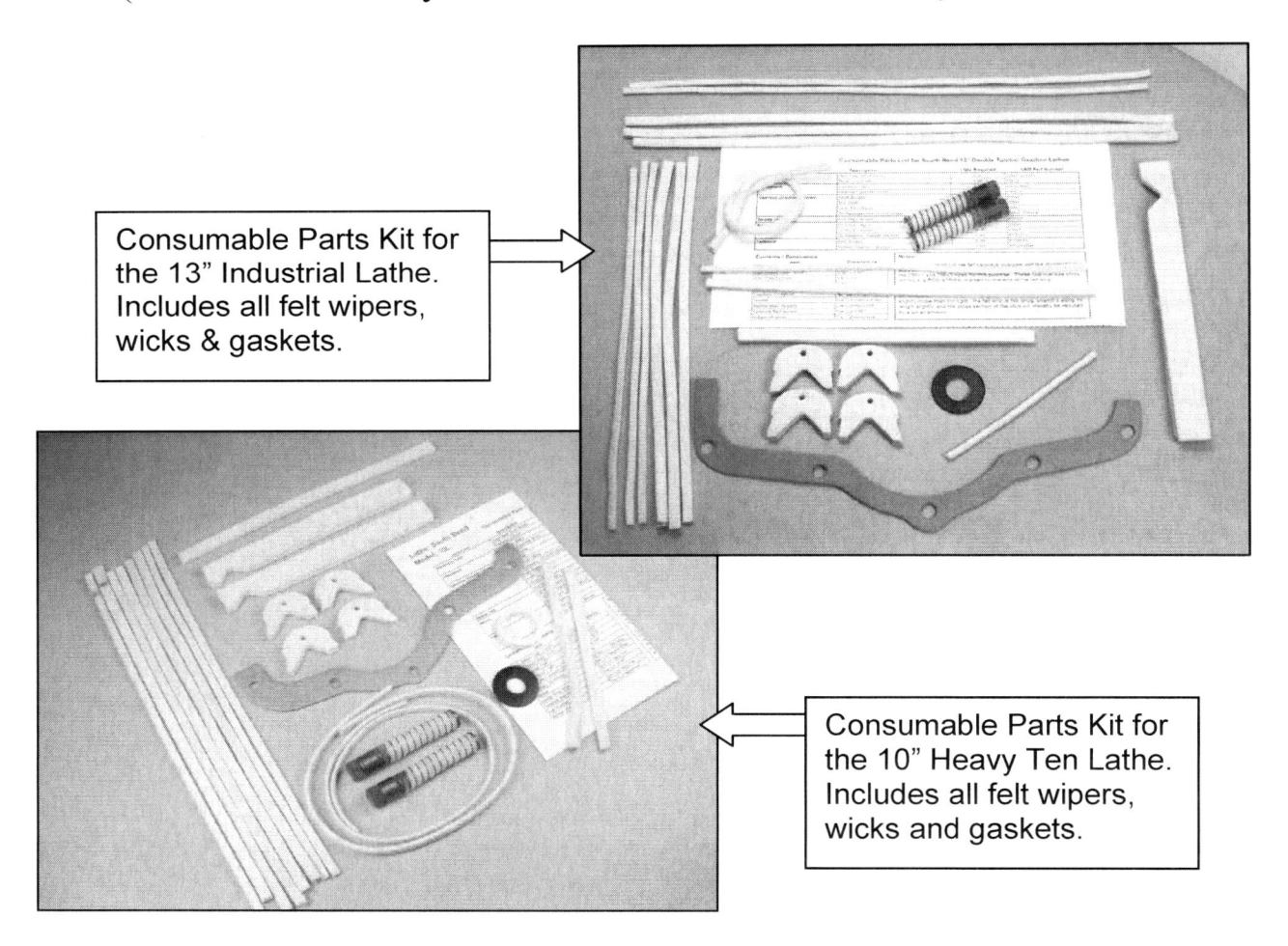

Consumable Parts Kit for the 13" Industrial Lathe. Includes all felt wipers, wicks & gaskets.

Consumable Parts Kit for the 10" Heavy Ten Lathe. Includes all felt wipers, wicks and gaskets.

Note: Although all of these aftermarket components are manufactured to be compatible with the original lathe specifications, they are not represented as original South Bend Lathe® parts.

Replacement Gits® Oil Hole Covers

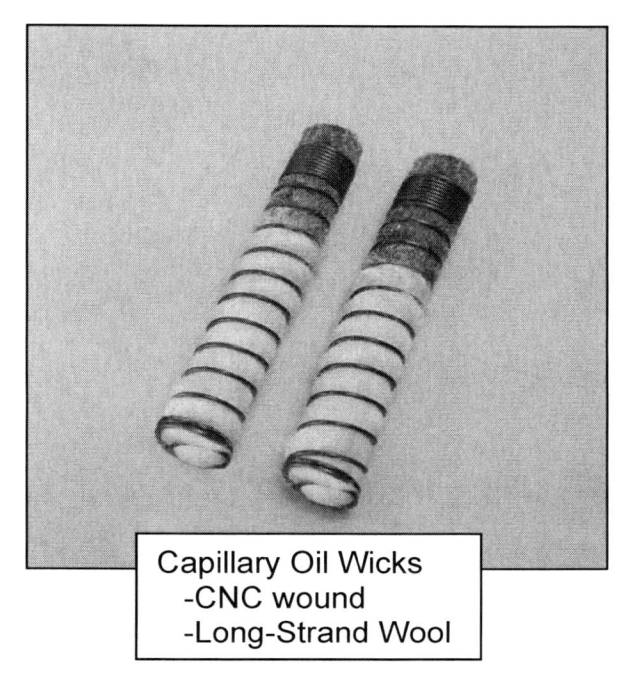

Capillary Oil Wicks
-CNC wound
-Long-Strand Wool

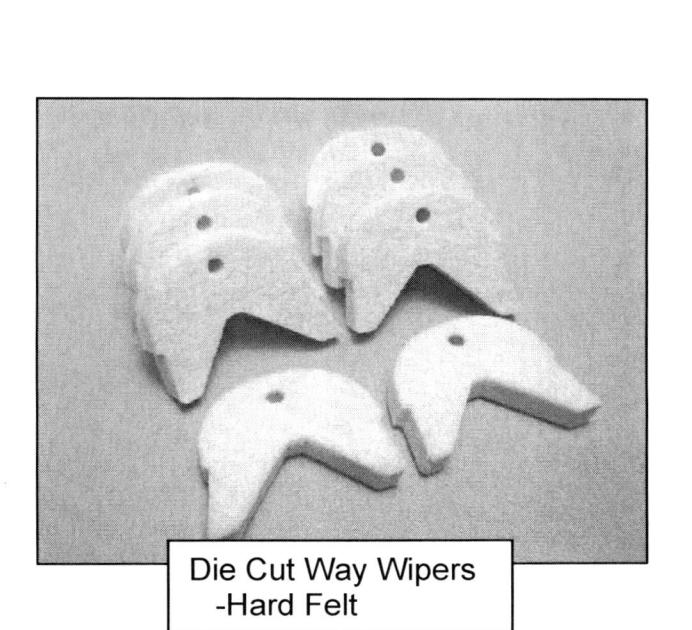

Die Cut Way Wipers
-Hard Felt

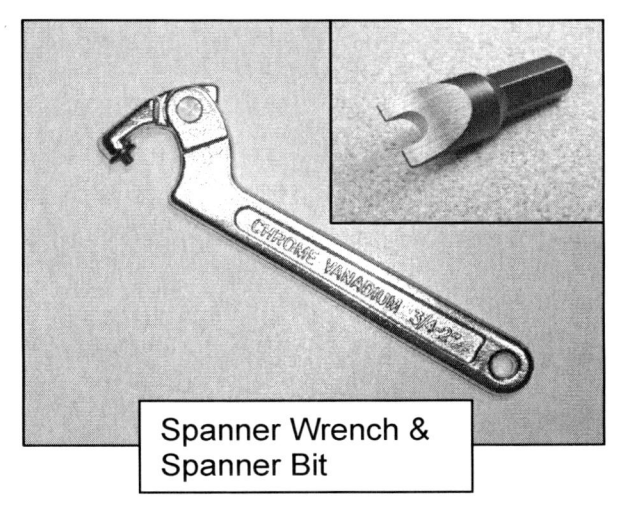

Spanner Wrench & Spanner Bit

Note: Although all of these aftermarket components are manufactured to be compatible with the original lathe specifications, they are not represented as original South Bend Lathe® parts.

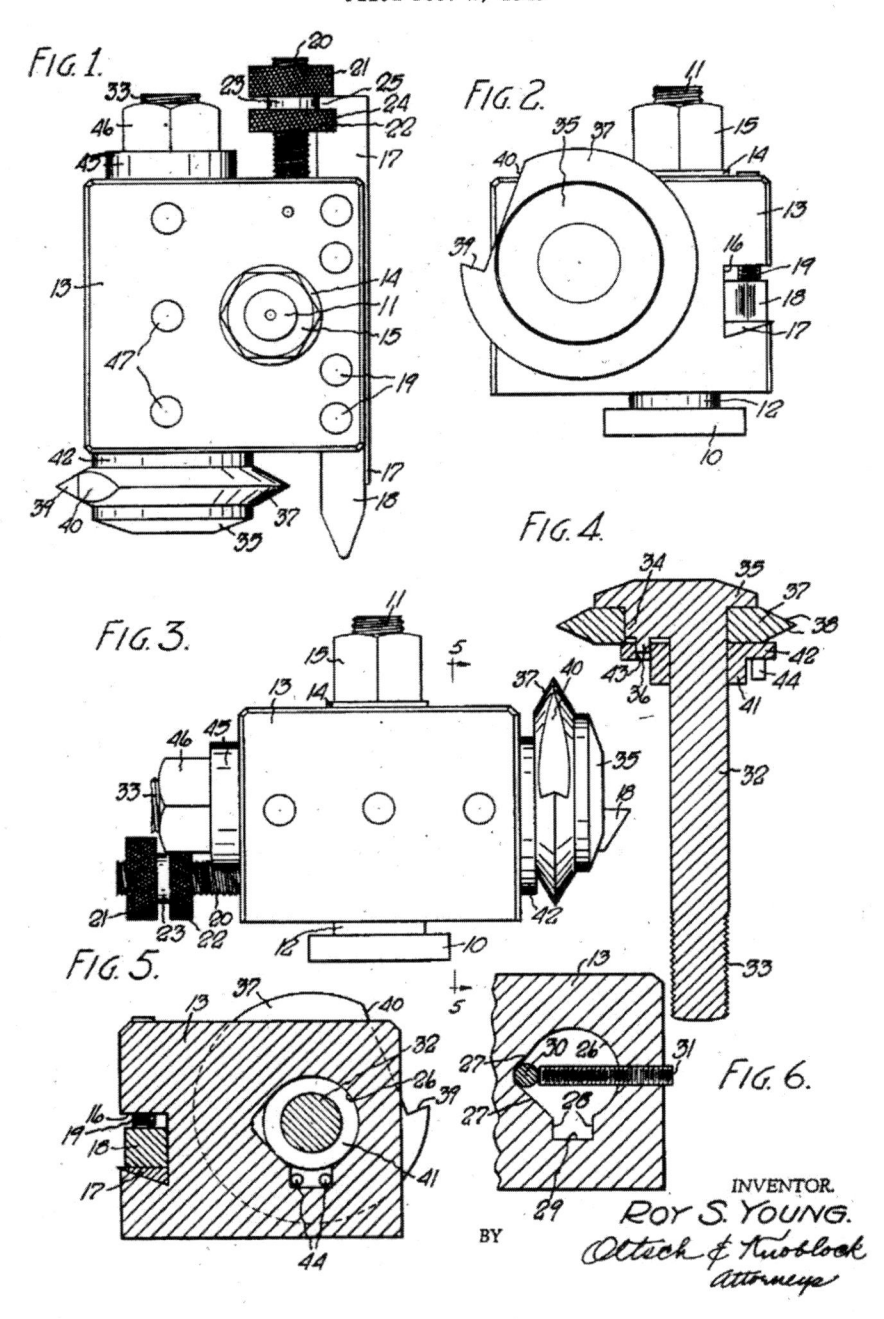

1942 South Bend Patent for a
multi-functional tool post.

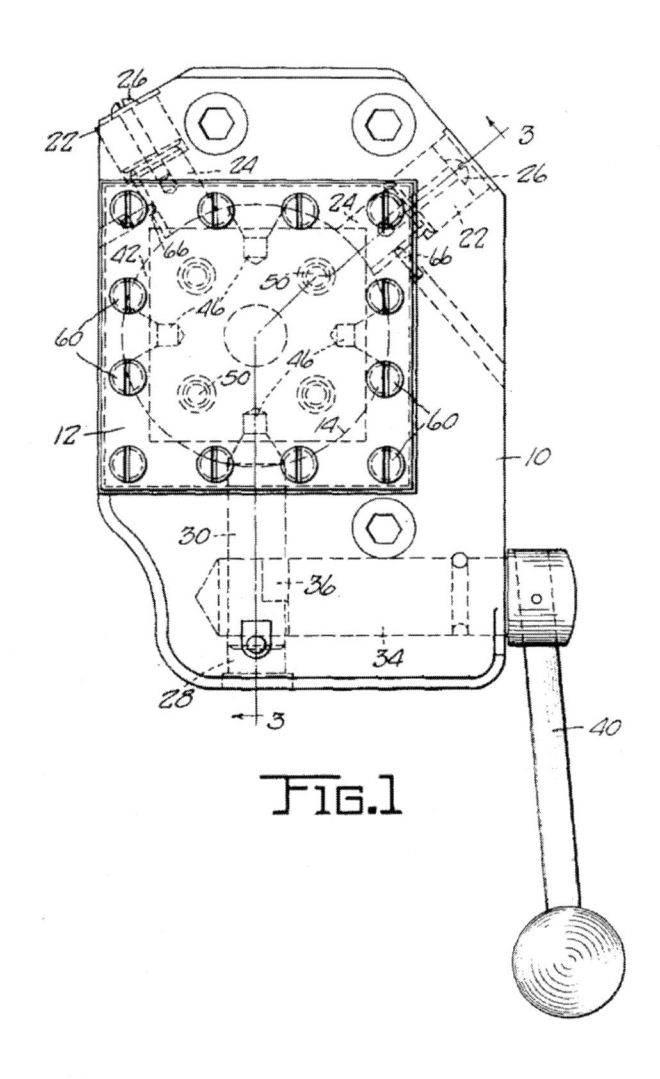

FIG.1

RUSSEL E. FRUSHOUR.
INVENTOR.

BY *Altsch & Knoblock*

ATTORNEYS.

1950 South Bend Patent for a turret tool post (Page 1 of 2)

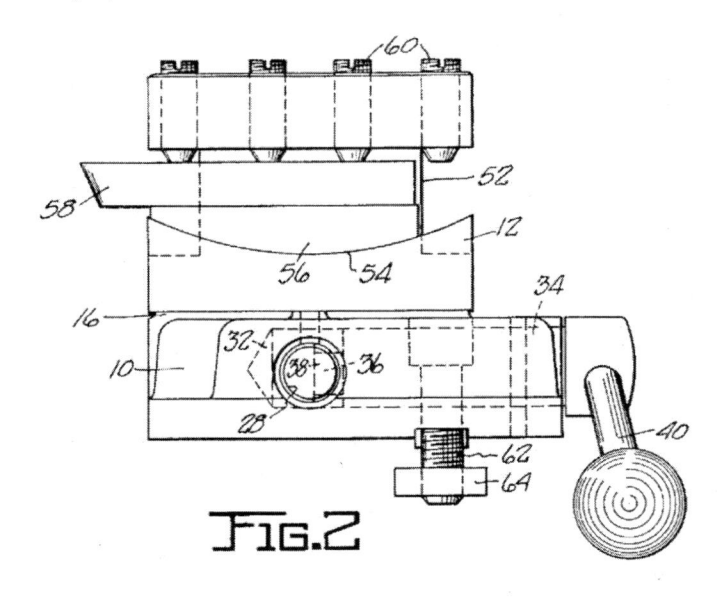

FIG.2

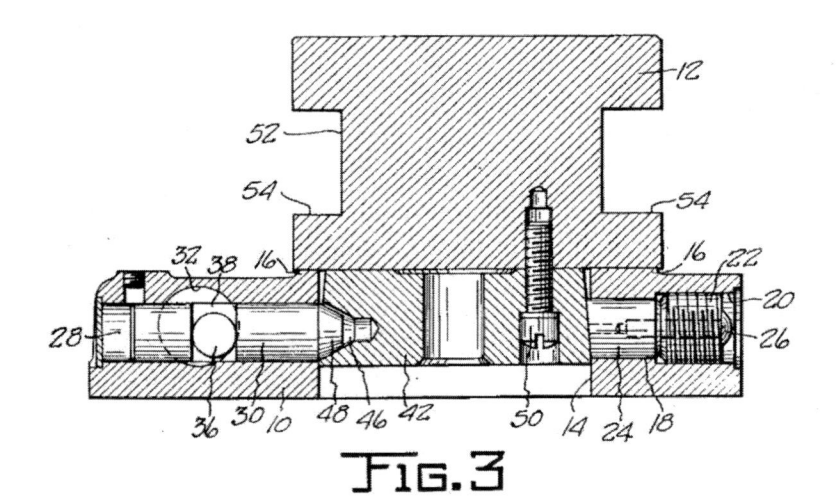

FIG.3

RUSSEL E. FRUSHOUR.
INVENTOR.

BY Oltsch & Knoblock

ATTORNEYS.

1950 South Bend Patent for a
turret tool post (Page 2 of 2)